Transmission and Display
of
Pictorial Information

TRANSMISSION AND DISPLAY
OF PICTORIAL INFORMATION

D. E. Pearson, *Ph.D., D.I.C.*

*Department of Electrical Engineering Science,
University of Essex*

PENTECH PRESS
London

First Published 1975
by Pentech Press Limited
London: 8 John Street, WC1N 2HY

© Pentech Press Limited, 1975

ISBN 0 7273 2101 3

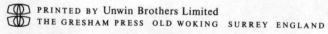 PRINTED BY Unwin Brothers Limited
THE GRESHAM PRESS OLD WOKING SURREY ENGLAND

Produced by 'Uneoprint'

A member of the Staples Printing Group

621.388
PEA

CONTENTS

Page

1. The Mathematical Analysis of Images: An Introduction   1

1.1   Image transmission as a communication process   1
1.2   Representation of images   2
1.3   Multidimensional functions   3
1.4   The two-dimensional Fourier transform   5
1.5   Extension of Woodward's notation to two dimensions   9
1.6   Separability   14
1.7   Circular symmetry   15
1.8   Convolution   16
1.9   Sampling   19
1.10 Two-dimensional bandwidth and the sampling theorem   19
1.11 Probabilistic signals in two dimensions   23
1.12 Further developments in two-dimensional Fourier theory   27
1.13 The three-dimensional Fourier transform   28

2. Properties of the Eye Affecting System Design   31

2.1   Angle subtended at the eye   31
2.2   Response to radiant energy   32
2.3   Response to spatial patterns   42
2.4   Response to temporal patterns   45
2.5   Relevance of the spatio-temporal sine-wave response for system design   47

3. Scanning   51

3.1   Types of scan   51
3.2   Scanning as a sampling process   54
3.3   Ideal scanning   55
3.4   Pre-scan bandlimitation   60
3.5   Some parameters of practical scanning systems   69
3.6   The video signal   76
3.7   Spatial carrier modulation   88

Page

4. Reception and Display of Monochrome Pictures   **91**

    4. 1   Line broadening   91
    4. 2   Kell factor   94
    4. 3   Phosphors   95
    4. 4   Visibility of sine-wave interference   97
    4. 5   Visibility of random noise   105
    4. 6   Grey scale and gamma   108
    4. 7   Visibility of noise over the grey scale   109

5. Transmission of Monochrome Information   **111**

    5. 1   Introduction   111
    5. 2   Analogue baseband transmission   111
    5. 3   Transmission by carrier modulation   114
    5. 4   Digital transmission   114
    5. 5   Image restoration and enhancement   121
    5. 6   Information theory and picture coding   122

6. Displays in Colour   **125**

    6. 1   Introduction   125
    6. 2   The CIE system of colour measurement   126
    6. 3   Perceived colour   141

7. Transmission of Colour Information   **162**

    7. 1   Principles of colour reproduction   162
    7. 2   Analogue transmission   177
    7. 3   Digital transmission   196

8. Subjective Assessment of Picture Quality   **199**

    8. 1   Relationship between picture quality and
            channel capacity   199
    8. 2   A numerical scale for picture quality   199
    8. 3   Category-judgement methods   201
    8. 4   Comparison methods   204
    8. 5   Waveform testing   208

References   209

Index   219

PREFACE

The book is an attempt to set down and explain the fundamental
principles of electronic systems which process, store or transmit
one particular kind of information, namely that which ultimately
enters the human eye. These principles are common to a variety of
systems including broadcast and cable television, facsimile, videotelephone systems, computer-generated visual displays and scanning
electron microscopes. The material is addressed primarily to communication engineers, whose job requires an understanding of the
nature of video signals and their efficient transmission. The book in
fact evolved from a series of lectures given to students attending the
M.Sc. course in Telecommunication Systems at the University of
Essex over the past few years.

Traditional communication engineering makes fairly extensive use of
Fourier concepts such as frequency spectrum and bandwidth. These
concepts may also usefully be applied to an understanding of pictorial
information processing. Chapter 1 is an introduction to Fourier mathematics and its application to pictures. The reader who is unfamiliar
with basic Fourier theory may like to skim this chapter briefly to
obtain a qualitative grasp of some of the ideas such as spatial frequency, and then proceed to Chapter 2. Large sections of the book
are not dependent on a detailed understanding of the first chapter.

Many, if not all, of the parameters of a picture transmission system
are related in some way to properties of human vision. Chapter 2 is
therefore a second introductory chapter with the purpose of acquaint-
ing the reader with some of the basic facts of vision, particularly with
current views of the eye as a low-pass spatio-temporal filter in the
Fourier domain. There follows in Chapter 3 a treatment of scanning;
in Chapter 4, monochrome displays; and in Chapter 5, analogue and
digital coding and transmission methods for monochrome signals.
Chapters 6 and 7 deal with colour and Chapter 8 with subjective
assessment. The text overall is more concerned with principles than
with practice, but from time to time I have illustrated the principles
by reference to practice in the United Kingdom and the United States,
in which countries my own practical experience has been gained.

I am very grateful to a number of people who have helped to shape the
form and content of the book by providing me with information about
their own and their institution's work, some of it unpublished. Among
these are, in no particular order of merit: in the U. K., Mr. I. F.
Macdiarmid, Mr. J. W. Allnatt and Dr. J. E. Thompson of the British
Post Office Research Department, Dr. F. W. Campbell and Dr. J. G.
Robson of the Physiological Laboratory, University of Cambridge,
Mr. A. N. Heightman of the Marconi Company, Mr. W. N. Sproson of
the B.B.C. Research Department, Dr. A. H. Robinson of the Inter-

national Publishing Corporation, and Dr. G. B. Townsend of the Independent Broadcasting Authority; in the U.S.A., a large number—too numerous to name—of my former colleagues at Bell Laboratories, Dr. O. H. Schade of R.C.A., Dr. C. J. Bartleson and Dr. E. J. Breneman of the Kollmorgen Corporation, Professors W. F. Schreiber, T. S. Huang (now at Purdue) and O. J. Tretiak of M.I.T. and Dr. L. S. Golding and Dr. R. K. Garlow of Comsat Laboratories.—My special thanks go to Dr. John Limb and Mr. Charles Rubinstein of Bell Laboratories and to Professor Herbert Voelcker of the University of Rochester, who read sections of the first draft of the manuscript and made a number of helpful suggestions; also to Mrs. Jan Harrison and Mrs. Noël Finney, who typed the manuscript.

D. E. PEARSON
Wivenhoe Park
Colchester
Essex

Chapter 1

THE MATHEMATICAL ANALYSIS OF IMAGES: AN INTRODUCTION TO MULTIDIMENSIONAL FOURIER THEORY

1.1 Image Transmission as a Communication Process

In the transmission of information about the visual appearance of an object or scene to a distant point, it is common practice first to form an *image* of the scene. The process of image formation by means of a lens is a familiar one; what is produced is a representation of the original which is reduced in size and in which three spatial dimensions are compressed into two, but in which the essential visual information such as the relative sizes, shapes and positions of objects are preserved. Most visual communication systems do this as a first step with the exception of some systems such as facsimile, where the object may be scanned directly. It is the same first step which we ourselves use in seeing: the formation of an image on the retina of the eye.

To transmit the image it is usual to scan it electronically, producing an electrical signal which carries the essential information and from which a reconstruction can be made at the receiver. When the image is thus reconstructed and displayed on a cathode ray tube (CRT) or other display device, it is termed a *picture*, paralleling the usage in painting and photography. However, *picture* and *image* are used almost interchangeably in much of the literature on the subject.

The analysis of image scanning, transmission and display may be carried out using many of the concepts familiar to communication engineers, such as filtering and sampling. The purpose of this analysis is to be able better to understand the process by which the image is converted into an electrical signal (the *video* signal) and reconverted for display at the receiver. The communication engineer is faced with the problem of transmitting this signal over transmission channels of various kinds, analogue and digital, satellite, cable and radio; he is concerned to know therefore how video signals differ from speech and data signals, how much bandwidth they require and how they are affected by noise. When transmission over digital channels is required, he is concerned to encode them efficiently without sacrificing quality. Insight into these problems is gained through mathematical analysis, while bearing in mind that the ultimate receiver is the human eye and that not all of its characteristics are readily describable in mathematical terms.

The first step in the analysis which follows will be to attempt to

describe or represent an image using the mathematics of communication signal theory. What distinguishes image transmission mathematically from most other types of communication is the increased
dimensionality of the information source. A man can hear effectively
at a distance by arranging to transmit to him a unidimensional
representation of sound pressure, as a function of time, from a
convenient point near the sound source. To provide him with sight at
a distance he needs information about visible energy incident on the
image plane, not at one point, but over a whole area. For a scene
with moving objects, the changes in the incident energy as a function
of time must also be transmitted, so that the image representation
requires a total of three dimensions compared with one for speech.
In the case of stereo, additional information is needed in both cases.

1.2   Representation of Images

Communication theorists tend to spend a good deal of time devising
representations of the source of signals, and with good reason, since
the understanding of communication processes has been much
advanced by this attitude. One of the most successful representations
of unidimensional source signals, from this standpoint, has been the
Fourier transform:

$$G(f) = \int_{-\infty}^{\infty} g(t)e^{-j2\pi ft}\ dt$$

with its inverse

$$g(t) = \int_{-\infty}^{\infty} G(f)e^{+j2\pi ft}\ df$$

where $g(t)$ is the waveform or time-domain description of the source
signal. The transform or spectrum $G(f)$ allows us to consider $g(t)$
as the sum or integral of a large number of sine waves of various
frequencies f, and leads to the concept of bandwidth, which is a basic
term in the language of communication engineers. Also, by using
$G(f)$ rather than $g(t)$ to represent the signal, operations such as filtering become tractable. The action on $G(f)$ of several cascaded filters is simply obtained as a mathematical product, whereas in the
time domain the equivalent process is multiple convolution (Bracewell,
1965).

The power of the Fourier transform has been increased over the past
few decades by the work of mathematicians such as Temple (1955) and
Lighthill (1958) on generalised functions,* so that it is now possible

---

* The generalised function approach allows us to describe, manipulate
  and transform, with confidence, 'difficult' functions like $\delta(t)$, the unit
  impulse or delta function, by treating each function as the limit of a
  sequence of functions. For an introductory account, consult Bracewell (1965).

to find spectra for almost every communication signal of interest. The Fourier approach has greatly illuminated processes such as modulation, sampling, quantisation and pulse transmission (Bracewell, 1965; Bennett and Davey, 1965; Carlson, 1968; Cattermole, 1969). Similar insights into the processes involved in image transmission are obtained through the use of multidimensional Fourier transforms, and this chapter provides an introduction to the subject. An attempt has been made to keep the mathematical notation simple, and to pursue mathematical niceties only as far as may be helpful for a grasp of the concepts.

1.3   Multidimensional Functions

The equivalent of the time-domain representation $g(t)$, which is used for, say, speech signals, is the space-and-time or spatio-temporal domain representation $g(x, y, t)$ for images and pictures, where x and y are horizontal and vertical spatial dimensions respectively in the plane of the image, and t is time (Figure 1.1). The assumption which

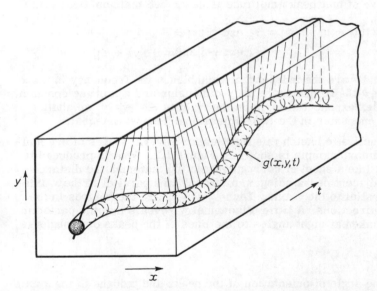

Figure 1.1   Representation of a monochrome image of a swinging pendulum as a function $g(x, y, t)$ in x, y, t space.

is made in this description is that $g(x, y, t)$ represents the *illuminance* of the image plane or the *luminance* of the display. These photometric concepts are explained a little further in Chapter 2; for the moment suppose that we have ignored colour in the image and have represented something which, in everyday language, would be called the intensity or strength of the light. As we shall be concerned with ordinary scenes illuminated by daylight or the more common types of artificial light, the light forming the image will be assumed to be incoherent, making $g(x,y,t)$ a real, non-negative-valuea function. This restriction plays an important part in the analysis and synthesis of filtering operations on such images, since, for example, the impulse response of a realisable filter cannot go negative at any point, as this would correspond to negative light output. Further, in the analysis of optical systems using Fourier concepts, it should be noted that two underlying assumptions are those of *linearity* and *space-time* invariancy. The former implies that the principle of superposition holds, and the latter that the system response is independent of both time and spatial position in the image plane. These are simple extensions of the concepts of linearity and time invariancy in unidimensional communication systems (Bennett, 1970).

As in the case of the unidimensional transform, the multidimensional Fourier transform of $g(x,y,t)$ is a representation in terms of sine or cosine waves of various frequencies and phases. A two-dimensional cosine wave of unit peak amplitude is described mathematically as

$$\cos\left[2\pi(ux + vy) + \phi\right] = \tfrac{1}{2}\exp\left\{j[2\pi(ux + vy) + \phi]\right\} + \tfrac{1}{2}\exp\left\{-j[2\pi(ux + vy) + \phi]\right\}$$

where x and y are the independent variables, u the frequency in the x dimension, v the frequency in the y dimension and ϕ a phase constant. The complex exponential form on the right is that which we shall presently encounter in the two-dimensional Fourier integral.

It is instructive to sketch this function for several values of u, v and ϕ; a particular example is shown in Figure 1.2. What is produced is something like a sheet of corrugated roofing material, the distance between adjacent peaks being $\tfrac{1}{u}$ along any line parallel to the x axis and $\tfrac{1}{v}$ parallel to the y axis. Thus $\tfrac{1}{u}$ and $\tfrac{1}{v}$ are the periods in the two axial directions. A little trigonometry reveals that the period in a section taken at right angles to the lines of the peaks or troughs is

$$\lambda = (u^2 + v^2)^{-\tfrac{1}{2}}$$

and that the angle of orientation of the peaks and troughs to the x axis is

$$\theta = \arctan\frac{u}{v}$$

In the Fourier transform, negative values of frequency arise. If the sign of u is opposite to that of v the angle θ becomes negative; in which case Figure 1.2 must be rotated to form an angle θ with the x axis in the opposite sense shown.

In our usage of the two-dimensional sine wave, x and y will commonly represent distance along horizontal and vertical axes respectively in an image or picture, with the amplitude representing illuminance or luminance. In this usage u becomes the *horizontal spatial frequency* and v the *vertical spatial frequency,* measured in cycles per millimetre or, when we have the human observer in mind, in cycles per degree subtended at the eye. Spatial frequency is also termed *wave number*.

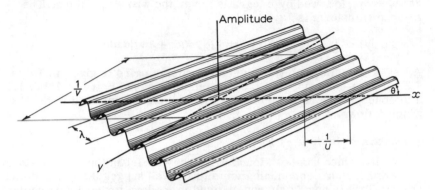

Figure 1.2 A two-dimensional sine wave.

Three-dimensional sine waves

The extension of these concepts to three dimensions gives the three-dimensional cosinusoid

$$\cos\left[2\pi(ux + vy + ft) + \phi\right] = \tfrac{1}{2}\exp\left\{j[2\pi(ux + vy + ft) + \phi]\right\}$$
$$+ \tfrac{1}{2}\exp\left\{-j[2\pi(ux + vy + ft) + \phi]\right\}$$

where t is the third dimension and f the frequency along the t axis. This is more difficult to imagine than the two-dimensional case, but can be likened to a variation of density in a solid or gas in three-dimensional space, the dense regions being in regular strata along straight lines

$$ux + vy + ft + \phi/2\pi = 0$$

Another interpretation is obtained if the corrugated sheet in Figure 1.2 is considered to move at a constant velocity equal to λf in a direction at right angles to the lines of its peaks and troughs. Any chosen point in the xy plane then oscillates in amplitude at a frequency equal to f hertz.

1.4   The Two-dimensional Fourier Transform

The Fourier transform of a two-dimensional function $g(x, y)$, which might represent a monochrome image of a stationary scene, is defined as

$$G(u,v) = \int_{-\infty}^{\infty} \int_{-\infty}^{\infty} g(x,y) \exp\left[-j2\pi(ux + vy)\right]dx\,dy$$

The form is seen to be similar to that of the unidimensional Fourier transform, involving multiplication of the function to be transformed by the negative complex exponential half of the real cosinusoid cos $2\pi(ux + vy)$, followed by integration over the whole x,y plane. The inverse transform is

$$g(x,y) = \int_{-\infty}^{\infty} \int_{-\infty}^{\infty} G(u,v) \exp\left[+j2\pi(ux + vy)\right]du\,dv$$

A list of two-dimensional Fourier transform pairs is given in Table 1.2 with, for comparison, a table of unidimensional pairs in Table 1.1. The concepts and notation used in the tables are explained in the text which follows.

Woodward's notation

A notation which has been found to be very useful in the representation of unidimensional communication signals was suggested by Woodward (1953). This is now fairly widely used in modern textbooks on communication signal theory (Carlson, 1968; Cattermole, 1969; Bennett, (1970), to which the reader is referred for examples.

Woodward's notation covers four frequently used functions:

(1)   rect $(t) = 1, |t| < \frac{1}{2}$

$ = 0, |t| > \frac{1}{2}$

$ = \frac{1}{2}, |t| = \frac{1}{2}$

(2)   sinc $(t) = \dfrac{\sin \pi t}{\pi t}$

(3) $\text{rep}_T\left[g(t)\right] = \displaystyle\sum_{n=-\infty}^{\infty} g(t - nT)$

(4) $\text{comb}_T\left[g(t)\right] = \displaystyle\sum_{n=-\infty}^{\infty} g(nT)\,\delta\,(t - nT)$

The first two of these functions, (1) and (2), are Fourier transforms of each other and, with adjustment of the scaling constants, so are (3) and (4) (see Table 1.1). Woodward's notation is particularly helpful in describing sampling, and since the basis of our approach to scanning is to represent it as a sampling process, we consider an extension of Woodward's notation to two dimensions. A similar approach has been taken by authors of texts on modern optics (e.g. Goodman, 1968). We later consider the extension to three dimensions.

Table 1.1   Unidimensional Fourier transforms

Description	Function	Transform
1 Definition	$g(t)$	$G(f) = \int_{-\infty}^{\infty} g(t)\mathrm{e}^{-\mathrm{j}2\pi ft}\,\mathrm{d}t$
2 Scaling	$g(t/T)$	$\|T\| \cdot G(fT)$
3 Time shift	$g(t - T)$	$G(f) \cdot \mathrm{e}^{-\mathrm{j}2\pi fT}$
4 Frequency shift	$g(t) \cdot \mathrm{e}^{\mathrm{j}2\pi Ft}$	$G(f - F)$
5 Complex conjugate	$g^*(t)$	$G^*(-f)$
6 Temporal derivative	$\dfrac{\mathrm{d}^n}{\mathrm{d}t^n} \cdot g(t)$	$(\mathrm{j}2\pi f)^n \cdot G(f)$
7 Spectral derivative	$(-\mathrm{j}2\pi t)^n \cdot g(t)$	$\dfrac{\mathrm{d}^n}{\mathrm{d}f^n} \cdot G(f)$
8 Reciprocity	$G(t)$	$g(-f)$
9 Addition	$A.g(t) + B.h(t)$	$A.G(f) + B.H(f)$
10 Multiplication	$g(t) \cdot h(t)$	$G(f) * H(f)$
11 Convolution	$g(t) * h(t)$	$G(f) \cdot H(f)$
12 Delta function	$\delta(t)$	1
13 Constant	1	$\delta(f)$
14 Rectangular function	$\mathrm{rect}\,(t)$	$\mathrm{sinc}\,(f)$
15 Sinc function	$\mathrm{sinc}\,(t)$	$\mathrm{rect}\,(f)$
16 Unit step function	$u(t)$	$\frac{1}{2}\,\delta(f) - \dfrac{\mathrm{j}}{2\pi f}$
17 Signum function	$\mathrm{sgn}(t)$	$-\dfrac{\mathrm{j}}{\pi f}$
18 Decaying exponential, two-sided	$\mathrm{e}^{-\|t\|}$	$\dfrac{2}{1 + (2\pi f)^2}$
19 Decaying exponential, one-sided	$\mathrm{e}^{-\|t\|} \cdot u(t)$	$\dfrac{1 - \mathrm{j}2\pi f}{1 + (2\pi f)^2}$
20 Gaussian function	$\mathrm{e}^{-\pi t^2}$	$\mathrm{e}^{-\pi f^2}$
21 Repeated function	$\mathrm{rep}_T[g(t)]$	$\left\|\dfrac{1}{T}\right\|\,\mathrm{comb}_{1/T}\,[G(f)]$
22 Sampled function	$\mathrm{comb}_T[g(t)]$	$\left\|\dfrac{1}{T}\right\|\,\mathrm{rep}_{1/T}\,[G(f)]$

Table 1.2 Two-dimensional Fourier transforms

Description	Function	Transform
1 Definition	$g(x,y)$	$G(u,v) = \int_{-\infty}^{\infty} \int_{-\infty}^{\infty} g(x,y) \cdot \exp\left[-j2\pi(ux+vy)\right]dx\,dy$
2 Scaling	$g(x/A, y/B)$	$\lvert AB \rvert\, G(Au, Bv)$
3 Spatial shift	$g(x-A, y-B)$	$G(u,v) \cdot \exp\left[-j2\pi(Au+Bv)\right]$
4 Frequency shift	$g(x,y) \cdot \exp\left[j2\pi(Cx+Dy)\right]$	$G(u-C, v-D)$
5 Complex conjugate	$g^*(x,y)$	$G^*(-u,-v)$
6 Spatial derivative	$\left(\dfrac{\partial}{\partial x}\right)^m \left(\dfrac{\partial}{\partial y}\right)^n g(x,y)$	$(j2\pi u)^m \, (j2\pi v)^n \, G(u,v)$
7 Spectral derivative	$(-j2\pi x)^m \, (-j2\pi y)^n \, g(x,y)$	$\left(\dfrac{\partial}{\partial u}\right)^m \left(\dfrac{\partial}{\partial v}\right)^n G(u,v)$
8 Reciprocity	$G(x,y)$	$g(-u,-v)$
9 Addition	$A.g(x,y) + B.h(x,y)$	$A.G(u,v) + B.H(u,v)$
10 Multiplication	$g(x,y) \cdot h(x,y)$	$G(u,v) * H(u,v)$
11 Convolution	$g(x,y) * h(x,y)$	$G(u,v) \cdot H(u,v)$
12 Delta function	$\delta(x,y) = \delta(x) \cdot \delta(y)$	1
13 Constant	1	$\delta(u,v) = \delta(u) \cdot \delta(v)$
14 Separable function	$g(x,y) = g_1(x) \cdot g_2(y)$	$G(u,v) = G_1(u) \cdot G_2(v)$
15 Rectangular function	$\mathrm{rect}\,(x,y)$	$\mathrm{sinc}\,(u,v)$
16 Sinc function	$\mathrm{sinc}\,(x,y)$	$\mathrm{rect}\,(u,v)$
17 Repeated function	$\mathrm{rep}_{X,Y}[g(x,y)]$	$\dfrac{1}{\lvert XY \rvert}\,\mathrm{comb}_{1/X,\,1/Y}[G(u,v)]$
18 Sampled function	$\mathrm{comb}_{X,Y}[g(x,y)]$	$\dfrac{1}{\lvert XY \rvert}\,\mathrm{rep}_{1/X,\,1/Y}[G(u,v)]$
19 Functions with circular symmetry	$r^2 = x^2 + y^2$	$\rho^2 = u^2 + v^2$
20 Gaussian function	$e^{-\pi r^2}$	$e^{-\pi \rho^2}$

Table 1.2 (contd.)

Description	Function	Transform
21 Circular function	$\mathrm{rect}\left(\dfrac{r}{2R}\right)$	$\dfrac{R}{\rho} \cdot J_1(2\pi R\rho)$
22 First-order Bessel	$\dfrac{P}{r} \cdot J_1(2\pi\, Pr)$	$\mathrm{rect}\ \dfrac{\rho}{2P}$
23 Ring	$\delta(r - R)$	$2\pi R \cdot J_0\,(2\pi\, R\rho)$
24 Zero-order Bessel	$2\pi\, P \cdot J_0(2\pi\, Fr)$	$\delta(\rho - P)$

1.5   Extension of Woodward's Notation to Two Dimensions

We define the following four functions:

(1)   rect $(x,y) = $ rect (x) . rect (y)

This function has the value 1 when both x and y are less than $\tfrac{1}{2}$ and 0 when either x or y is greater than $\tfrac{1}{2}$. We may stretch the extent over which the function has the value unity by dividing x and y by constants A and B, giving

$$\mathrm{rect}\left(\frac{x}{A},\ \frac{y}{B}\right) = \mathrm{rect}\left(\frac{x}{A}\right).\ \mathrm{rect}\left(\frac{y}{B}\right)$$

which has the value 1 inside a rectangle of dimensions $A \times B$ (Figure 1.3), and 0 outside. It could represent, say, an image of a white rectangle on a black background.

(2)   sinc $(x,y) = $ sinc (x) . sinc (y)

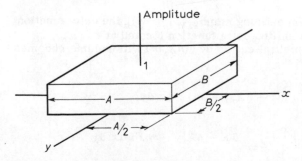

Figure 1.3 The function rect $(x/A, y/B)$

Figure 1.4 shows a sketch of sinc $(x/A, y/B)$, which has zeros on the x axis at $\pm A, \pm 2A, \pm 3A, \ldots\ldots\ldots$ and on the y axis at $\pm B, \pm 2B, \pm 3B,$ $\ldots\ldots\ldots$.

$$(3)\ \mathrm{rep}_{X,\,Y}\,[g(x,y)] = \sum_{n=-\infty}^{\infty}\ \sum_{m=-\infty}^{\infty}\ g(x - nX, y - mY)$$

This function is a repeated version of the basic function $g(x, y)$, the repetitions being at intervals X along the x axis and Y along the y axis (Figure 1.5).

$$(4)\quad \mathrm{comb}_{X,\,Y}\,[g(x,y)] = \sum_{n=-\infty}^{\infty}\ \sum_{m=-\infty}^{\infty}\ g(nX, mY)\,\delta\,(x - nX, y - mY)$$

The delta function in two dimensions $\delta\,(x, y)$ may be regarded in a similar way to the unidimensional delta function, as a generalised function, i.e. as the limit of a sequence of two-dimensional functions (Goodman, 1968). It may also be written as

$$\delta\,(x, y) = \delta\,(x)\ .\ \delta\,(y)$$

when the multiplication is interpreted in terms of the limiting sequence. The individual delta functions $\delta\,(x)$ and $\delta\,(y)$ are to be considered here as two-dimensional functions. Thus $\delta\,(x)$ has a discontinuity at $x = 0$ irrespective of the value of y and can be regarded as an *impulse plane* or *impulse sheet* erected over the y axis in the xy plane. Similarly $\delta(y)$ is an impulse sheet erected over the x axis.

The volume under $\delta(x, y)$ is unity, since

$$\int_{-\infty}^{\infty}\ \int_{-\infty}^{\infty}\ \delta(x, y)\ \mathrm{d}x\ \mathrm{d}y = \int_{-\infty}^{\infty}\ \delta(x)\ \mathrm{d}x\ .\ \int_{-\infty}^{\infty}\ \delta(y)\,\mathrm{d}y$$

$$= 1\ .\ 1 = 1$$

In the double summation defining $\mathrm{comb}_{X\,.\,Y}\,[g(x, y)]$, the delta function $\delta(x - nX, y - mY)$ is a shifted delta function located at $x = nX$, $y = mY$. By virtue of multiplication by $g(nX, mY)$ its volume becomes $g(nX, mY)$, since

$$\int_{-\infty}^{\infty}\ \int_{-\infty}^{\infty}\ g(nX, mY)\ \delta(x - nX, y - mY)\ \mathrm{d}x\ \mathrm{d}y$$

$$= g(nX, mY) \int_{-\infty}^{\infty}\ \int_{-\infty}^{\infty}\ \delta(x - nX, y - mY)\ \mathrm{d}x\ \mathrm{d}y$$

$$= g(nX, mY)$$

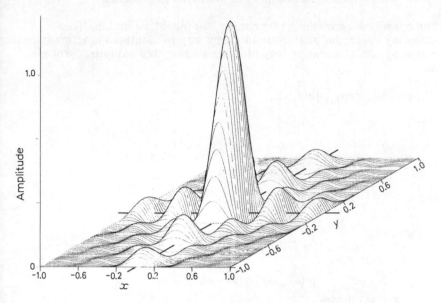

Figure 1.4   Computer-drawn representation of $\text{sinc}\left(\dfrac{x}{A}, \dfrac{y}{B}\right)$ on normalized axes of x and y. In the figure $A = B = 0.2$, so that the zeros of the function occur at intervals of 0.2 along both x and y axes, except at $x = 0, y = 0$.

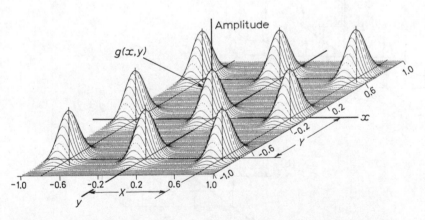

Figure 1.5   The function $\text{rep}_{X,Y}[g(x,y)]$. The basic function $g(x,y)$ is normally that located at $x = 0, y = 0$ i.e. the central one in the figure; however, any of the other displaced versions may be regarded as $g(x,y)$ with the same result. In the figure the repetition distance along the x axis is $X = 0.8$ and along the y axis $Y = 0.7$.

The operation represented by $comb_{XY}$ is therefore an idealised sampling operation, analogous in every way to idealised unidimensional sampling. An alternative way of representing this sampling process is

$$g(x,y) \cdot rep_{X,Y}\left[\delta(x,y)\right],$$

since

$$rep_{X,Y}\left[\delta(x,y)\right] = \sum_{n=-\infty}^{\infty} \sum_{m=-\infty}^{\infty} \delta(x-nX, y-mY)$$

and

$$g(x,y) \cdot \sum_{n=-\infty}^{\infty} \sum_{m=-\infty}^{\infty} \delta(x-nX, y-mY)$$

$$= \sum_{n=-\infty}^{\infty} \sum_{m=-\infty}^{\infty} g(nX, mY)\, \delta(x-nX, y-mY)$$

The only values of $g(x,y)$ affecting the volumes under the delta functions are at their infinite discontinuities, i.e. at $x=nX, y=mY$.

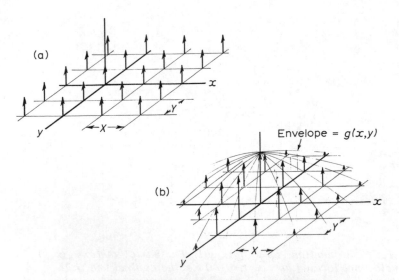

Figure 1.6   (a) The sampling function $rep_{X,Y}\left[\delta(x,y)\right]$ *and (b) the sampled function* $comb_{X,Y}\left[g(x,y)\right] = g(x,y) \cdot rep_{X,Y}\left[\delta(x,y)\right].$

The sampling function $\text{rep}_{X,Y}[\delta(x,y)]$ is illustrated in Figure 1.6a and the sampled function $\text{comb}_{X,Y}[g(x,y)]$ in Figure 1.6b. The delta functions are drawn such that the height of the arrow represents the volume under the delta function, since their amplitudes are all infinite and it is their volumes which are of interest.

Two illustrations are shown in Figure 1.7 of the use of Woodward's notation in describing simple pictures and in finding their two-dimensional transforms with the aid of Table 1.2. Other, equivalent, descriptions can be given for the same figures, and ingenuity is sometimes required to find the most easily transformable description. Frequently the transforms of equivalent descriptions appear to differ from one another, but with manipulation turn out, as they should do, to be identical.

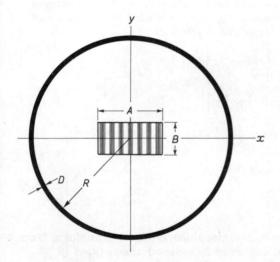

Figure 1.7 (a) A simple test card with sinusoidal vertical bars. The annulus is described as the difference of two circles.

$$g(x,y) = \cos 2\pi u_0 x \cdot rect\left(\frac{x}{A}, \frac{y}{B}\right) + rect\left[\frac{(x^2 + y^2)^{1/2}}{2(R + D)}\right]$$

$$- rect\left[\frac{(x^2 + y^2)^{1/2}}{2R}\right]$$

$$G(u,v) = \frac{AB}{2}\left\{[sinc\ [A(u - u_0), Bv] + sinc\ [A(u + u_0), Bv]\right\}$$

$$+ (u^2 + v^2)^{-1/2}\left\{(R + D)J_1[2\pi(R + D)(u^2 + v^2)^{1/2}]\right.$$

$$\left. - RJ_1[2\pi R(u^2 + v^2)^{1/2}]\right\}$$

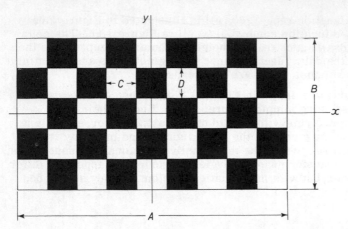

Figure 1.7 (b) A black-and-white chequerboard. A white rectangle and another shifted rectangle are together repeated in xy space and then truncated by a larger rectangle function.

$$g(x, y) = rect\left(\frac{x}{A}, \frac{y}{B}\right) \left\{ rep_{2C, 2D}\left[rect\left(\frac{x}{C}, \frac{y}{D}\right)\right.\right.$$

$$\left.\left. + rect\left(\frac{x - C}{C}, \frac{y - D}{D}\right)\right]\right\}$$

$$G(U, v) = AB \, sinc \, (Au, Bv) * \frac{1}{4} \, comb_{\frac{1}{2C}, \frac{1}{2D}} \{sinc \, (Cu, Dv).$$

$$(1 + exp \, [-j2\pi(Cu + Dv)]\}$$

1.6   Separability

In evaluating any particular two-dimensional Fourier transform from the basic integral, a simplification is introduced when $g(x, y)$ is *separable;* i.e. when

$$g(x, y) = g_1(x) \cdot g_2(y),$$

where $g_1(x)$ and $g_2(y)$ are unidimensional functions of x and y respectively. Substitution in the defining equation for the Fourier transform gives

$$G(u, v) = \int_{-\infty}^{\infty} \int_{-\infty}^{\infty} g(x, y) \, exp \, [-j2\pi(ux + vy)] \, dx \, dy$$

$$= \int_{-\infty}^{\infty} g_1(x) \, exp \, (-j2\pi u x) \, dx \cdot \int_{-\infty}^{\infty} g_2(y) \, exp \, (-j2\pi v y) \, dy$$

$$= G_1(u) \cdot G_2(v)$$

This is a very useful result, since many two-dimensional functions of interest *are* separable, including the functions just defined using Woodward's notation. For example, if

$$g(x,y) = \text{rect}\left(\frac{x}{A}, \frac{y}{B}\right)$$

$$= \text{rect}\left(\frac{x}{A}\right) \cdot \text{rect}\left(\frac{y}{B}\right)$$

then

$$G(u, v) = G_1(u) \cdot G_2(v)$$

$$= |A| \text{ sinc } (Au) \cdot |B| \text{ sinc } (Bv)$$

$$= |AB| \text{ sinc } (Au, Bv)$$

This result is also obtained with the aid of Table 1.2, pairs 2 and 15. The transform of the two-dimensional delta function $\delta(x,y)$ is similarly derived and is equal to unity over the whole u, v plane.

We note that if $g(x,y)$ is separable, then both $\text{rep}_{X,Y}[g(x,y)]$ and $\text{comb}_{X,Y}[g(x,y)]$ are separable, for

$$\text{rep}_{X,Y}[g(x,y)] = \sum_{n=-\infty}^{\infty} \sum_{m=-\infty}^{\infty} g_1(x - nX)g_2(y - mY)$$

$$= \sum_{n=-\infty}^{\infty} g_1(x - nX) \sum_{m=-\infty}^{\infty} g_2(y - mY)$$

$$= \text{rep}_X[g_1(x)] \cdot \text{rep}_Y[g_2(y)]$$

and

$$\text{comb}_{X,Y}[g(x,y)] = \sum_{n=-\infty}^{\infty} \sum_{m=-\infty}^{\infty} g_1(nX)g_2(mY)\,\delta(x - nX)\,\delta(y - mY)$$

$$= \sum_{n=-\infty}^{\infty} g_1(nX)\delta(x - nX) \sum_{m=-\infty}^{\infty} g_2(mY)\delta(y - mY)$$

$$= \text{comb}_X[g_1(x)] \cdot \text{comb}_Y[g_2(y)]$$

1.7   Circular Symmetry

A scanning spot traversing an image may have approximate circular symmetry. In the analysis of scanning we will have cause to examine the effect of the size and shape of the scanning spot on the transmitted

image and we will be involved in taking the Fourier transform of the
function representing the spot. To find the Fourier transform of a
circularly symmetric function, substitute

$$x = r \cos \theta \qquad y = r \sin \theta$$

$$u = \rho \cos \phi \qquad v = \rho \sin \phi$$

These substitutions generate new functions $g_0(r)$ and $G_0(\rho)$ from
$g(x,y)$ and $G(u,v)$ respectively, with

$$G_0(\rho) = \int_{r=0}^{\infty} g_0(r) \int_{\theta=0}^{2\pi} \exp\left(-j2\pi\rho r \cos\theta\right) d\theta \; r \; dr$$

Some transforms of this type are given in the lower part of Table 1.2.
Since

$$\frac{1}{2\pi} \int_0^{2\pi} \exp\left(-jx \cos\theta\right) d\theta = J_0(x),$$

the zero-order Bessel function of the first kind, we may write

$$G_0(\rho) = 2\pi \int_0^{\infty} g_0(r) \, J_0(2\pi\rho r) \, r \; dr$$

Transforms of this type are referred to as *Fourier-Bessel transforms*
or *Hankel transforms of zero order*. For our purposes they are no
more than special cases of the two-dimensional Fourier transform.

1.8   Convolution

When a signal $f(t)$ is filtered by a linear filter whose impulse response
is $h(t)$, it is known (Carlson, 1968) that the output of the filter $g(t)$ is
the convolution of $f(t)$ with $h(t)$, i.e.

$$g(t) = f(t) * h(t)$$

$$= \int_{-\infty}^{\infty} f(t-x) \, h(x) \, dx$$

In our characterisation of image scanning and transmission we shall
find that two-dimensional convolution crops up fairly frequently. This
is because many operations on the image are describable as *spatial
filtering*. In the frequency domain, spatial filtering involves a
modification of the spectrum of an image $F(u,v)$ by a filter function
$H(u,v)$, the process being representable as

$$G(u,v) = F(u,v) \cdot H(u,v)$$

where $G(u,v)$ is the spectrum of the modified image $g(x,y)$. A simple
example of spatial filtering occurs when an image is defocused

(Herriott, 1958). In this case $H(u, v)$ is a function which attenuates the high-frequency components in the image, i.e. $H(u, v)$ represents a spatial low-pass filter.

The space-domain equivalent of two-dimensional filtering is two-dimensional convolution, written as

$$g(x, y) = f(x, y) * h(x, y)$$

$$= \int_{-\infty}^{\infty} \int_{-\infty}^{\infty} f(x - w, y - z) \, h(w, z) \, dw \, dz$$

where w and z are dummy variables of integration. The proof of this result may be obtained by taking the Fourier transform of $g(x, y)$:

$$G(u, v) = \int_{-\infty}^{\infty} \int_{-\infty}^{\infty} [f(x, y) * h(x, y)] \exp[-j2\pi(ux + vy)] \, dx \, dy$$

$$= \int_{-\infty}^{\infty} \int_{-\infty}^{\infty} \int_{-\infty}^{\infty} \int_{-\infty}^{\infty} f(x - w, y - z) \, h(w, z) dw \, dz \ .$$

$$\exp[-j2\pi(ux + vy)] \, dx \, dy$$

Changing the order of integration, we have

$$G(u, v) = \int_{-\infty}^{\infty} \int_{-\infty}^{\infty} h(w, z).$$

$$\left\{ \int_{-\infty}^{\infty} \int_{-\infty}^{\infty} f(x - w, y - z) \exp[-j2\pi(ux + vy)] \, dx \, dy \right\} dw \, dz$$

The double integral inside the brackets is the Fourier transform of $f(x, y)$ shifted to $x = w, y = z$ and, when evaluated, is equal to $F(u, v)$. $\exp[-j2\pi(wu + zv)]$ (Table 1.2, No. 3). This gives us

$$G(u, v) = F(u, v) . \int_{-\infty}^{\infty} \int_{-\infty}^{\infty} h(w, z) \exp[-j2\pi(wu + zv)] \, dw \, dz$$

$$= F(u, v) . H(u, v)$$

Two-dimensional convolution may be interpreted graphically on the wz plane as shown in Figure 1.8. One of the functions, say $f(w, z)$ is shifted from the origin to the point $w = x, z = y$. It is then rotated through 180°, followed by multiplication with the other function $h(w, z)$. The volume under the resultant surface is the value of the convolution integral for the particular values of x and y chosen.

It is instructive to note that the shift of $f(x, y)$ to a point $x = A$, $y = B$ can itself be represented as a convolution:

$$f(x - A, y - B) = f(x, y) * \delta(x - A, y - B)$$

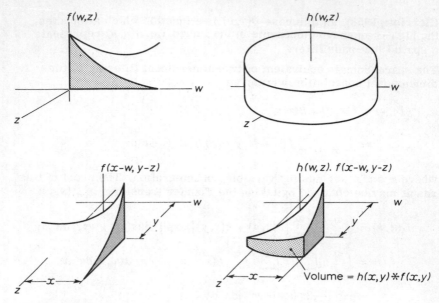

Figure 1.8 Graphical representation of two-dimensional convolution.

the delta function being located at the point to which the desired shift is required. This result follows from the *sifting property* of the delta function (Bracewell, 1965), the two-dimensional sifting property being derivable from the one-dimensional case as follows:

$$f(x,y) * \delta(x - A, y - B)$$

$$= \int_{-\infty}^{\infty} \int_{-\infty}^{\infty} f(w, z)\, \delta[(x - A) - w, (y - B) - z]\mathrm{d}w\ \mathrm{d}z$$

$$= \int_{-\infty}^{\infty} \delta[(y - B) - z] \int_{-\infty}^{\infty} f(w, z)\, \delta[(x - A) - w]\mathrm{d}w\ \mathrm{d}z$$

$$= \int_{-\infty}^{\infty} \delta[(y - B) - z]\, f(x - A, z)\mathrm{d}z$$

$$= f(x - A, y - B)$$

Some useful two-dimensional relations whose proof is left as an exercise to the reader are:

(i) $\delta(x) * \delta(y) = 1$

(ii) $\mathrm{rep}_{X,Y}[g(x,y)] = g(x,y) * \mathrm{rep}_{X,Y}[\delta(x,y)]$

1.9   Sampling

The fundamental process of scanning, by which an image is trans-mitted over a channel or input to a computer for processing, is describable in idealised form as multidimensional sampling. Two-dimensional sampling can be written mathematically as

$$\text{comb}_{X,Y}[g(x,y)] = g(x,y) \cdot \text{rep}_{X,Y}[\delta(x,y)]$$

The spectrum of $\text{comb}_{X,Y}[g(x,y)]$ is found by using the relationship that multiplication in the x,y domain is equivalent to convolution in the u,v domain. If we let

$$f(x,y) = \text{comb}_{X,Y}[g(x,y)]$$

and

$$d(x,y) = \text{rep}_{X,Y}[\delta(x,y)]$$

then

$$F(u,v) = G(u,v) * D(u,v)$$

Since $d(x,y)$ is a separable function it may be written

$$d(x,y) = \text{rep}_X[\delta(x)] \cdot \text{rep}_Y[\delta(y)]$$

Hence, from Table 1.1,

$$D(u,v) = \frac{1}{|X|} \text{comb}_{1/X}[1] \cdot \frac{1}{|Y|} \text{comb}_{1/Y}[1]$$

$$= \frac{1}{|X|} \text{rep}_{1/X}[\delta(u)] \cdot \frac{1}{|Y|} \text{rep}_{1/Y}[\delta(v)]$$

$$= \frac{1}{|XY|} \text{rep}_{1/X,\,1/Y}[\delta(u,v)]$$

$$\therefore F(u,v) = \frac{1}{|XY|} \text{rep}_{1/X,\,1/Y}[G(u,v)]$$

The effect of two-dimensional sampling is to cause $G(u,v)$ to be replicated throughout the u,v plane, the replications being at

$$u = 0, \pm \frac{1}{X}, \pm \frac{2}{X}, \pm \frac{3}{X} \ldots, v = 0, \pm \frac{1}{Y}, \pm \frac{2}{Y}, \pm \frac{3}{Y}, \ldots$$

The analogy with unidimensional sampling is apparent.

1.10   Two-dimensional Bandwidth and the Sampling Theorem

In forming an image $g(x,y)$ of a scene by means of a lens, it is found that very fine detail in the original scene does not appear in the image.

The better the lens, the better it is able to resolve this fine detail, but there comes a point, however good the lens may be and however sharply it may be focused, when the fineness of the detail exceeds the resolving power of the lens and the detail is lost. There is therefore, another significant difference between an image and the original scene which we have not yet considered and that is that an image has a limited *spatial bandwidth* (Hopkins, 1962). We could attempt to measure the filtering action of the lens by putting a card with a two-dimensional sinusoidal variation of reflectance in the field of view and illuminating it uniformly, then the luminance of the card will be given by $\cos[2\pi(ux + vy) + \phi]$ as in Figure 1.2. We could then proceed to measure the spatial bandwidth W in cycles per centimetre by increasing the spatial frequency $(u^2 + v^2)^{1/2}$ (e.g. by using a set of cards with different spatial frequencies and noting the fall-off in the amplitude of the sinusoidal variation of illuminance in the image). We would have to specify a criterion of some sort in order to fix the bandwidth W. This might be the 3 dB or 20 dB point or perhaps the cut-off point, when the lens completely failed to resolve the stripes and the image was uniformly grey. Measurements would have to be taken with an objective measuring technique, e.g. by scanning the stripes in the image with a fine spot and measuring the amplitude of the electrical sinusoid, since judgement by eye could lead to error, the eye being itself a spatial low-pass filter.

The ratio of the amplitudes of the imaged and original spatial sine waves, plotted as a function of sine wave frequency, is termed the frequency response or *modulation transfer function* (MTF) of the lens or optical system. Practical methods for measuring the MTF of lenses are a little more sophisticated than the one just mentioned (Herriott, 1958; Hopkins, 1962; Sproson and Hacking, 1963) and take account of the variation in response as a function of the position of the spatial sine wave in the field of view of the lens. The MTF may typically decrease with increasing distance from the optical axis and may depend on whether the angular alignment of the sine wave is sagittal or tangential. If the effect of spatial displacement on the frequency response is negligible (strictly zero), the response is said to be *space-invariant* or *isoplanatic* (Fellgett and Linfoot, 1955). Although this condition seldom holds in practical cases, an average or weighted MTF is sometimes used as single figure for the whole lens. Lenses may also exhibit a response (spurious resolution) beyond the first point of cut-off due to ripples in the amplitude and phase characteristic.

The bandwidth of the image spectrum $G(u, v)$ is determined both by the nature of the scene and the filtering properties of the lens. In the general case the bandwidth of $G(u, v)$ must be specified for every angle θ (Figure 1.9) but in special cases may be reduced to one or, more commonly, two numbers. When $G(u, v)$ is circularly symmetric, one number W suffices to describe its bandwidth, while if it is rectangular (often because it is separable into two components $G_1(u)$

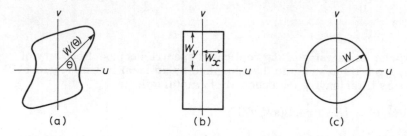

Figure 1.9 Image spectra $G(u, v)$. In (a) the bandwidth must be specified as a function $W(\theta)$ of the angle θ; in (b), $G(u, v)$ is rectangular and two number W_x and W_y suffice; in (c) a single number W describes bandwidth for a circularly symmetric function.

and $G_2(v)$) two numbers, W_x and W_y, suffice. The numerical value of the bandwidth is taken as half of the total width or extent of the figure, as in Figure 1.9 b. The negative frequency components merely mirror the positive frequency components, for $g(x, y)$ real.

When $g(x, y)$ is sampled, its spectrum $G(u, v)$ is replicated in u, v space. The sampling theorem in two dimensions is a little more complicated than in one dimension (Peterson and Middleton, 1962). The simple case is that of Figure 1.9 b, when the bandwidth is given by two numbers W_x and W_y. The analysis of this case follows. In the case of spectra of the type in Figure 1.9 a and Figure 1.9 c a rectangular sampling lattice may not be the most efficient one. The problem is to devise a sampling lattice and corresponding replication lattice which pack as many replications as possible into a given area of u, v space without overlap or *aliasing*. The solution to this problem is dependent on the exact shape of $G(u, v)$ and may only be derivable by inspection.

Rectangular sampling

Consider the two-dimensional sampling of a function $g(x, y)$ which is strictly bandlimited to W_x, W_y; i.e.

$$G(u, v) = 0, \ |u| > W_x$$

$$= 0, \ |v| > W_y$$

Sampling of $g(x, y)$ at intervals of X along the x axis and Y along the y axis causes replication of $G(u, v)$ at intervals of $1/X$ and $1/Y$ along the u and v axes respectively. Clearly, if

$$W_x < \frac{1}{2X}$$

and $W_\mathrm{y} < \dfrac{1}{2Y}$

no overlap or aliasing of the replicated spectra occurs. Recovery of $g(x,y)$ from its samples is then possible by an ideal two-dimensional low-pass filter having the spectral characteristic

$$H(u, v) = |XY| \text{ rect } (uX, vY)$$

the amplification factor $|XY|$ being necessary to restore the original amplitude of $g(x,y)$. If $F(u, v)$ is the spectrum of the sampled function, the output of the filter is

$$F(u, v) . H(u, v)$$

$$= \frac{1}{|XY|} \text{ rep}_{1/X, \, 1/Y} [G(u,v)] . |XY| \text{ rect } (uX, vY)$$

$$= G(u, v)$$

This is shown in Figure 1.10. In the space domain, ideal low-pass filtering becomes (Table 1.2, Nos. 2, 11, and 16)

$$g(x,y) = f(x,y) * h(x,y)$$

$$= \text{comb}_{X, Y} [g(x,y)] * \text{sinc} \left(\frac{x}{X}, \frac{y}{Y} \right)$$

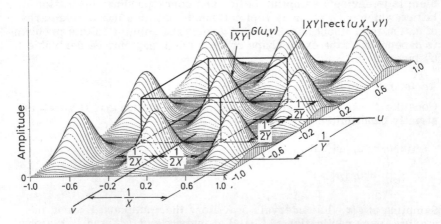

Figure 1.10 Spectral representation of the recovery of a function from its samples by two-dimensional low-pass filtering. The rectangular box is an ideal low-pass filter which excludes all replications except the baseband one centred on $u = 0, v = 0$.

To recover $g(x,y)$ from its samples, therefore, an interpolation function of the form sinc $(x/X, y/Y)$ must be superimposed on every sample. This function has the value unity at $x = 0, y = 0$ and is zero at all other sampling points $x = nX, y = mY, n = \pm1, \pm2, \pm3 \ldots$, $m = \pm1, \pm2, \pm3, \ldots$

Point-spread and line-spread functions

The function $h(x,y) = $ sinc $(x/Y, y/Y)$ can be regarded as the two-dimensional impulse response of the low-pass filter $H(u,v)$, since this is the filter ouput for a delta function input $\delta(x,y)$. The two-dimensional impulse response is often called the *point-spread function*, since $\delta(x,y)$ represents a point of light, which would appear as $h(x,y)$ at the far end of an optical system having the transfer function $H(u,v)$.

The *line-spread function* is the response of the system of an infinitely thin line of light, represented by an impulse sheet $\delta(x)$ or $\delta(y)$. It is just the unidimensional response in a given spatial direction expressed in two-dimensional terms; its use is appropriate when $H(u,v)$ is separable.

The unidimensional Fourier transform of the line-spread function is termed the *optical transfer function* (OTF). It is in general a complex function $H_1(u)$ or $H_2(v)$, depending on the axial direction being considered; its modulus is the *modulation transfer function* (MTF) which we previously mentioned in connection with lenses. When the line-spread function is an even function of space, the OTF is real and equal to the MTF.

Images of finite spatial extent

It should be noted that the sampling theorem in two dimensions can never apply exactly to practical images which are of finite spatial extent. It is a property of the Fourier transform that when a function is truncated in the spatial domain its spectrum extends to infinity and cannot therefore be strictly bandlimited. This can be seen by multiplying a bandlimited image of infinite extent by the truncating function rect $(x/A, y/B)$, A and B being constants. In the frequency domain this results in convolution of the image spectrum with $|AB|$ sinc (Au, Bv), a function which is infinite in extent in both u and v directions. Consideration of the nature of convolution (Figure 1.8) leads to the conclusion that the truncated image spectrum also extends to infinity.

1.11   Probabilistic Signals in Two Dimensions

Communication signals are not in general describable as deterministic functions, since to convey information they need to behave with some unpredictability. This is also true of images and video signals. The deterministic representation $g(x,y)$ or $g(x,y,t)$ for specific images is useful in analysing the system response, but an alternative probabilistic approach has been found to be useful too, particularly in the field of image coding. Probabilistic representations allow in- : formation—theoretic descriptions and also serve to characterise noise.

Entropy of images

Shannon (1948) introduced the concept of average self-information or *entropy* into the language of communication engineering. In the case of a source generating statistically independent symbols from an ensemble of values, where the outcome is a random variable X with probability density function $p(x)$, the entropy $H(X)$ is given by

$$H(X) = -\int_x p(x) \log p(x) \mathrm{d}x$$

or in the case of source with nth-order statistical dependence between symbols, by

$$H(X) = -\int_{x_1} \int_{x_2} \dots \int_{x_n} p(x_1, x_2, \dots x_n).$$

$$\log p(x_1, x_2 \dots x_n) \mathrm{d}x_1 \, \mathrm{d}x_2 \dots \mathrm{d}x_n$$

where $p(x_1, x_2, \dots x_n)$ is the joint probability density function of a block of n symbols. These expressions can be written with summation signs in place of the integral signs in the special case where X is a discrete random variable.

In the application of these concepts to images, it is difficult to identify the appropriate ensemble of source signals. In a simple description, we could specify the first-order probability density function for illuminance in the image or luminance in the display, for which we have previously used the letter g. This would give us a function $p(g), g \geqslant 0$. We might note, however, that this simple description does not take into account the statistical dependency or correlation that is observed in practice between points near to one another in the image (the probabilistic equivalent of the predominance of low spatial frequencies in images). Elaborating, therefore, we might specify the nth-order joint probability density function (PDF) $p(g_1, g_2, \dots g_n)$ for n points in the image at Nyquist sample spacings. To encompass all the samples in the image, however, n needs to be very large and the description becomes intractable.

In practice probabilistic descriptions in terms of joint PDFs are used and have been estimated (Kretzmer, 1952; Schreiber, 1956) for a small number n of spatially adjacent picture elements. From these estimates it is possible to calculate the entropy of picture signals on a limited basis and evaluate the possibilities for statistical encoding. However, because of the difficulties of compiling comprehensive statistics, especially when the third dimension of time is involved as

well, it has not been possible, with any generality, to evaluate the
information content of images in the Shannon sense. In the practical
evaluations of entropy it has proved to be more helpful first to perform an irreversible operation on the image to define its source
ensemble and only thereafter to attempt to calculate entropy and
coding procedures. These operations have become known as source
encoding and channel encoding respectively, the first being guided
by the properties of vision so as to minimise the subjective error.
We will pursue these considerations in later chapters.

Autocorrelation functions, energy and power density spectra

An alternative approach relies on the *autocorrelation function,*
which has the advantage that it leads directly to the power spectrum.
Recalling the unidimensional case (Bracewell, 1965), the autocorrelation function of a stochastic finite-energy signal $g(t)$ is

$$r(\tau) = \int_{-\infty}^{\infty} g(t)\, g(t + \tau) \mathrm{d}t$$

which is a kind of rough practical measure of the degree in which
values of $g(t)$ at an interval τ are statistically dependent on one
another. The unidimensional Fourier transform of $r(\tau)$ is the energy
density spectrum:

$$|G(f)|^2 = \int_{-\infty}^{\infty} r(\tau) \mathrm{e}^{-\mathrm{j}2\pi f \tau} \mathrm{d}\tau$$

Proceeding analogously to the two-dimensional case, we characterise
the random signal or noise by $g(x,y)$. Our interest again turns to
whether spatially adjacent values of $g(x,y)$ are statistically dependent
or independent. This time, however, we may be interested in the
dependency between any two points in the x,y plane. We therefore
define the *two-dimensional autocorrelation function* for a finite-energy
signal $g(x,y)$ as

$$r(\alpha,\beta) = \int_{-\infty}^{\infty} \int_{-\infty}^{\infty} g(x,y)\, g(x + \alpha, y + \beta) \mathrm{d}x\, \mathrm{d}y$$

which in turn gives us the *two-dimensional energy density spectrum*
as its Fourier transform:

$$|G(u,v)|^2 = \int_{-\infty}^{\infty} \int_{-\infty}^{\infty} r(\alpha,\beta)\, \exp\left[-\mathrm{j}2\pi\,(\alpha u + \beta v)\right] \mathrm{d}\alpha\, \mathrm{d}\beta$$

Two-dimensional noise

For infinite-energy signals the autocorrelation function is defined as:

$$r(\alpha,\beta) = \lim_{X \to \infty} \lim_{X \to \infty} \frac{1}{XY} \int_{-Y/2}^{Y/2} \int_{-X/2}^{X/2} g(x,y) g(x + \alpha, y + \beta)\, \mathrm{d}x\, \mathrm{d}y$$

Table 1.3 Three-dimensional Fourier transforms

Description	Function	Transform
1 Definition	$g(x, y, t)$	$G(u, v, f) =$ $\int_{-\infty}^{\infty} \int_{-\infty}^{\infty} \int_{-\infty}^{\infty} g(x, y, t) .$ $\exp[-j2\pi(ux + vy + ft)]$ $dx\ dy\ dt$
2 Scaling	$g(x/A, y/B, t/T)$	$\|ABT\| . G(u, v, f)$
3 Spatio-temporal shift	$g(x - A, y - B, t - T)$	$G(u, v, f) .$ $\exp[-j2\pi(Au + Bv + Tf)]$
4 Frequency shift	$g(x, y, t) .$ $\exp[j2\pi(Cx + Dy + Ff)]$	$G(u - C, v - D, f - F)$
5 Complex conjugate	$g^*(x, y, t)$	$G^*(-u, -v, -f)$
6 Reciprocity	$G(x, y, t)$	$g(-u, -v, -f)$
7 Addition	$A . g(x, y, t) + B . h(x, y, t)$	$A . G(u, v, f) + B . H(u, v, f)$
8 Multiplication	$g(x, y, t) . h(x, y, t)$	$G(u, v, f) * H(u, v, f)$
9 Convolution	$g(x, y, t) * h(x, y, t)$	$G(u, v, f) . H(u, v, f)$
10 Delta function	$\delta(x, y, t)$	1
11 Constant	1	$\delta(u, v, f)$
12 Separable function	$g(x, y, t) = g_1(x) . g_2(y) . g_3(t)$	$G(u, v, f) = G_1(u) . G_2(v) . G_3(f)$
13 Rectangular function	$\text{rect}(x, y, t)$	$\text{rect sinc}(u, v, f)$
14 Sinc function	$\text{sinc}(x, y, t)$	$\text{rect}(u, v, f)$
15 Repeated function	$\text{rep}_{X, Y, T}[g(x, y, t)]$	$\dfrac{1}{\|XYT\|} . \text{comb}_{\frac{1}{X}, \frac{1}{Y}, \frac{1}{T}}[G(u, v, f)]$
16 Sampled function	$\text{comb}_{X, Y, T}[g(x, y, t)]$	$\dfrac{1}{\|XYT\|} . \text{rep}_{\frac{1}{X}, \frac{1}{Y}, \frac{1}{T}}[G(u, v, f)]$

Table 1.3 (contd.)

Description	Function	Transform
Functions with cylindrical symmetry		
$r^2 = x^2 + y^2$		$\rho^2 = u^2 + v^2$
17 Cylinder	$\text{rect}\left(\dfrac{r}{2R}\right) \cdot \text{rect}(t)$	$\dfrac{R}{\rho} \cdot J_1(2\pi R\rho) \cdot \text{sinc}(f)$
Functions with spherical symmetry		
	$q^2 = x^2 + y^2 + t^2$	$s^2 = u^2 + v^2 + f^2$
18 Gaussian function	$e^{-\pi q^2}$	$e^{-\pi s^2}$
19 Sphere	$\text{rect}\left(\dfrac{q}{2}\right)$	$\dfrac{\sin 2\pi s - 2\pi s \cos 2\pi s}{2\pi^2 s^3}$

and the *two-dimensional power density spectrum* $S(u, v)$ as its Fourier transform, by the Wiener-Kinchine theorem. Through this concept we can describe the spectral distribution of noise power in the u, v plane and the degree to which the noise may be filtered to reduce its overall power and visibility. As a special case, if

$$r(\alpha, \beta) = \delta(\alpha, \beta)$$

then

$$S(u, v) = 1$$

by Table 1.2, No. 12. This noise has a constant power density spectrum for all values of u, v and is termed *two-dimensional white noise*.

Imagine that an optical system having a spatial frequency response rect $(u/2W_x, v/2W_y)$ is presented at its input with white noise, i.e. a picture with random perturbations of luminance in all directions, having an impulsive autocorrelation function. If, say, $W_x \ll W_y$ the output of the system will be another random picture but with a good deal of statistical dependency introduced in the x direction, less in the y. The visual appearance of computer-generated pictures of this kind is illustrated in a paper by Julesz (1962). Changes in the degree of correlation in a random picture change its texture and also its visibility when regarded as an interfering pattern.

1.12   Further Developments in Two-dimensional Fourier Theory

There are a number of other concepts in unidimensional Fourier theory which carry over quite easily into two dimensions, for example, conservation of energy, represented by Parseval's theorem, the use of moments for partial information about spectral decay, one-sided spectra, analytic signals, etc. Many of these concepts can be derived with the aid of Table 1.2. Some interesting relationships stem from the reciprocity between spatial and frequency domains (Table 1.2, No. 8).

1.13   The Three-dimensional Fourier Transform

The three-dimensional Fourier transform of a function $g(x, y, t)$, which might represent an image of a scene containing moving objects, is given by

$$G(u, v, f) = \int_{\infty}^{-\infty} \int_{-\infty}^{-\infty} \int_{-\infty}^{-\infty} g(x, y, t) \exp \left[-j2\pi(ux + vy + ft)\right] dx\, dy\, dt$$

and the inverse transform by

$$g(x, y, t) = \int_{-\infty}^{\infty} \int_{-\infty}^{\infty} \int_{-\infty}^{\infty} G(u, v, f) \exp \left[+j2\pi(ux + vy + ft)\right] du\, dv\, df$$

A list of three-dimensional transforms is given in Table 1.3. With an understanding of the previous sections dealing with two-dimensional transforms, the table should be readily interpretable. Simplifications again result when the function $g(x, y, t)$ is separable, either as

$$g(x, y, t) = g_1(x) \cdot g_2(y) \cdot g_3(t)$$

or in combinations such as

$$g(x, y, t) = g_0(x, y) \cdot g_3(t)$$

Extension of Woodward's notation to three dimensions

Woodward's notation is readily extended to the third dimension, with definitions

(1)   rect (x, y, t) = rect (x) . rect (y) . rect (t)

$\qquad\qquad$ = rect (x, y) . rect (t)

(2)   sinc (x, y, t) = sinc (x) . sinc (y) . sinc (t)

$\qquad\qquad$ = sinc (x, y) . sinc (t)

(3) $\text{rep}_{X, Y, T} \left[g(x, y, t)\right] =$

$$\sum_{n=-\infty}^{\infty} \sum_{m=-\infty}^{\infty} \sum_{k=-\infty}^{\infty} g(x - nX, y - mY, t - kT)$$

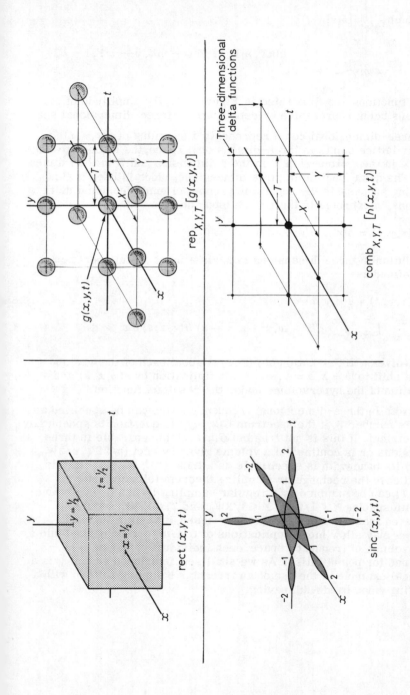

Figure 1.11 Representation of the four Woodward functions in three-dimensional form.

(4) $\text{comb}_{X,Y,T}\left[h(x,y,t)\right]$

$$= \sum_{n=-\infty}^{\infty} \sum_{m=-\infty}^{\infty} \sum_{k=-\infty}^{\infty} h(nX, mY, kT)\delta(x - mX, y - mY, t - kT)$$

These functions are illustrated in Figure 1.11, the amplitude of the functions being represented by density in the three-dimensional space.

The three-dimensional comb represents a sampling of $g(x,y,t)$ at regular lattice points in three-dimensional space, the lattice spacings being X in the x dimension, Y in the y dimension and T in the t dimension. The delta function in three dimensions, which is used in this sampling process, is the separable product of unidimensional delta functions, interpreted in the generalised-function sense:

$$\delta(x,y,t) = \delta(x) \, . \, \delta(y) \, . \, \delta(t)$$

Convolution in three dimensions is again a most useful operation. It is defined as

$$f(x,y,t) * h(x,y,t)$$

$$=\int_{-\infty}^{\infty} \int_{-\infty}^{\infty} \int_{-\infty}^{\infty} f(x-w, y-z, t-s) \, h(w,z,s) \, \mathrm{d}w \, \mathrm{d}z \, \mathrm{d}s$$

and involves a 180° rotation of $f(w,z,s)$ about each of the w, z and s axes, a shift to $w = x, z = y, s = t$, multiplication by $h(w,z,s)$ and evaluation of the hypervolume under the resultant function.

Bandwidth in three-dimensional frequency space can be specified as a single number W if the spectrum $G(u,v,f)$ in question is spherically symmetrical. If this is not true but $G(u,v,f)$ is separable in three dimensions or is confined to a volume given by rect $(u/2W_x, v/2W_y, f/2W_t)$ its bandwidth is specifiable as a triad (W_x, W_y, W_t). In this second case the rectangular sampling theorem tells us that $g(x,y,t)$ can be sampled by a regular sampling lattice or comb function with spacing $X < 1/2W_x$, $Y < 1/2W_y$ and $T < 1/2W_t$ and fully recovered from its samples. In other cases, irregular sampling patterns may allow more replications of $G(u,v,f)$ to be packed into a given volume of frequency space; each individual case has to be examined for possibilities. As we shall see, interlaced scanning is a practical example of the use of an irregular sampling pattern with a resulting video bandwidth saving.

Chapter 2

PROPERTIES OF THE EYE AFFECTING
SYSTEM DESIGN

It is a well-established principle in the design of systems for the transmission or display of pictorial information, that what the eye does not see, the system need not transmit or display. To transmit a physical description of an image which is overspecified in terms of what the human observer can perceive is to waste channel bandwidth and money. The guiding principle is one of *economy of representation*, and before we can proceed to an examination of the requirements for the scanning, coding, transmission and display of pictorial information, we need to look at the human receiver of that information. From the point of view of our understanding it is encouraging that engineering concepts such as filtering and Fourier analysis are being used by psychologists and physiologists in their descriptions of visual processes (Campbell, 1968; Levinson, 1972).

In a brief treatment of this kind it is necessary to resort to over-simplification. The eye is in reality an instrument of fascinating complexity, whose physiology and interconnection with the brain are subjects of active research and experimentation. We shall attempt only to abstract from the wealth of existing data a few essential properties that are relevant to our purposes. It is as well to bear in mind that simplifications need qualifications, the qualifications being in this case those of restricted values of stimulus luminance, angular subtense and so on. In engineering terms, the eye is not a linear device, either in its temporal or spatial response, but may be treated as approximately linear under restricted viewing conditions.

2.1 Angle Subtended at the Eye

Displayed pictures are of various sizes and are viewed at various distances. A large picture viewed at a large distance can produce an image on the retina which is the same size as that of small picture viewed at a short distance. The retina can resolve detail better when the retinal image is larger and spread over more of its photoreceptors; so the angle θ subtended at the eye by the display (Figure 2.1), which determines the retinal image size, is an important parameter in indicating how well the eye is likely to resolve detail in the picture. For this reason spatial frequencies in a picture are often expressed in cycles per degree or cycles per radian rather than in cycles per centimetre, if an experimenter has the human viewer in mind. Table 2.1 lists some conversion figures.

The retina is not a homogeneous structure (Le Grand, 1968; Davson,

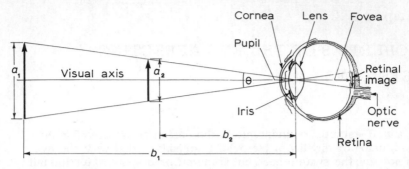

Figure 2.1 Showing how the angle subtended by a display at the eye $\theta = 2\ arctan\ (a_1/2_{b_1}) = 2\ arctan\ (a_2/2_{b_2})$ *determines the retinal image size.*

1972) the central area or *fovea* being capable of high resolution (and good colour vision) with a fall-off in performance in the extra-foveal region.

The foveal area subtends an angle which is estimated to be between 1° and 2°; a finger held up at arm's length subtends roughly this angle and constitutes an engineer's guide to foveal vision. It is readily verified by this means that domestic television displays subtend 5-15° at typical viewing distances and are therefore seen largely with extrafoveal vision. Since, in the transmission of pictures, the transmitter does not usually know how many viewers are watching the picture or where they are looking at any particular time, the system designer has to arrange that resolution over the whole picture satisfies foveal vision. Feedback systems with tracking of the viewer's eye movements have not yet been found to be practicable.

2.2   Response to Radiant Energy

The V_λ curve

Light is a form of radiated electromagnetic energy. The physical description of radiant energy is usually made in terms of certain concepts and units which were agreed by the *Commission Internationale de l'Eclairage* (CIE) in 1957 and have since been incorporated in the International System of Units (SI). A summary of these radiometric concepts and units is given in Table 2.2

The band of radiant energy which is visible to the eye is quite narrow, extending from approximately 400 to 700 nanometres (nm). Energy near the centre of this band produces a greater sensation of brightness than does energy near the extremities. Careful measurements of the relative response of the eye to monochromatic light of various wavelengths have been made by various research workers and, although variability of response is encountered from subject to subject,

Table 2.1 Conversion between spatial frequency in cycles per centimetre and cycles per degree subtended at the eye. The function tabulated is $u/[2 \arctan(1/200D)]$, where D is the viewing distance in meters and u the spatial frequency in cycles per centimetre. The table entries in italics are frequencies beyond the eye's cut-off frequency under average display viewing conditions.

Spatial frequency (cycles/cm)	Viewing distance (metres)									
	0.5	1	1.5	2	3	4	5	10	20	50
	Spatial frequency (cycles/degree)									
0.01	0.01	0.02	0.03	0.03	0.05	0.07	0.09	0.17	0.35	0.87
0.05	0.04	0.09	0.13	0.17	0.26	0.35	0.44	0.87	1.7	4.4
0.1	0.09	0.17	0.26	0.35	0.52	0.70	0.87	1.7	3.5	8.7
0.2	0.17	0.35	0.52	0.70	1.0	1.4	1.7	3.5	7.0	17
0.4	0.35	0.70	1.0	1.4	2.1	2.8	3.5	7.0	14	35
0.6	0.52	1.0	1.6	2.1	3.1	4.2	5.2	10	21	52
0.8	0.70	1.4	2.1	2.8	4.2	5.6	7.0	14	28	70
1	0.87	1.7	2.6	3.5	5.2	7.0	8.7	17	35	87
2	1.7	3.5	5.2	7.0	10	14	17	35	70	175
4	3.5	7.0	10	14	21	28	35	70	140	349
6	5.2	10	16	21	31	42	52	105	209	524
8	7.0	14	21	28	42	56	70	140	279	698
10	8.7	17	26	35	52	70	87	175	349	873
20	17	35	52	70	105	140	175	349	698	—
40	35	70	105	140	209	279	349	698	—	—
60	52	105	157	209	314	419	524	—	—	—
80	70	140	209	279	419	559	698	—	—	—
100	87	175	262	349	524	698	873	—	—	—

Table 2.2   Radiometric Concepts and units

Concept	Symbol	SI unit*	Qualitative description
Radiant flux	P_e	watt (W)	total radiated power emitted from a given surface or falling on that surface
Irradiance	E_e	W/m²	radiant flux received per unit surface area
Radiant emittance	M_e	W/m²	radiant flux emitted per unit surface area
Radiant intensity	I_e	W/steradian (sr)	radiant flux emitted from a point source per unit solid angle in a given direction
Radiance	L_e	W/(m² sr)	extension of the concept of radiant intensity to extended sources; the radiant intensity per unit area normal to the given direction.

*   British Standards Institution BS 3763: 1970 *The International System of Units (SI)*

this is small enough to have made possible the specification by the CIE of the response of a *standard observer*. This response is termed the relative luminous efficiency curve of the standard observer, or the V_λ curve, which is tabulated in Table 2.3 and illustrated in Figure 2.2, both for the case of 2 degree vision, which is substantially foveal, and 10 degree vision which is substantially extrafoveal and is more appropriate for large areas in displays.

In engineering terms, the eye acts as a bandpass filter to radiant energy, the peak response being obtained at 555 nm.

Photometry

If an electrical bandpass filter having a response $|H(\lambda)|^2$ identical to that in Figure 2.2 were presented, not with a sinusoidal input, but with a signal having a continuous power density spectrum $|F(\lambda)|^2$, the power density spectrum of the output $|G(\lambda)|^2$ would be given by†

$$|G(\lambda)|^2 = |H(\lambda)|^2 \cdot |F(\lambda)|^2$$

† The spectra here are specified as functions of wavelength λ rather than frequency to correspond to the conventional practice in photometry.

Table 2.3 Selected ordinates of the relative luminous efficiency curves for the 1931 CIE standard (2 degree) observer and the 1964 CIE supplementary large-field (10 degree) observer.

Wavelength λ (nm)	2 degree field	10 degree field
380	0.0000	0.0000
400	0.0004	0.0020
420	0.0040	0.0214
440	0.0230	0.0621
460	0.0600	0.1282
480	0.1390	0.2536
500	0.3230	0.4608
520	0.7100	0.7618
540	0.9540	0.9620
560	0.9950	0.9973
580	0.8700	0.8689
600	0.6310	0.6583
620	0.3810	0.3981
640	0.1750	0.1798
660	0.0610	0.0603
680	0.0170	0.0159
700	0.0041	0.0037
720	0.0010	0.0008
740	0.0002	0.0002
760	0.0001	0.0000
780	0.0000	0.0000

provided the filter was linear and the principle of superposition applied. It is fortunate and remarkable that the eye turns out to be very nearly linear under typical viewing conditions and that we may indeed calculate its output in this way. The total power at the output of the filter is

$$\int_0^\infty |G(\lambda)|^2 d\lambda = \int_0^\infty |H(\lambda)|^2 \, |F(\lambda)|^2 d\lambda$$

which, in the conventional notation of photometry, becomes

$$L = k_m \int_0^\infty V_\lambda L_{e\lambda} d\lambda$$

k_m being a constant, and V_λ being the function illustrated in Figure 2.2 (the 2 degree function unless otherwise stated) and $L_{e\lambda}$ being the

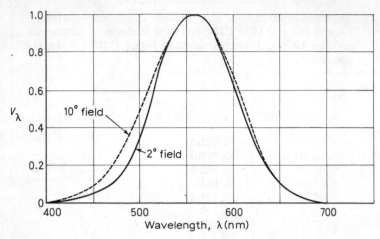

Figure 2.2 The CIE relative luminous efficiency curve V_λ for the standard observer, for both 2 degree and 10 degree photopic (daylight) vision.

radiance density of the stimulus as a function of λ. The quality L is termed the *luminance* of the stimulus. It is a single number representing the brightness as seen by the standard observer, whose responses will be close to that of most observers with normal vision. If k_m is made equal to $680\,\text{lm/W}$, L will be in candelas per square metre. This value of k_m does not define the candela; rather it is itself determined from the definition of the candela. Table 2.4 gives a table of photometric concepts and units which are related to the radiometric units of Table 2.2 by integral equations of this sort, e.g. illuminance E is given by

$$E = k_m \int_0^\infty V_\lambda E_{e\lambda}\,\mathrm{d}\lambda$$

where $E_{e\lambda}$ is the irradiance density as a function of wavelength.

In using the filter analogy for the response of the eye, it should be borne in mind that the filter output is not radiant energy, but a subjective sensation or response. A system such as this in which the input is a physically measurable quantity and the output a psychological response is termed a *psychophysical* system. To measure the psychological response we have to ask the subject questions or make him perform tasks, but the techniques for doing this have become quite sophisticated and reliable. By *defining* the psychological (brightness) response of a standard observer to light of various wavelengths, the CIE has made luminance into an *objective* measure, something which can be read from an instrument without the need for psychological tests. Therein lies its usefulness.

Table 2.4   Photometric concepts and units

Concept	Symbol	SI unit	Related radiometric concept
Luminous flux	F	lumen (lm) (a uniform point source having $I = 1$ candela emits 1 lumen per steradian)	radiant flux
Illuminance	E	lux (lx) (1 lux = 1 lm/m^2)	irradiance
Luminous emittance	M	lux	radiant emittance
Luminous intensity	I	candela (cd) (A blackbody radiator of area $(1/6) \times 10^{-5}$ m^2 at the temperature of freezing platinum and under pressure of 101 325 N/m^2 has a luminous intensity normal to the surface of 1 candela)	radiant intensity
Luminance	L	cd/m^2	radiance

Useful conversion factors
1 footlambert (fL) = 3.426 cd/m^2
1 millilambert (mL) = 3.183 cd/m^2
1 footcandle (fcd) = 10.76 lux

In addition to a sensation of brightness the eye sees both monochromatic stimuli and continuous spectral distributions as having *colour*. In a later chapter we shall see that, interestingly enough, colour can be specified for a standard observer using the same linear bandpass filter approach.

It should now be apparent why the photometric concept of illuminance is used to characterise light falling on the image plane rather than irradiance. Light with a high irradiance may be barely visible, but light with a high illuminance appears bright to all humans with normal vision. In the same way, luminance is used in preference to radiance to specify the output of a luminous source such as a CRT display. The luminances encountered in typical CRT displays fall in the range 0.1-1000 cd/m^2, the lower figure corresponding to the very dark parts of a low-level display and the upper figure to the highlights of a bright display (in any one display the ratio of maximum to minimum luminance is unlikely to be much more than 100 : 1 or 2 log units and is typically less than this). This luminance range spans the accepted division between *mesopic* and *photopic* vision, mesopic vision (10^{-3}–10 cd/m^2) involving both rods and cones and photopic vision (>10 cd/m^2) cones only (Judd and Wyszecki, 1963; Le Grand, 1968). For low-level displays the V_λ curve may not give an accurate result, since the rods increase the eye's sensitivity at the blue end of the spectrum (the *Purkinje* effect); in this case some weighted average of photopic and *scotopic* (rod only) luminous efficiency curves (Le Grand, 1968), may be appropriate.

Brightness

Luminance is an important factor but not the sole factor in determining whether an area in the picture is seen as light or dark. The luminance of other surrounding areas (the *surround*), including the viewing room, also plays a part. If a luminous area has a surround of much higher luminance, the area appears dark, while the opposite is true if the surround is of low luminance.

Luminance is, as we have seen, an objective measure, in the sense that we can obtain its numerical value from a calibrated photosensitive instrument. *Brightness* is the term used to denote our *subjective* response to light, the impression we have of the light source being bright or dim. Brightness, also commonly termed *luminosity*, is used for self-luminous objects such as CRT displays, while the similar concept of *lightness* is used for non-self-luminous objects such as reflecting grey scale charts.

If brightness and lightness are subjective responses inside a person's head, how can they be measured? There are two measurements of interest, relating to two types of application in display engineering. An important factor in ensuring a high display quality is good *tone reproduction*, that is, the rendition of whites, greys and blacks as distinct and pleasing. In this case the interest lies in knowing what the subject regards as equal steps on his scale of brightness. In another application such as amplitude quantisation of the video signal, the concern might be to make the quantal steps of such a size as to be invisible or just visible; here it is the subject's *luminance difference threshold* or *contrast threshold* that is of interest. *Contrast* is a term commonly used to describe differences in luminance, such as at borders.

To ascertain what a subject regards as equal steps in brightness as a function of luminance, he could be given say, an electronically generated grey scale on a display CRT and allowed to adjust the steps until they appeared equal. A similar task, involving the selection of a certain number of paint chips from a large variety ranging from black through grey to white, could be used to ascertain equal steps in lightness. The determination of contrast threshold can be made by one of a number of techniques which attempt to discover the value of luminance difference which will be seen in 50% of the observations which a subject makes, this being the way in which a threshold is usually defined.

The classic result for threshold contrast is known as *Weber's law* or sometimes as the *Weber-Fechner law*. If a visual field of luminance L is divided into two parts along some border and the luminance of one part is increased by an amount ΔL to produce threshold contrast, Weber's law says that

$$\frac{\Delta L}{L} = k$$

where k is a constant known as the Weber Fraction. Weber's law holds approximately over most of the range of luminances likely to be encountered in typical displays ($0.1-1000\,\text{cd/m}^2$) where its value is about $0.01-0.02$, but there is a gradual increase in k in the lower part of this range (below about $1\,\text{cd/m}^2$) as the luminance is decreased.

It may be imagined that a simple relationship exists between contrast threshold measurements and grey scale (suprathreshold) measurements; however, experiment shows this is not so (Bartleson, 1968). Threshold differences, in which noise in the human visual system may be influential, cannot simply be integrated to give information about large differences. Thus if, as Fechner did, we interpret Weber's law as $dB = a\,dL/L$, where dB is the increase in brightness due to an infinitesimal increase dL in luminance, a being a constant, then by integration we obtain $B = a \log L + \text{constant}$. However, the actual form of the curve obtained for a complex scene (Bartleson and Breneman, 1967b) is shown in Figure 2.3, which is seen to be significantly different from a simple logarithmic relationship, this being a straight line in the figure.

The more complex situation in the case of a displayed picture may be appreciated by reference to Figure 2.4. Weber's law assumes the observer is *adapted* to the luminance L. Adaptation is an important mechanism which allows us a high contrast sensitivity over an enormous range of scene luminances. In viewing a picture we tend to adapt to some surround luminance level L_0 which is a weighted average of the room luminance L_r and the picture luminance L_p. Both the room and the picture luminance will generally vary as functions of spatial position but may be represented, in so far as their adaptation effect is concerned, by equivalent uniform fields (Moon and Spencer, 1945; Rubinstein and Pearson, 1970). Thus in viewing a border between two small areas L and $L + \Delta L$ as shown, we are generally adapted to a luminance other than L. If our adaptation level is high in relation to L, both the small areas appear dark or black. When the surround luminance is high, this tends to increase the adaptation level resulting in a depression of the brightness curve in Figure 2.3 for the bright surround condition.

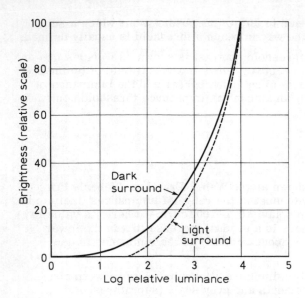

Figure 2.3 General relationship between perceived brightness and log luminance in a complex scene (after Bartleson and Breneman, 1967b).

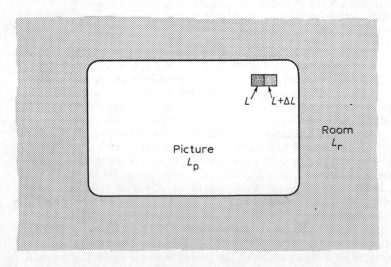

Figure 2.4 Factors affecting brightness perception in displays.

A number of research workers have attempted to characterise the relationship between brightness or lightness and luminance (see Wyszecki and Stiles, 1967). Most of these formulations are not general enough for display engineering purposes as they assume some fixed value of surround luminance and do not allow for the complexity of the viewing conditions represented in Figure 2.4. Of the more general formulations, that of Stevens (1957) is a power-law relationship of the form $B = aL^{\gamma}$ where B is absolute brightness, a is a constant and γ is an exponent which is adjusted to allow for the viewing conditions. Bartleson and Breneman (1967b) have suggested a form $B = aL^{\gamma}/f(L)$ where $f(L)$ is a function of luminance with parameters determined by the viewing conditions, which produces a slower rate of rise of brightness than a simple power law at higher luminances. Judd (1940) used a form $B = aL(L_0 + b)/(L + L_0)$ where a and b are constants and L_0 the surround luminance; this has been applied with some success in complex scenes (Rubinstein and Pearson, 1970).

Engineers are often satisfied with approximate relationships. While brightness perception in displays is a continuing subject of research, it is possible to say, from accumulated experimental evidence, that

$$B = aL^{\gamma}, \text{ with } \gamma \simeq 1/3, \text{ dark surround}$$
$$\simeq 1/2, \text{ bright surround}$$

provides a simple though approximate relationship* between brightness B and luminance L. This law is a straight line when log brightness is plotted against log luminance.

Studies of the overall subjective quality of displayed pictures with various tone scales have produced evidence that quality is maximised if the relative perceived brightness in the display is the same as that in the original scene (Bartleson and Breneman, 1967a). If a viewer at the original scene has an adaptation level giving rise to a relationship $B = a_1 L_1^{\gamma 1}$ and at the end display, with different viewing conditions, the relationship is $B = a_2 L_2^{\gamma 2}$, then for the original and reproduced luminance to produce the same relative brightness, we should have $a_2 L_2^{\gamma 2} = a_1 L_1^{\gamma 1}$ or

$$L_2 = aL_1^{\gamma_s}$$

where $a = (a_1/a_2)^{1/\gamma_2}$ and $\gamma_s = \gamma_1/\gamma_2$. The exponent γ_s in this relationship is referred to as the *system gamma* and is the slope of the curve relating log display luminance to log scene luminance. It is a

---

* If it is required that $B = 0$ for black-appearing objects, the relationship has to be modified to $B = a(L - L_t)^{\gamma}$ in cases where L_t, the threshold luminance, is non-negligible.

parameter which features frequently in the analysis of image transmission systems. As we shall see in Chapter 4, γ_S needs to be different for different surround conditions at the display.

Retinal illuminance

In the same way as the eye's ability to resolve detail in an image is
affected by the size of the retinal image rather than the size of the
external object, so the perception of brightness is determined by the
illuminance of the retina, rather than the luminance of the external
object. The amount of light reaching the retina is regulated to some
extent by the pupil, whose diameter can vary between about 2 and
8 mm. This regulation is not very effective over the enormous range
of light levels (10^{-6} to 10^6 cd/m^2) over which the eye can function,
but does serve to optimise visual acuity (Campbell and Gregory,
1960).

A special unit of illuminance, the *troland,* has been introduced to
account for pupil variation, which is often encountered in referring to
data on the eye. From a consideration of the dioptrics of the eye, it
can be shown (Le Grand, 1968) that when an external object has a
luminance L candelas per square meter, the retinal illuminance E
in lux is given by

$$E = 3.6\ LS\tau_\lambda \times 10^{-3}$$

where S is the area of the pupil in square millimetres and τ_λ a factor
which allows for the transparency of the ocular media, varying between about 0.1 at 400 nm and 0.7 at 700 nm. The retinal illuminance
is said to be 1 troland when the pupil area is 1 mm^2 and the external
source of luminance 1 cd/m^2. A conversion table has been given by
Le Grand (1968), from which it may be inferred that the pupil area
under typical display conditions is between about 5 mm^2 (high surround
luminance) and 15 mm^2 (low surround luminance), making troland
figures 5-15 times as much as candela per square metre figures.

2.3   Response to Spatial Patterns

The spatial-frequency response (modulation transfer function) of the
eye may be measured by a technique similar to that previously cited
for measuring the spatial bandwidth of a lens. A technique which has
been used in practice is to generate the spatial sinusoids directly on
the face of a CRT, allowing easy control of both frequency and amplitude. This may be done by intensity modulating the electron beam of
a raster display with the output a sine-wave signal generator. For
measuring the horizontal frequency response, for example, the signal
generator is arranged to be locked to the horizontal line rate so that
the intensity pattern is repeated from line to line and a vertical set of
stripes is produced. For the stripes to have a strictly sinusoidal
variation of luminance in the horizontal direction, the output of the

signal generator may have to be predistorted to compensate for non-linearities in the luminance/input-voltage characteristic of the display tube. A large number of lines are used in the raster so that the stripes appear continuous in the vertical direction.

In measuring the spatial-frequency response of the eye, we are again confronted with a psychophysical system. We cannot merely plot the ratio of input to output amplitudes, as we would for an electrical filter, because the output is a sensory impression (of vertical stripes) inside a person's head. To overcome this difficulty, we note that in practice, as the amplitude of the input is decreased, the stripes become more and more difficult to see, until finally they appear as a uniform grey field. This particular point is quite accurately measurable by psychometric techniques and is termed the threshold for the perception of contrast in the stripes.

The spatial frequency response of the human visual system can now be deduced on the assumption that we are dealing with a linear filter followed by a peak threshold detector, as shown in Figure 2.5. For if the input has to be very large to bring the output above threshold, we can conclude that the filter is attenuating strongly at that spatial frequency.

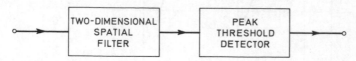

Figure 2.5 Assumptive model for the eye in measuring its spatial frequency response.

The results of an experiment of this kind carried out by Campbell and Robson (1968) are reproduced in Figure 2.6. Campbell and Robson used vertically oriented sinusoidal gratings of the form

$$L + \Delta L \cos(2\pi u x)$$

where L is the average luminance, ΔL the peak luminance deviation and u the spatial frequency of the grating. Two values of L were used, $500 \, cd/m^2$ and $0.05 \, cd/m^2$, and the value of ΔL at the threshold was determined for a number of spatial frequencies. The ratio $\Delta L/L$, which is akin to the Weber fraction, was taken as defining the contrast of the grating at threshold; its reciprocal $L/\Delta L$ was plotted as the *contrast sensitivity* of the visual system as a function of spatial frequency and so appears in Figure 2.6.

The two luminances used by Campbell and Robson happen to correspond roughly to the limits found in typical CRT displays. For bright displays ($500 \, cd/m^2$) we see that the eye has a peak sensitivity at about 3-4 cycles/degree with a fall-off in sensitivity at both higher and lower frequencies. Cut-off is reached at a little over 50 cycles/ degree. As the luminance is lowered, the frequency of peak sensitivity and the sensitivity itself are reduced with cut-off being reached at a lower spatial frequency.

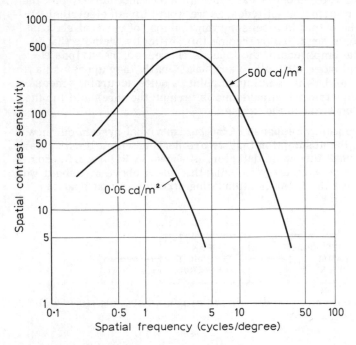

Figure 2.6   Contrast sensitivity of the eye for sine wave gratings (after Campbell and Robson, 1968). The pupil diameter was 2.5 mm.

The sensitivity in Figure 2.6 relates to monocular vision; with bin-ocular vision, which is more usual in viewing displays, the sensitivity at any spatial frequency is increased by a factor of $\sqrt{2}$ or 1.4, and the cut-off bandwidth for high-brightness displays to about 60 cycles/ degree (Campbell and Green, 1965). The results obtained with horizontally oriented gratings are similar, but at 45° the bandwidth is reduced by 10-20% (Higgins and Stultz, 1948). The assumptions of linearity and threshold detection in the filter model of Figure 2.5 have been confirmed by Campbell, Carpenter and Levinson (1969). They found that the threshold visibility of non-sinusoidal patterns and edges could be predicted by considering them as a sum of Fourier sine wave components. Often it is only the fundamental and first harmonic of a repetitive pattern which affect its visibility as the higher frequency components fall outside the eye's passband. By

inverse Fourier transforming the response of Figure 2. 6, Campbell,
Carpenter and Levinson arrived at an estimate of the line-spread
function of the visual system (Figure 2. 7). The filtering action of
the eye on any spatial pattern is computable by convolving the
pattern with the line spread function.

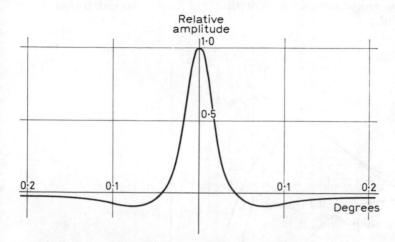

*Figure 2.7   Line-spread function of the human eye (after Campbell,
Carpenter and Levinson, 1969).*

It is possible to say, therefore, that the eye acts as a two-dimensional
low-pass filter for spatial patterns. Its response cuts off at about
60 cycles/degree in foveal vision, less in peripheral vision. It has a
peak response around 3 cycles/degree at average display luminances
and a substantially attenuated response at very low spatial frequencies.
In a transmission system, any high or very low spatial frequencies
in the source image may safely be 'maltreated' or omitted (Schreiber,
1967), whereas spatial frequencies around 3 cycles/degree require
more delicate consideration. Moreover, interference or noise in the
communication channel which gives rise to spatial frequencies in the
display near 3 cycles/degree will be at peak visibility.

2.4   Response to Temporal Patterns

The temporal bandwidth of the eye may be measured by a technique
analogous to that for spatial bandwidth. A point source of light (in
practice a small uniform luminance area) is caused to fluctuate
sinusoidally about a mean value of luminance L. The description of
the stimulus is:

$$L + \Delta L \cos (2\pi f t)$$

where ΔL is the peak amplitude of the fluctuation and f its frequency. If ΔL is large enough and f is not too high, such a source appears to *flicker*. For any given value of f, the value of ΔL which produces a threshold sensation of flicker may be determined experimentally. Flicker threshold is normally expressed in terms of the fraction $\Delta L/L$, termed the temporal contrast; it is usual to plot its inverse $L/\Delta L$, the *temporal contrast sensitivity* of *flicker sensitivity*, as a function of f.

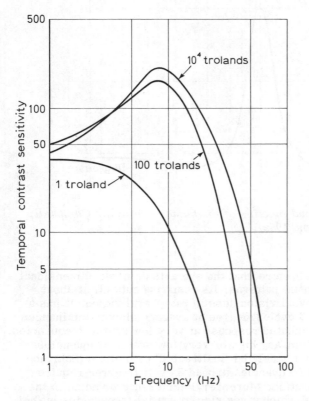

Figure 2.8 Flicker sensitivity of the eye for a 2 degree field at various values of retinal illuminance (after de Lange, 1958). As a very rough approximation for display viewing, 100 trolands is equivalent to about 10 cd/m^2 in the display.

A set of curves obtained in this way by de Lange (1958) is plotted in Figure 2.8. Similar determinations have been made by others (e.g. Kelly, 1961). The curves show that the eye is noticeably more sensitive to flicker at high luminances than at low luminances and their shape indicates that the eye acts as a low-pass filter for temporal

frequencies. The 10 000 troland curve is appropriate for the highlights of bright CRT displays, and it can be seen that the filter
characteristic peaks at about 8 Hz. Cut-off is reached at about 70 Hz
and there is a substantial fall-off at low frequencies. The 1 troland
curve, appropriate for the dark parts of low-level displays, shows a
much reduced sensitivity to flicker and lower bandwidth. It is
curious that the shape of these curves is very similar to the eye's
spatial frequency response (Figure 2. 6) and that the numerical
values are nearly the same when the frequency is measured in
cycles per degree in the spatial case and hertz in the temporal case.

Tests of the validity of a linear-filter and peak-threshold detector
assumption for the temporal case have been made by studying the
visibility of non-sinusoidal repetitive stimuli and flashes. These
results lend support to an approximate analysis procedure wherein
the temporal waveform describing the luminance variation is analysed
into its Fourier components and the filter output obtained by superposition.

While Figure 2. 8 summarises many of the important characteristics
of flicker, additional factors such as stimulus size, eccentricity and
colour also affect flicker sensitivity (Le Grand, 1968) with fairly
complex interactions. Sensitivity increases gradually with increasing
stimulus area; it is less for peripheral vision than for foveal vision,
except for large-area or low-luminance stimuli, when it is greater.

2. 5   Relevance of the Spatio-temporal Sine-wave Response for System Design

Our response to a picture is certainly more complex than is describable by the sum total of our responses to its individual Fourier sine-
wave components. We are involved in the perception and form and
movement (Cherry, 1962) and discrimination of signal from noise.
If we understand how humans perform the acts of perception and
cognition associated with vision, we might be able to build electronic
equivalents. We might be able to recognise trees or faces electronically and by so doing economise on the representation of images
(Gabor and Hill, 1961; Kolers, 1972). Instead of transmitting the
amplitude of each picture sample to describe an object we could
merely transmit a few salient details including, for example, the
spatial location and orientation of the object. The future hold out
exciting possibilities in this field, some of which may eventually be
realised through the efforts of current research in picture coding.

The sine-wave responses of the eye in space and time as portrayed
in Figures 2. 6 and 2. 8 are based on measurements made at threshold
with stationary fixation, and caution is needed in applying the results
to displays. Although, in a well designed system, distortion and noise
will be near threshold, the Fourier components of the picture will be
above threshold. The complexities previously mentioned in connection
with brightness perception also apply. For suprathreshold conditions,

the eye's response may be nonlinear and this typically occurs at a boundary between two different luminance levels in a picture. The presence of a sharp change in luminance, in either space or time, can markedly reduce the visibility of small luminance changes in its vicinity. This effect is known as spatial or temporal *masking* (Le Grand, 1968). Spatial masking is taken account of in coding edges in pictures, and temporal masking in the rate of presentation of new information after a complete scene change (Seyler and Budrikis, 1965; Budrikis, 1972). Again, tracking of a moving object in the picture can affect the eye's response to the Fourier components.

Another limitation of the sine wave response data we have to date is the lack of phase information. If the Fourier components of a pattern are reproduced with incorrect relative phases, this can cause a marked alteration in the appearance of the pattern. The eye is sensitive to quite small phase changes and in this respect is quite unlike the ear. For this and other reasons, some engineers have advocated a waveform approach to systems analysis, on the grounds that system distortions can more readily be assessed in the space and time domains than in the frequency domain (Lewis, 1954). The frequency response of the eye provides a complementary viewpoint (Schade, 1964) with useful design considerations and insight; however some phenomena, such as effects at boundaries, may best be treated in the space or time domain.

Studies have been made of the eye's response to patterns which vary as a function of both space and time. Brainard (1967) used moving sine waves of the type $L + \Delta L \cos 2\pi(ux + vy + ft)$ and Robson (1966) flickering gratings given by $L + \Delta L (\cos 2\pi ux) \cos(2\pi ft)$, where u and v are horizontal and vertical spatial frequencies respectively and f temporal frequency. Their results indicate some interaction between spatial and temporal responses, so that the spatiotemporal response is not separable into a simple product of the spatial response of Figure 2.6 and the temporal response of Figure 2.8. At high temporal frequencies the spatial contrast sensitivity is reduced and there is no peak in the curve. This result is relevant to the reproduction of detail in moving objects. Similarly at high spatial frequencies there is an overall reduction and a nearly monotic fall-off in flicker sensitivity; this result is used in interlaced scanning.

From the Fourier standpoint therefore, the eye is effectively a *three-dimensional low-pass filter* whose cut-off bandwidth for bright displays is about 60 cycles/degree in both horizontal and vertical spatial frequency and about 70 Hz in temporal frequency. For dim displays these figures are lower. The fact that any visual output which the system may produce is low-pass filtered by the eye immediately suggests the basic economy of representation which all practical picture transmission systems make use of, namely that the image may be similarly bandlimited before transmission. If this bandlimitation is introduced at the transmitter, the image may be *sampled* in each dimension. By the sampling theorem, provided the sampling frequency exceeds twice the bandwidth in each dimension, the image is fully recoverable at the receiver; indeed, the eye itself will perform the necessary low-pass filtering to obtain recovery of the image and there is no need for electro-optical low-pass filtering. The number of samples needed for an image of dimensions 1 degree × 1 degree × 1 second is approximately:

$$(2 \times 60) \times (2 \times 60) \times (2 \times 70) \simeq 2 \times 10^6 \text{ samples}$$

in this idealised case. In practice a lower sampling density is used, as we shall see in the next chapter, partly by reducing the sampling frequency in each dimension to the point where it is at or below the visual cut-off frequency, rather than at twice this frequency, and partly by exploiting the eye's relative insensitivity at frequencies which are high in both space and time, through interlacing.

Two-level patterns

Because of the low-pass filtering action of the eye, pictorial information can be displayed with only two luminance levels and yet appear to have a continuum of brightness levels over the grey scale (Knowlton and Harmon, 1972). This is illustrated in Figure 2.9. The displayed pattern of black and white squares in Figure 2.9a has a basic repetition frequency substantially beyond the eye's cut-off

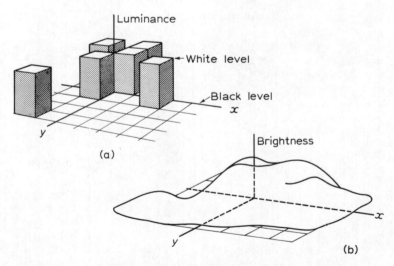

Figure 2.9 (a) Pattern of high-density black or white squares. (b) Perceived distribution of brightness after low-pass filtering by the eye.

frequency; what is seen therefore is the low-pass filtered version in Figure 2.9b, which is Figure 2.9a convolved with the point-spread function of the eye. The amplitude of the filtered function is continuous and is related to the density of squares in the original pattern. Although the figure is drawn for two dimensions, the principle applies equally well in three dimensions.

Chapter 3

SCANNING

3.1 Types of Scan

Scanning is the process whereby the three dimensions of an image are converted to a one-dimensional signal for transmission over a single channel. Physically, a scanning spot traverses the image in zig-zag lines, termed collectively a *raster*, sensing the image illuminance at every point in its path (Figure 3.1). When the spot reaches the bottom it returns and commences another scan. This process may be regarded as the periodic sampling of a matrix of chosen resolution elements, termed *picture elements*, sometimes abbreviated to *pels* or *pixels*. The number of such elements needed is related to the spatial bandwidth of the image, the conditions of viewing at the display and the required quality of reproduction. We shall examine the influence of these factors in due course.

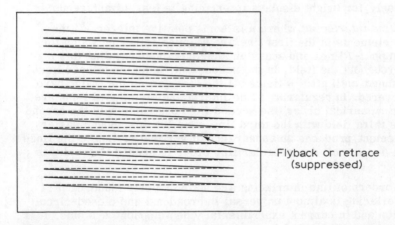

Flyback or retrace
(suppressed)

Figure 3.1 A line-continuous, noninterlaced scanning raster.
The left-to-right slope is negligible with a large number of lines.

For any given number of picture elements, a large number of different scanning patterns are possible. The pattern illustrated in Figure 3.1, in which the picture elements are scanned in progressive order along a line and progressively line by line, is termed *sequential* or *noninterlaced* scanning. It is instrumentally the simplest form and is appropriate for scanning still pictures where considerations of flicker do not arise (for example, where the picture is effectively stored at the receiver, as in wirephoto, facsimile and other 'hard copy' systems). However, for pictures viewed on CRT displays where the picture flickers if the scan rate is too low, many other patterns have been considered with a view to reducing the required scan rate in picture elements per second and the video transmission bandwidth. Most of these have involved scanning a fraction only (a *field*) of the total number of elements (a *frame* or *picture*) in a single scan and returning to scan the remaining elements in subsequent scans. This type of scanning is termed *interlaced* scanning, in that each field, in a well chosen pattern, is spatially interlaced with the previous one. Each field comprises a sampling of the image at a spatial density below that required for adequate reproduction of spatial detail and if viewed singly this would be apparent. However, one field is followed rapidly, at a rate which is usually 50 or 60 per second, by another interlaced field, and the missing spatial information is rapidly built up. What suffers in this process, as we shall see, is the reproduction of moving objects with a high spatial-frequency content, but since the eye is relatively insensitive at high combined spatio-temporal frequencies, a modest degree of interlacing can be successful. Since the spatio-temporal bandwidth of the eye is lower for lower luminances, higher orders of interlacing (more fields per frame) for a given number of fields per second can be successful for low-level displays. Conversely, for bright displays interlacing is less advantageous.

In *n : 1 line interlacing,* where *n* is some positive integer, all the picture elements in the first line are scanned, following which the spot jumps *n-1* lines and scans another full line, repeating this process throughout the field. In the subsequent fields the missed lines are scanned, until after *n* fields all the elements in the frame have been covered. In regular *n : 1* line interlacing the missed lines are taken in numerical order (the second field beginning with the second line, the third field with the third line, etc.) but this, though easier to implement, produces an appearance of vertical motion of the lines termed *line crawl*. An irregular line order is needed to avoid this effect.

Higher orders of line interlacing are not commonly found, but 2 : 1 line interlacing is almost universal in broadcast and closed-circuit television and in current experimental videotelephone systems. It is for this reason that a 2 : 1 line-interlaced picture is often termed simply *interlaced*. If a noninterlaced picture at a frame rate of 50 or 60 frames per second is converted to an interlaced picture at 50 or 60 fields per second, the transmission rate in picture elements per second is halved. However, a price is paid in picture quality (Maurice, 1958). Since the frame rate is halved, flicker appears at 25 or 30 Hz. This occurs at a high spatial frequency and is therefore minimally visible, but it does degrade the picture and make fine spatial detail difficult to see. Brown (1967) measured the bandwidth advantage due to interlacing by getting subjects to compare interlaced pictures with noninterlaced pictures in terms of quality. He lowered the quality of the noninterlaced pictures by reducing their spatial resolution, thereby also reducing their bandwidth. He found that for the pictures he tested, namely 30 frame per second 225-line low-resolution still pictures, the bandwidth advantage of interlacing was 37% at a screen highlight luminance of 140 cd/m² but only 6% at 340 cd/m², where flicker is more visible. Since the line spacing in Brown's experiment was coarse, these figures for interlacing advantage may be low in comparison with those which might be obtained for broadcast television; on the other hand, still lower figures would be expected for similar pictures containing motion or at the European 25 frames per second rate, flicker being more visible at this frequency.

Interlacing can also be carried out in the horizontal direction. This is termed *dot interlacing* (Gouriet, 1952; Jesty, 1952) and is illustrated in Figure 3.2. In dot-interlaced scanning the scanning beam is blanked by a high-frequency rectangular gating wave to produce the dot pattern as shown in the figure. By a suitable choice of the rectangular wave frequency, the next scan over the same spatial path can produce a dot pattern interlaced with the first. This is *2:1 dot interlace*. Normally, alternate lines of dots in a 2:1 dot-interlaced field are displaced relative to one another, as shown in the figure, to reduce the dot pattern visibility.

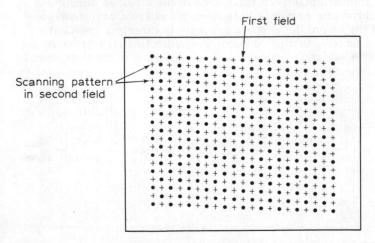

Figure 3.2 One field of a 2:1 dot-interlaced scan. In the second field the spot dot-scans the gaps in the first field.

If the mark-space ratio of the rectangular wave is altered to produce an interval between dots equal to *n* times the picture element spacing, then *n:1 dot interlacing* is obtained. As with line interlacing, many forms of *n:1* dot interlacing are possible, corresponding to various patterns of selecting the dots in any one field. A generalisation of dot interlacing to include any irregular pattern of dots in a field has been termed *pseudo-random dot scanning* (Deutsch, 1971). For maximum effectiveness the pattern is not just random but needs to be selected to have low visibility (Brainard, Mounts and Prasada, 1967). This can be achieved by concentrating the energy content of the pattern in the high spatio-temporal frequencies. With the medium- or low-resolution scanning used in most practical television systems, it is found that dot interlacing and pseudo-random dot scanning increase the visibility of an already rather visible scanning raster; they are therefore hardly ever used except for low-luminance or low-quality displays.

3.2   Scanning as a Sampling Process

The transmission of a monochrome picture by scanning can be described by the chain of operations represented in Figure 3.3. The formation of the image and the extraction of luminance is carried out by the camera. A lens system forms an image of the scene on the photosensitive surface of the camera tube which is scanned by an electron beam or other means. Although in theory an optical filter should be placed in the light path which, in combination with the spectral sensitivity of the lens and camera tube, has the V_λ response of the CIE standard observer, for monochrome pictures almost any broad, panchromatic response is found to be satisfactory. Low-pass filtering of the image in the spatial domain is largely a result of finite spot size but can also be accomplished optically; storage on the photosensitive surface provides low-pass filtering in the time domain.

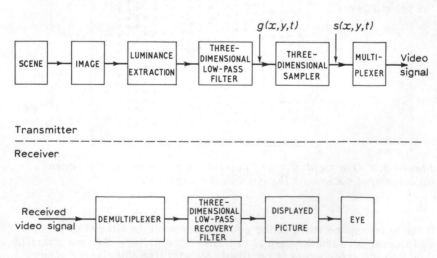

Figure 3.3 Transmission of a monochrome picture by scanning.

All the types of scanning just discussed can be subsumed under the general description of *three-dimensional sampling* followed by *time-division multiplexing* of the samples. In terms of this description the picture elements, if they are of infinitesimal width, may be regarded as samples. The action of the scanning spot is to multiplex the samples into a single electrical signal, the *video signal*. If each frame is divided into a large number of elements and if the scanning spot scans a large number of complete frames every second, this results in a large total of elements scanned per second and a high rate of transmission of video samples. The *sampling density* in space-time is said to be high in this case. The higher the sampling density, the better the system is able to resolve spatial details and movement.

Some practical scanning devices, e.g. charge-coupled arrays (Tompsett, 1972), take discrete samples in all three dimensions of the image, but in others such as vidicons and plumbicons, scanning is continuous in the horizontal spatial dimension, as in Figure 3.1. It is possible to treat the general form of scanning as discrete in all three dimensions, provided the sampling theorem is obeyed and there is no aliasing. Continuity can be introduced, if desired at any stage, by an ideal low-pass filtering operation. We shall later consider a sampling description which is continuous in x and show that this produces identical results to the discrete treatment.

3.3 Ideal Scanning

In studying the properties of practical scanners, it is useful first to describe an ideal form of scanning and then to introduce the practical imperfections one by one. In ideal scanning we shall assume that the image is strictly bandlimited in three-dimensional spatio-temporal frequency space and that it is possible to scan it with a spot of infinitesimal width which can be represented as a delta function. The simple case is that of a noninterlaced scan which takes discrete samples of the image $g(x, y, t)$ at regular spacings X, Y and T in the horizontal spatial, vertical spatial and temporal dimensions respectively. This requires either scanning a frame in an infinitesimal time and then waiting an interval T, or storing the image while the scan takes place. In either case the sampled signal can be written as

$$s(x, y, t) = \text{comb}_{X, Y, T}[g(x, y, t)]$$

With X, Y and T assumed to be positive numbers, the spectrum of $s(x, y, t)$ is (from Table 1.3)

$$S(u, v, f) = \frac{1}{XYT} \, \text{rep}_{1/X, 1/Y, 1/T} \, [G(u, v, f)]$$

Interpreted, this means that the spectrum of the sampled signal is a scaled version of the spectrum of the image $G(u, v, f)$ repeated at intervals $1/X, 1/Y$ and $1/T$ throughout the frequency space u, v, f, the scaling factor $1/XYT$ being equal to the sampling density.

What sampling density is necessary to recover the image $g(x, y, t)$ from its samples without impairment? This is given by the rectangular sampling theorem in three dimensions, namely that $g(x, y, t)$ can be recovered provided it is bandlimited in advance of sampling to

$$W_x < \frac{1}{2X},\ W_y < \frac{1}{2Y},\ W_t < \frac{1}{2T}$$

Alternatively stated, the sampling frequency must be greater than $2W_x$ in the x dimension, $2W_y$ in the y dimension and $2W_t$ in the t dimension, giving an overall sampling density $\rho > 8\ W_x W_y W_t$. If any of these conditions is not fulfilled, aliasing results, as shown in Figure 3.4. In the figure the amplitude of the transform $G(u, v, f)$ and

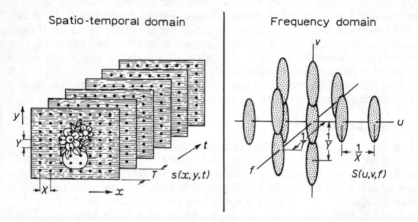

Figure 3.4 An image sample at too low a sampling frequency in the vertical spatial dimension, producing aliasing.

its replications are represented as densities in u, v, f space. As drawn, the figure shows that the sampling frequency in the y or vertical spatial dimension is too low, whereas the x and t sampling frequencies are adequate. The remedy is to decrease Y, i.e. to make the scanning lines closer together. If this is not done some spurious high vertical spatial frequencies will appear in the recovered image, e.g. as Moiré patterns. Similarly, if both temporal and spatial aliasing were to occur, spurious spatio-temporal frequencies would appear in the image, e.g. wagon wheels appearing to turn backwards.

Recovery of $g(x, y, t)$ from $s(x, y, t)$ requires an ideal low-pass filter in the frequency domain, together with appropriate scaling:

$$G(u, v, f) = S(u, v, f)\ .XYT\ \text{rect}(Xu, Yv, Tf)$$

In the time domain this becomes, by inverse Fourier transformation,

$$g(x, y, t) = s(x, y, t) * \text{sinc}\left(\frac{x}{X}, \frac{y}{Y}, \frac{t}{T}\right)$$

This convolution implies an interpolation between the delta-function samples by three-dimensional sinc functions to recover $g(x, y, t)$, each sinc function having the value unity at the sample in question and zero at every other sample point in the x, y, t space.

Line-continuous scanning

It is possible to give a mathematical description to scanning which allows for the more usual continuity of scan along a line (Robinson 1973). An array of scanning lines which is continuous in the x dimension but discontinuous in the y and t dimensions is describable as

$$d(x, y, t) = \text{rep}_{Y, T}\left[\delta(y, t)\right]$$

Where Y and T are the line spacings in the y and t dimensions. The function on the right is an array of delta functions in the y, t plane which are invariant with x, forming impulse lines in three-dimensional space. Its Fourier transform may be found by writing it as a separable product

$$d(x, y, t) = 1 \cdot \text{rep}_{Y, T}\left[\delta(y, t)\right]$$

whence, from Tables 1.1-1.3

$$D(u, v, f) = \delta(u) \cdot \frac{1}{YT} \text{comb}_{1/Y, 1/T}[1]$$

$$= \frac{\delta(u)}{YT} \text{rep}_{1/Y, 1/T}\left[\delta(v, f)\right]$$

This is a two-dimensional array of three-dimensional delta functions in the $u = 0$ plane. In scanning an image $g(x, y, t)$, the impulse lines $d(x, y, t)$ sample the image function in the y and t dimensions but leave the function unaffected in the x dimension. Thus

$$s(x, y, t) = g(x, y, t) \cdot \text{rep}_{Y, T}\left[\delta(y, t)\right]$$

$$= \text{comb}_{Y, T}\left[g(x, y, t)\right]$$

The transform of the scanned image is (from Table 1.3)

$$S(u, v, f) = G(u, v, f) * D(u, v, f)$$

The effect of this convolution is to replicate $G(u, v, f)$ at intervals of $v = 1/Y$ and $f = 1/T$ in the plane $u = 0$. The spectrum for a line-continuous scanned image therefore differs from the all-discrete case previously considered in that there is no replication of $G(u, v, f)$ in the u dimension. The all-discrete case can be converted into the line-continuous case by an ideal low-pass filter in the u dimension of a bandwidth such as to exclude all replications but leave the baseband spectrum untouched. Conversely, the line-continuous case is converted to the all-discrete case by sampling of the video signal after scanning.

Interlaced scanning

As we have seen, a variety of interlaced patterns are possible. We shall consider, by way of an example, the most common form, which is 2 : 1 line interlacing. The pattern of scanning in the y, t plane is shown in Figure 3.5. In comparison with noninterlaced scanning, half

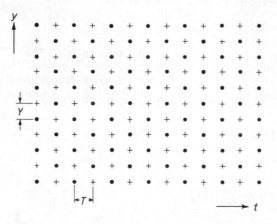

Figure 3.5 Cross-section of 2 : 1 line-interlaced scanning in the y, t plane. The missing lines, in comparison with noninterlaced scanning, are indicated by crosses.

the dots or delta functions are missing. To convert the description for noninterlaced scanning to one for interlaced scanning, we multiply by a two-dimensional function which is zero at the points where we wish to eliminate dots and unity where we wish to leave them alone. There are many such functions but a simple one is

$$\tfrac{1}{2} + \tfrac{1}{2} \cos 2\pi\Big(\frac{y}{2Y} + \frac{t}{2T}\Big)$$

which is a raised cosine wave tilted at 45 degrees. The scanned image becomes modified to

$$s(x, y, t) = \text{comb}_{X, Y, T}\ \left\{[g(x, y, t)] \cdot \left[\tfrac{1}{2} + \tfrac{1}{2} \cos 2\pi\Big(\frac{y}{2Y} + \frac{t}{2T}\Big)\right]\right\}$$

This transforms into

$$S(u,v,f) = \frac{1}{XYT} \; \text{rep}_{1/X,1/Y,1/T} \left\{ [G(u,v,f)] \; * \; \left[(\tfrac{1}{2} \; \delta(u,v,f) \right. \right.$$

$$\left. \left. + \; \delta(u) \; \left\{ \tfrac{1}{4} \; \delta\!\left(v - \frac{1}{2Y}, f - \frac{1}{2T}\right) + \tfrac{1}{4} \; \delta\!\left(v + \frac{1}{2Y}, f + \frac{1}{2T}\right) \right\} \right] \right\}$$

This expression is obtained by noting that multiplication becomes convolution in the transform domain and further by expressing the cosine in exponential form, whence it transforms using Table 1.2, No. 4, together with the separability rule. Simplifying, we have

$$S(u,v,f) = \frac{1}{2XYT} \; \text{rep}_{1/X,1/Y,1/T} \left[G(u,v,f) \right.$$

$$\left. + \frac{1}{2} \; G\!\left(u, v - \frac{1}{2Y}, f - \frac{1}{2T}\right) + \frac{1}{2} \; G\!\left(u, v + \frac{1}{2Y}, f + \frac{1}{2T}\right) \right]$$

Convolution with a delta function merely shifts a function to the location of the delta function; therefore the spectrum in this case, ignoring scaling constants, comprises the original noninterlaced spectrum $\text{rep}_{1/X,1/Y,1/T} \left[G(u,v,f) \right]$ to which are added two displaced versions of half amplitude. The situation is illustrated in Figure 3.6 by a

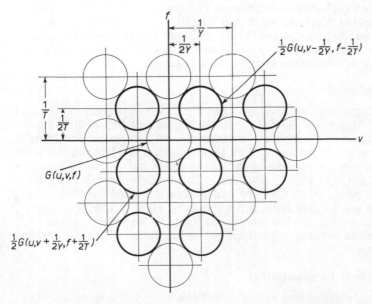

Figure 3.6 Cross-section of the three-dimensional Fourier spectrum of an image scanned by the 2:1 line-interlaced scan of Figure 3.5. The contributions added due to the interlacing are shown in bold lines.

cross-section of $S(u, v, f)$ taken in the v, f plane. $S(u, v, f)$ is portrayed as deficient in frequencies which are high simultaneously in the vertical spatial and temporal dimensions, so that its cross-section is approximately circular. As we have seen, the eye has a relatively poor response to these frequencies and we suppose that they have been cleverly eliminated from $G(u, v, f)$ by filtering, or that the scene does not contain them.

Also shown in Figure 3.6 is a situation where the basic sampling frequencies $1/Y$ and $1/T$ have been chosen to be a little higher than they need be from aliasing considerations, perhaps because the designer has tried to reduce the visibility of the scanning lines and of flicker. This is close to the practical case. We then see that, with these assumptions, the additional replications in v, f space caused by the interlacing can be fitted in without overlapping the baseband spectrum. To recover the image from the interlaced samples we now need a filter with a circular rather than a rectangular cross-section.

Thus horizontal 2:1 line-interlaced scanning succeeds and is appropriate for images which do not have objects with fine vertical detail or sharp vertical edges moving in relation to the field of view of the camera. When this occurs, aliasing is visible, as happens in practical systems, noticeably when the camera zooms in on or pans upwards along an object with vertical edges. Interlacing in its ideal form is seen to be an exploitation of the non-rectangular shape of the spectrum in packing replications closer together in frequency space. Clearly, depending on the characteristic shape of the spectrum and the amount of pre-scan and post-scan filtering which is possible, other types of interlacing may be advantageous.

Direction of scan

In some circumstances, such as when the picture contains substantial amounts of high vertical-spatial-frequency energy or vertical movement, it may be advantageous, in medium- and low-resolution systems, to scan from top to bottom rather than from left to right. Since, however, we live on the surface of the earth where movement is largely horizontal, there is some advantage in the common practice of scanning horizontally. Also, viewers are generally seated and their head movements are largely from left to right or right to left; this movement can cause successive interlaced fields to lose their spatial interlacing and become superimposed on the retina if the scan direction is vertical.

3.4   Pre-scan Bandlimitation

If the image is defocused, either intentionally or because of imperfections in the lens system, this introduces spatial low-pass filtering. The filtering action is usually more of a gradual roll-off at high spatial frequencies than a sudden one, and may have ripples (Herriott,

1958). Because of this roll-off and aided by the predominance of low spatial frequencies in many natural scenes, the spectrum of the image generally has a gradual decay with increasing spatial frequency, as shown in Figure 3.7. An exception to this is the case of a page of printed or typewritten text, in which there are many sharp edges which contribute materially to the high-frequency content of the spectrum.

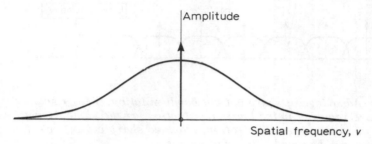

Figure 3.7 Cross-section along the vertical spatial-frequency axis of a typical image spectrum showing attenuation of high frequencies and an impulse at the origin.

Since the illuminance of the image plane $g(x, y)$ is a non-negative function of x and y, there is always a delta function at the origin of any image spectrum. This is evident if the mean or DC value and the AC value are separated to give

$$g(x, y) = g_0 + g_1 (x, y)$$

where g_0 is a constant and the mean value of $g_1 (x, y)$ is zero. Transforming with the aid of Table 1.2, this gives

$$G(u, v) = g_0 \, \delta(u, v) + G_1 (u, v)$$

The delta function is illustrated in Figure 3.7; it turns out to be a nuisance in image scanning, since when the image is sampled the delta function is replicated along with the rest of the spectrum (Figure 3.8). This makes exact recovery of the image from its samples more difficult, as the recovery filter has to attenuate a high concentration of energy at the sampling frequency and its harmonics. Those readers familiar with the design of electronic circuits for sampling will know of the advantage to be gained by AC-coupling the signal into the sampler to avoid this same problem.

The practical result of a slow roll-off in the image spectrum and an impulse at the sampling frequency $1/Y$ is that in many systems more scanning lines are used than are strictly necessary. Figure 3.8

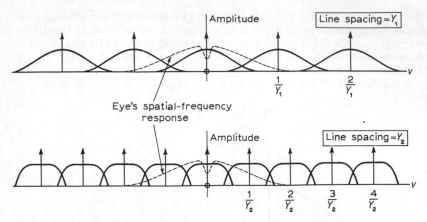

*Figure 3.8 Advantage of sharp optical bandlimitation. Fewer scan-
ning lines are required in the lower illustration for the same degree
of aliasing as in the upper illustration, provided sharp cut-off recovery filters can be found.*

shows the vertical spectra of two scanned images both having the
same 3 dB bandwidth, one with a slow and the other with a fast vertical spatial-frequency cut-off. In the latter case fewer scanning lines
are needed for a given aliasing tolerance, provided appropriate fast
cut-off recovery filters can be employed at the receiver. It is the
absence of such filters in practice (corresponding to more complex
line-broadening or spot-wobble techniques in the spatial domain) and
a reliance on the eye to perform the required filtering, that make the
upper illustration in Figure 3.8 more nearly representative of
scanning practice. Improvements in spatial filtering techniques, both
for the pre-sampling filter and the recovery filter, will allow lower
spatial sampling rates and more efficient scanning. A similar analysis and similar conclusions apply to temporal filtering and sampling
of the image, where the decay of typical phosphors provides a very
weak temporal low-pass filtering action, and reliance must be placed
on the eye in practice to perform the necessary low-pass filtering.

Finite spot size and the aperture effect

The main source of spatial bandlimitation is more likely to be spot
size than optical imperfections. Lateral leakage of charge on the
photoconductive camera target can also be a factor. For a spot of
finite diameter, the expressions for ideal scanning (Section 3.3) must
be modified. If the spot has a profile given by $h_0(x, y)$, its sampling
action at a particular point $x = x_0, y = y_0$ is

$$s(x_0, y_0) = \int_{-\infty}^{\infty} \int_{-\infty}^{\infty} g(x, y) h_0(x-x_0, y-y_0) dx\ dy$$

Thus the sample that is taken of the image $g(x, y)$ is a weighted average over the spatial extent of the spot. The above expression may be rewritten as a convolution integral by letting $h(x, y) = h_0 (-x, -y)$; i.e. $h_0(x, y)$ rotated through 180°. Then

$$s(x_0, y_0) = \int_{-\infty}^{\infty} \int_{-\infty}^{\infty} g(x, y) \, h(x_0-x, y_0-y) \mathrm{d}x \, \mathrm{d}y$$

$$= [g(x, y) * h(x, y)]_x = x_0, y = y_0$$

where the right-hand side of the equation is the convolution of the image function and the rotated spot profile evaluated at $x = x_0, y = y_0$. In the case of a symmetrical spot profile, $h_0(x, y)$ may be used in place of $h(x, y)$ in the convolution.

When scanning is considered to be discrete in both x and y, the convolution is evaluated at all points x_0, y_0 at which a sample of the image is taken. Equivalently, the convolution may be evaluated for all values of x and y, and the resulting function sampled at the appropriate points. This gives the sampled image in the finite spot size case as

$$s(x, y) = \mathrm{comb}_{X, Y} \, [g(x, y) * h(x, y)]$$

The spectrum of $s(x, y)$ is found from Table 1.2:

$$S(u, v) = \frac{1}{XY} \, \mathrm{rep}_{1/X, \, 1/Y} [G(u, v) \, . \, H(u, v)]$$

with X and Y (assumed positive) being the sample spacings in the x and y dimensions respectively and convolution becoming multiplication in the frequency domain. This expression is the same as that for ideal scanning, with the exception that the image spectrum is multiplied by $H(u, v)$, the transform of the rotated spot profile. By the properties of Fourier transforms, if $h_0(x, y)$ is broad, then $H(u, v)$ is narrow and $G(u, v)$ is severely low-pass filtered. If the spot is small, $H(u, v)$ is broad and the filtering is gentle. In the limit, as the spot size decreases to a point, $h(x, y) \rightarrow \delta(x, y)$ and $H(u, v) \rightarrow 1$. In this case there is no spatial filtering of the image.

The analysis may also be carried out for scanning which is continuous in the x dimension and discrete in the y dimension (Robinson, 1973). In this case the scanned image is

$$s(x, y) = \mathrm{comb} \, {}_Y[g(x, y) * h(x, y)]$$

where the notation indicates that after convolution with the rotated spot profile, the image is sampled with impulse sheets oriented in the x direction and spaced Y apart in the y direction. The impulse sheet for any particular value of y is modulated by the convolved

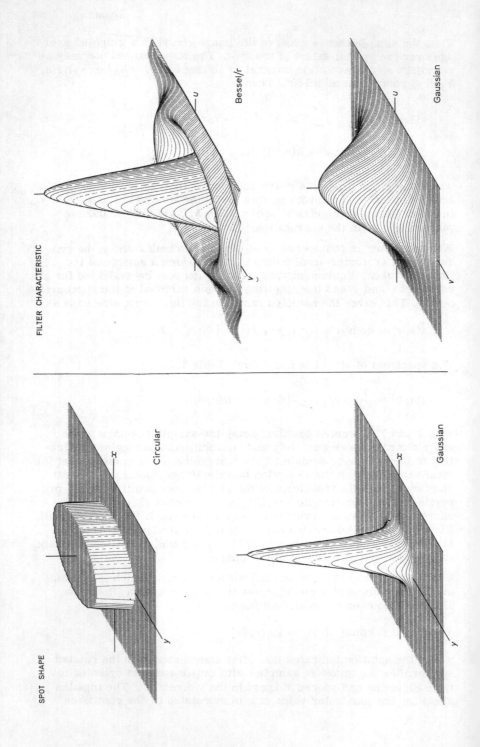

SPOT SHAPE

Circular

x

y

Gaussian

x

y

FILTER CHARACTERISTIC

Bessel/r

u

v

Gaussian

u

v

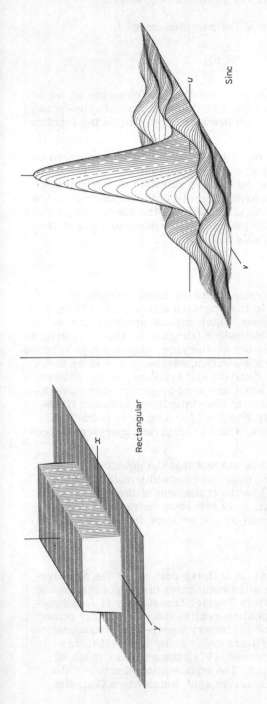

Figure 3.9 Some scanning spot shapes and their filtering action in the spatial frequency domain due to the aperture effect.

image function. The spectrum of the sampled image is

$$S(u, v) = \frac{1}{Y} \, \text{rep}_{1/Y}[G(u, v) \, . \, H(u, v)]$$

In both x-continuous and x-discrete scanning therefore the effect on the baseband image spectrum $G(u, v)$ is the same, namely low-pass spatial filtering in both x and y dimensions according to the function $H(u, v)$.

The low-pass filtering action of a finite-diameter spot is termed the *aperture effect,* since the spot is effectively a hole or aperture in the image plane through which the light is admitted to a photosensitive device behind it. It is the averaging of the illuminance over the aperture which gives rise to the attenuation of the higher frequencies. Some spot shapes and their filtering characteristics are shown in Figure 3.9, as derived from Table 1.2.

Aperture correction

It is the practice in broadcast-standard television cameras to equalise the low-pass roll-off due to the aperture effect, particularly with camera tubes such as plumbicons, which without aperture correction do not have sufficient spatial bandwidth (Heightman, 1967). Aperture correction is normally carried out on the video signal and is relatively simple to implement in the x direction, assuming this to be the direction of scan, but is more difficult and expensive in the y direction, where line-period delay lines are used to give access to vertically adjacent picture elements. In line-interlaced systems, field-period delays are theoretically required for such access but for reasons of cost line-period delays are used, giving aperture correction within each field only.

From the previous analysis, it is evident that the equalisation characteristic required is $1/H(u, v)$ over the bandwidth of the baseband image spectrum, where $H(u, v)$ is the transform of the rotated spot profile. If the spot profile $h_0(x, y)$ is invariant under a 180 degree rotation i.e. $h(x, y) = h_0(x, y) = h(-x, -y)$, we have, from Table 1.2

$$H(u, v) = H_0(u, v) = H(-u, -v)$$

For this to be true $H(u, v)$ must be entirely real, since the negative-frequency components are complex conjugates of the corresponding positive-frequency components in Fourier transforms of real functions. An all-real $H(u, v)$ suggests a realisation using linear phase and so under conditions of spot symmetry linear-phase equalisation is used (Thiele, 1970). Comb filters using delay lines fulfil this requirement (de Mouilpied Fremont, 1971), though other types of linear-phase filters can be used. The equalisation characteristic often approximates that of a Gaussian spot, which has a Gaussian filtering effect (Figure 3.9), though the characteristic is sometimes made variable and is adjusted for optimum visual effect. The spread of the scanning spot varies with the current density, being wider with higher current densities. Aperture correction selectively enhances high spatial-frequency noise generated with the video signal, but automatic circuits can be arranged to reduce or eliminate the equalisation for low levels of the video signal, corresponding to the darker parts of the picture, where the noise tends to be most visible (Heightman, 1972). As the eye's spatial bandwidth is reduced at low luminances, increased blurring can be tolerated.

Target storage

The physical nature of photosensitive camera targets is such that a flash of light is stored for some time, with a gradual decay. The form and rate of decay depends in practice on the type of camera tube and its operating conditions.

Neglecting spatial dimensions, a flash is describable as $L\delta(t)$. If the camera target response is of the form

$$h(t) = kLe^{-t/T} \quad t \geqslant 0$$
$$= 0 \quad t < 0$$

where k is a scale factor, then its filtering action may be calculated as the Fourier transform of this impulse response. From Table 1.1,

$$H(f) = kLT \cdot \frac{1 - j2\pi f T}{1 + (2\pi f T)^2}$$

The amplitude of this function is shown in Figure 3.10. It is in fact

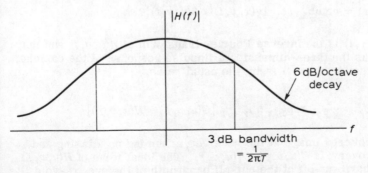

Figure 3.10 Temporal low-pass filtering action of a camera target with exponential decay, time constant T.

the equivalent of a simple RC low-pass filter with $T = RC$ and has a slow roll-off (6 dB/octave).

In a practical case the image may be continuously focused on the target which integrates the variations due to motion over a frame period. This action can be described as the convolution of the impulse response with the image prior to sampling. The effect of target storage is therefore to cause weak band limiting of the temporal frequencies in the image. The effect on any image will be dependent on the temporal spread of its Fourier spectrum, and this in turn will depend on the amount of movement in the scene.

For scenes with relatively little movement, e.g. videotelephone pictures, the spread may be small, but in cases where there is a lot of movement, perhaps accompanied by camera panning, e.g. rocket launches or sports fixtures, the spread will be large and bandlimiting will take place.

As in the spatial case, bandlimitation of the image before scanning is a necessity if aliasing is to be prevented. Leaky target storage is a rather feeble way of accomplishing this in the temporal dimension; a sharper cut-off in the temporal frequency domain would allow a lower temporal sampling (frame) rate, provided again that adequate interpolating phosphors could be employed at the receiver. The principle is identical to that illustrated in Figure 3. 8, but with the horizontal axes being temporal rather than spatial frequency.

Three-dimensional analysis

The spatial effects of optical imperfections, lateral target leakage and spot aperture may be combined with the temporal effect of target storage to give an overall description of image bandlimitation as some low-pass characteristic $H(u, v, f)$ in three-dimensional spatio-temporal frequency space. A more general description of the scanned image is therefore

$$s(x, y, t) = \text{comb}_{X, Y, T} \left[g(x, y, t) * h(x, y, t) \right]$$

where $h(x, y, t)$ is the inverse Fourier transform of $H(u, v, f)$ and may be viewed as the three-dimensional impulse response of the camera. The spectrum of $s(x, y, t)$ is, by the usual rules,

$$S(u, v, f) = \frac{1}{XYT} \text{rep}_{1/X, 1/Y, 1/T} \left[G(u, v, f) \cdot H(u, v, f) \right]$$

and the recovered image at the receiver, assuming no aliasing and perfect recovery, is $G(u, v, f) \cdot H(u, v, f)$. The ideal form of $H(u, v, f)$ is one of sharp cut-off at the cut-off bandwidth of the eye, to avoid aliasing but to allow the visible image components through the system without impairment.

3.5   Some Parameters of Practical Scanning Systems

We have previously seen that the eye's spatial bandwidth is about 60 cycles/degree and its temporal bandwidth about 70 Hz, for bright displays. At the Nyquist rate of two samples per cycle in each dimension, an ideal television system therefore requires 2×10^6 samples per square degree of displayed picture per second. However, for economic reasons, communication systems are rarely designed to be perfect; rather, they are designed such that impairments are kept within tolerable levels. These levels may be determined by subjective laboratory experiments linked by experience to the practical operation of such systems and, in the case of new systems, to marketing information and experimental trials.

In practical scanning systems therefore, the sampling density is invariably lower than 2×10^6. As the sampling density is lowered below this ideal there are two stages of impairment. In the first stage the picture quality falls off very slowly. The sampled picture appears to be continuous (although there may be no electro-optical interpolation at the display) since the sampling frequencies in both space and time are above the eye's cut-off. What are lost in this first stage are the very high spatial and temporal frequencies, which normally have low energy.

A threshold is reached when the sampling frequencies reach 60 samples per degree in space and 70 samples per second in time. Beyond this point the sampling structure itself becomes visible in the form of lines or dots in space and as flicker in time. Picture quality deteriorates more rapidly as the spatio-temporal continuity of the picture is destroyed. It is difficult to operate very far into this region without serious impairment, and steps must be taken such as the lowering of the display luminance. The sampling-visibility threshold is achieved at a density of approximately

$$60 \times 60 \times 70 = 2.5 \times 10^5 \text{ samples per degree}^2 \text{ second}$$

for bright pictures, and at lower densities as the luminance is decreased. This figure, which is a factor of eight reduced from the ideal, is approached by broadcast television systems.

Broadcast television

Some scanning parameters of broadcast television, System I, used in the United Kingdom and System M, used in the United States of America, are listed in Table 3.1.

In System I, line blanking occupies approximately 19% of the total line period and field blanking approximately 8% of the total field period. A wasteful total of $575 \times 12 \times 10^{-3} + 2 \times 1.612 = 10.12$ ms or 25.3%

of every frame period is used for blanking, this being necessary because of the slow retrace time of electromagnetic deflection systems used in domestic receivers. System M has a similar wastage figure.

Table 3.1   Parameters of CCIR 625-line System I and 525-line System M broadcast television

	System I	System M
Lines per frame	625	525
Active lines per frame	575	485 approximately
Frames per second	25	30
Line interlace	2 : 1	2 : 1
Line frequency	15 625 Hz	15 750 Hz
Aspect ratio (width/height)	4/3	4/3
Nominal video bandwidth	5. 5 MHz	4. 2 MHz
Line period	64 μs	63. 5 μs
Active line period	51. 7-52. 2 μs	52. 1-53. 3 μs
Line-blanking interval	11. 8-12. 3 μs	10. 2-11. 4 μs
Synchronising pulse width	4. 5-4. 9 μs	4. 19-5. 7 μs
Field period	20 ms	16. 667 ms
Active field period	18. 388 ms	15. 323-15. 450 ms
Field-blanking interval	1. 612 ms	1. 217-1. 344 ms
	(25 lines + 1 line-blanking interval)	(19-21 lines + 1 line-blanking interval)

Source: CCIR Conclusions, 1970, **5**, Part 2, Report 308-2, Characteristics of Monochrome Television Systems.

In Table 3.2 are listed some calculated values for the sampling frequency in each of the three dimensions of the image. These have been arrived at on the assumption that the viewer is sitting at a distance of either six or eight times the picture height from the screen, these being viewing distances which are used in the laboratory assessment of television pictures (CCIR Conclusions, 1970, **5**, Part 2, Report 405-1). The horizontal sampling frequency is arrived at by taking two samples per cycle of, in the case of System I, a 5. 5 MHz sine wave, this being the nominal bandwidth of the video signal. Thus the calculation for

Table 3.2 Sampling characteristics of broadcast television at viewing distances of six and eight times picture height

	System I (625 lines, 25 frames/s)		System M (525 lines, 30 frames/s)	
Viewing ratio (viewing distance/picture height)	6	8	6	8
Angle subtended at eye (width × height)	12.7° × 9.5°	9.5° × 7.2°	12.7° × 9.5°	9.5° × 7.2°
Picture size (samples wide × samples high)	572 × 575	572 × 575	443 × 485	443 × 485
Horizontal spatial sampling frequency (samples per degree)	45	60	35	47
Vertical spatial sampling frequency (samples per degree)	61	80	51	67
Temporal sampling frequency (samples per second)	50	50	60	60
Overall sampling density (samples per degree^2 second) with 2:1 line interlacing	6.9×10^4	1.2×10^5	5.4×10^4	9.4×10^4

System I at six times picture height is

$$\text{Horizontal sampling frequency} = \frac{\text{samples per active line time}}{\text{picture width in degrees}}$$

$$= \frac{2 \times 5.5 \times 10^6 \times 52 \times 10^{-6}}{12.7}$$

$$= 45 \text{ samples per degree}$$

The vertical sampling frequency is taken as the number of active lines per frame divided by the picture height in degrees and the temporal sampling frequency is taken as the field rate. The overall sampling density is calculated as the product of the three separate sampling frequencies, divided by two to allow for interlacing.

It may be seen from inspection of Table 3.2 that the sampling frequencies are comparable with the cut-off frequencies of the eye and that the overall sampling densities are of the same order of magnitude as the figure of 2.5×10^5 samples per degree^2 second, previously cited. In fact, were it not for 2:1 line interlacing, the overall sampling densities would approach this limit at eight times picture height in both System I and System M. The differences between the two systems are apparent from the table, which indicates that System I has higher spatial sampling frequencies than System M. System M, however, has a higher temporal sampling frequency and therefore brighter pictures are possible without visible flicker. It may be noted that in both systems the vertical sampling frequency is higher than the horizontal sampling frequency; this is because the samples are presented to the viewer without effective interpolation and it is therefore necessary to increase the vertical sampling frequency over parity with the horizontal sampling frequency. This is known as the *Kell effect,* and is discussed further in the next chapter. The high vertical sampling frequency serves both to provide spatial continuity and to reduce the visibility of interlacing flicker. In noninterlaced systems this frequency can be lower (Brown, 1967).

Visual telephone systems

At the time of writing several countries are experimenting with various forms of visual telephone systems. Table 3.3 shows the essential parameters of two such systems, the experimental UK *Viewphone* service (Gerrard and Thompson, 1973) and the US *Picturephone* service (Dorros, 1971; Crater 1971) together with calculations of sampling frequencies. In comparison with broadcast television, the visual telephone picture has a low spatial sampling density and therefore a more visible line structure as well as less resolution. The type of picture for which the systems are designed are head-and-shoulders pictures of people, which can be satisfactorily reproduced with a lower spatial bandwidth than is required for high-detail scenes, such

Table 3.3 Scanning parameters for the UK experimental *Viewphone* compared with the US *Picturephone* (monochrome) visual telephone services (reprinted with permission)

	Viewphone	*Picturephone*[†]
Lines per frame	319	267
Active lines per frame	303	251
Frames per second	25.08	29.96
Line interlace	2:1	2:1
Line frequency	8.0 kHz	8.0 kHz
Aspect ratio (width/height)	11/10	11/10
Nominal video bandwidth	1.0 MHz	1.0 MHz
Active line period	105.2 μs	105.5 μs
Screen size (width/height)	19.3 × 17.5 cm*	14 × 12.7 cm
Viewing distance	1.4 m	92 cm
Angle subtended at eye (width × height)	7.9° × 7.2°	8.7° × 7.8°
Picture size (samples wide × samples high)	210 × 303	211 × 251
Horizontal spatial sampling frequency (samples per degree)	27	24
Vertical spatial sampling frequency (samples per degree)	42	32
Temporal sampling frequency (samples per second)	50	60
Overall sampling density (samples per degree² second) with 2:1 line interlacing	2.8×10^4	2.3×10^4

* Pedestal model † Copyright 1971, American Telephone and Telegraph Company.

as crowd scenes, which are encountered in broadcast television. The larger angular subtense between scanning lines means, however, that interlacing flicker at the frame rate is more visible than at broadcast television standards. The problem is compounded by the need to view visual telephone pictures in bright surround conditions, since the viewer has to be seen by the distant party and must therefore be adequately illuminated. The preferred highlight luminance for Picturephone pictures is 275 cd/m² (Crater, 1971) compared with 70–170 cd/m² for monochrome broadcast television pictures at the same field rate (60/s) and 50 cd/m² at a field rate of 50/s (CCIR Conclusions, 1970, **5**, Part 2, Report 405-1).

Current visual telephone pictures therefore have lower sampling densities than broadcast television pictures when from visual considerations the use of brighter displays would suggest the advisability of higher densities. Considerations of cost, however, including the desire to utilise existing telephone cables for local transmission, have placed a practical limit on the video bandwidth at about 1 MHz. With this bandwidth limitation, it has proved to be better for face-to-face communication to provide a 7 or 8 degree picture of low resolution than a smaller picture of higher resolution.. Perhaps the future will see a demand for services such as medical consultation and diagnosis, education and shopping by television, computer interaction and document transmission, all over a wideband network. Advances in the coding and transmission of pictures as well as improved device technology, may make it possible to meet these demands more effectively and at a reasonable cost by alternative higher-resolution scanning standards.

Facsimile

Facsimile systems reproduce documents by low-speed scanning and video signal transmission over telephone lines. It is possible to calculate in advance the approximate number of samples per millimetre required to reproduce a document, on the assumption that it is held at a reading distance of, say, 40 cm. At this distance 1 sample/mm corresponds to about 7 samples/degree. Using a cut-off bandwidth for the eye of 60 cycles/degree, an ideal facsimile system will therefore have 2 × 60/7 or about 17 samples/mm and a system whose line structure is at the threshold of visibility will have half this number or about 8.5 samples/mm.

Common facsimile equipment, transmitting an A4 page (210 × 297 mm) over 3.4 kHz telephone lines in about 6 minutes, has a scanning density of 3.8 lines/mm, though variations about this figure are encountered. Costigan (1971) gives figures for line densities for various types of pictorial material: handwriting requires 3.1-3.8 lines/mm; fingerprints about 7.9 lines/mm (200 lines/in); photographs (wirephoto) 4-8 lines/mm. For newspaper pages about 16 lines/mm are needed for the text and a larger figure of 27 lines/mm for half-tone photographs appearing with the text (Huang, 1972a); the latter figure provides more resolution than the eye needs, but has to be used, in the absence of some suitable half-tone coding scheme, to avoid Moiré patterns caused by aliasing. A spatial sampling density for alphanumeric characters of 4.3 × 4.3 samples/mm = 18.5 samples/mm² is quoted by Arps, Erdmann, Neal and Schlaepfer (1969) for 97.5% legibility in a study of digital facsimile. Resolution along the direction of scan in facsimile systems is generally arranged to be equal to the vertical resolution, allowing for the Kell effect.

CRT displays of graphical material

CRT displays of graphical material, such as are used in computer-aided design and other computer-linked applications, are generally viewed at a closer distance than are broadcast television pictures. At an assumed viewing distance of 1 metre, 1 degree corresponds to 1.75 cm. The number of data points needed to provide as much spatial resolution as the eye can use is, for bright displays (500 cd/m^2 luminance, 60 cycles/degree visual cut-off), approximately

$$\frac{2 \times 60 \times 2 \times 60}{(1.75)^2} \simeq 4700 \text{ data points/cm}^2$$

Such displays can be presented in spatially discrete (dot) form and will be seen by the eye as spatially continuous. Continuity is preserved down to $4700/4 \simeq 1200$ data points per square centimetre. Lower sampling densities may be used at lower display luminances and larger viewing distances without the sampling structure being visible.

Shurtleff (1967) quotes the results of several studies of character legibility using scanned displays. For a high accuracy of identification (98-99% correct), alphanumeric symbols need to subtend a visual angle of at least 0.2-0.25 degrees and to be scanned at a minimum of 10-12 lines per symbol height. Taking the median figure in each of these ranges, this gives a line density of 49 lines/degree. For symbols subtending larger angles, accuracy of identification may be maintained at lower line densities; for example, symbols subtending 0.5 degrees require only 6 lines/symbol height for 99% accuracy of identification. Other factors such as the direction of scan (horizontal, vertical on 45 degree), white-on-black as opposed to black-on-white symbols and symbol fount were all found to have only a small effect on legibility.

The effects of important parameters such as whether there is interlacing, and what the scanning spot profile is, are not always brought out in reported studies. The difference between 6 lines/symbol and 10-12 lines/symbol for different angular sizes of symbol may be attributable to aperture effect. Marsh (1972) has pointed out that attention needs to be given to the criterion of legibility, with a disproportionate increase in display resolution being required for an increase from 99.0% to 99.9%. Thus in displays where the sampling structure is visible because there is ineffective interpolation between samples, complexities arise which probably require subjective assessment in each individual case. A sampling frequency of 60-120 samples/degree, derived from a consideration of the eye's bandwidth, is seen to provide an upper bound to practical design figures.

Aerial surveillance and space systems

A wide variety of standards have been used ranging from several hundred to several thousand scanning lines (Rechter, 1968; Eastman, 1970; Salomon, 1970). Television cameras with 10 000 lines have been produced, which allow considerable magnification of the pictures (Schade, 1971a).

3.6   The Video Signal

Bandwidth

The video signal may be in time-discrete form, as when the scanned samples are read into a computer or converted to PCM, or it may be continuous, as in the normal form of television camera where the scanning is continuous in the horizontal direction. In either event it can be viewed as a series of time-multiplexed image samples, the continuous case being produced by appropriate low-pass filtering of the discrete case.

If the sampling density of a scanner is ρ samples per degree^2 second and the image subtends α degrees $\times$ β degrees at the eye, the number of image samples to be transmitted per second is $\alpha\beta\rho$. If $1-\eta$ is the total fraction of time spent on line and frame or field blanking, the rate at which the image samples must be scanned during the active scanning periods is $\alpha\beta\rho/\eta$ samples per second. The minimum transmission bandwidth required for these samples is, by the sampling theorem, 0.5 Hz per sample per second. The bandwidth required for the video signal is therefore

$$W = \frac{\alpha\beta\rho}{2\eta}$$

As an example and a check on previous calculations, we compute the video bandwidth required for System I broadcast television signals. From Table 3.2 and using the previously computed figure of $1-\eta = 0.253$ or $\eta = 0.747$, we have

$$W = \frac{12.7 \times 9.5 \times 6.9 \times 10^4}{2 \times 0.747} = 5.57 \times 10^6 \text{ Hz}$$

which is within round-off accuracy of the nominal 5.5 MHz figure in Table 3.1.

The video transmission bandwidth is seen to be directly proportional to the spatio-temporal sampling density and to both the width and height of the picture. We have seen that in an ideal system ρ is about 2×10^6, but that it can be reduced to 2.5×10^5 without much deterioration of picture quality in many practical cases. Reduction by another order of magnitude is possible only by accepting noticeable loss of resolution. The figure of 2.5×10^5 gives rise to a video bandwidth of 167 kHz per square degree of picture size, assuming $\eta = 0.75$. It is clear therefore that even very small pictures require far larger transmission bandwidths than speech signals. Displayed picture size is an influential parameter in determining the video bandwidth since, assuming a fixed aspect ratio, the bandwidth is proportional to the square of the height or width of the picture. Picture size, as we have seen from the practical systems studied, needs to be at least 50 square degrees for effective visual communication and this in turn means bandwidths in megahertz. Despite advances in picture coding (Chapter 5) it is still not possible to provide effective visual communication much below 1 MHz or its digital equivalent. Of course in facsimile transmission, where there is no motion, the transmission rate and bandwidth may be as low as desired, subject only to the volume of material to be handled and the patience of the recipient at the receiving terminal.

Video spectrum

Within the bandwidth W, what distribution of video spectral energy results from scanning an image? This result is of fundamental importance in the study of image transmission, and was derived by Mertz and Gray (1934). The analysis may be carried through for both x-discrete and x-continuous scanning, but the video signal in the former case is just a sampled version of the video signal in the latter case, and its spectrum comprises replications along the video frequency axis of the spectrum of the continuous video signal. We therefore derive the simpler case of the video signal spectrum with x-continuous scanning.

Consider first a stationary image $g(x, y)$ of width A and height B, scanned by a spot of infinitesimal width in a noninterlaced scan with zero retrace time (Figure 3.11a). For mathematical convenience, the scanning lines will be considered to be oriented at a small angle θ to the horizontal, corresponding to the practical case where the vertical deflection of the spot is controlled by a sawtooth rather than a ratchet timebase. Later we consider the modifications required to deal with purely horizontal scanning lines, as well as the effects of interlacing, motion in the image, finite-diameter spots and blanking intervals. An equivalent description of the scan is illustrated in Figure 3.11b, in which there is only one scanning line, of infinite extent, scanning replications of the rotated image. In this case the scanning spot traces the same path across the image as in Figure 3.11a, provided that $\tan \theta = Y/A$, where Y is the vertical spacing of the scanning lines. Assuming this condition holds, let the multiple image of Figure 3.11b be represented by $r(x, y)$. Then the scanned signal $s(x)$, expressed as a function of x, is given by the cross-section of $r(x, y)$ taken along the x axis. This can be written mathematically as

$$s(x) = r(x, y) \,.\, \delta(y)$$

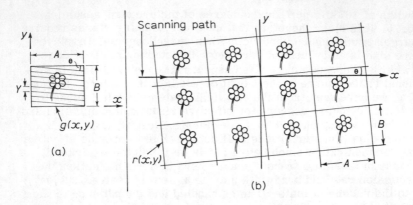

Figure 3.11 Equivalent scanning descriptions. In (a) the image is scanned by multiple scanning lines with a vertical spacing Y, inclined to the axis at θ = arctan (Y/A); in (b) the image is replicated in x, y space, rotated anticlockwise by θ and scanned by a single scanning line coincident with the x axis.

where $\delta(y)$ is an impulse sheet lying along the x axis. The video signal is the same as $s(x)$ apart from a scaling constant k linking x and t, which is equal to the spot velocity. For simplicity assume $k = 1$ and that we have adjusted the magnification of the image, i.e. the dimensions A and B, so that the spot scans across the width of the image in time T_L, the line period. We may then derive the video spectrum from the spatial spectrum $S(u)$ by substituting $f = u$, and $T_L \cos \theta = A$, where f is video signal frequency, and u the horizontal spatial frequency. Thus the dimensions of the image may be viewed as spatial or temporal, as suits our convenience. Following this procedure, the spectrum of $s(x)$ can be calculated by first writing $\delta(y)$ as a separable product. Thus

$$s(x) = r(x, y) \; . \; [\delta(y) \; . \; 1]$$

whence $S(u)$, by the usual rules, is

$$S(u) = R(u, v) * [1 \; . \; \delta(u)]$$

$$= R(u, v) * \delta(u)$$

We shall see that this expression can be given a simple graphical interpretation once $R(u, v)$ is known. $R(u, v)$ is the two-dimensional spectrum of the replicated and rotated image of Figure 3.11b. To evaluate it we need to write down a description for $r(x, y)$:

$$r(x, y) = \{\text{rep}_{A, B} \; [g(x, y)]\}_{\theta}$$

where the subscript θ indicates that the whole replicated image is rotated by an angle θ. To find the spectrum of $r(x, y)$, we use the result that if an image is rotated by θ in the x, y plane, its spectrum is similarly rotated by θ in the u, v plane (this may be proved by transforming to polar coordinates). Then

$$R(u, v) = \left\{ \frac{1}{AB} \, \mathrm{comb}_{1/A, 1/B} \left[G(u, v) \right] \right\}_\theta$$

Thus the spectrum of the 'polyphoto' image of Figure 3.11b is a sampled version of the image spectrum $G(u, v)$ rotated through an angle θ. Figure 3.12 shows a graphical representation of the convolution of $R(u, v)$ and $\delta(u)$. The impulse sheet $\delta(u)$, which is moved

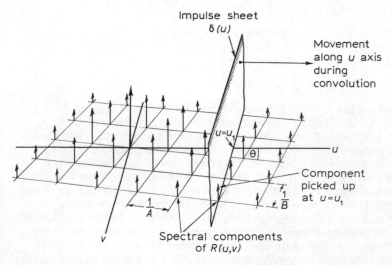

Figure 3.12 Graphical representation of $R(u, v) * \delta(u)$.

along the u axis in the convolution process, picks up and sums at $u = u_1$, all components $R(u_1, v)$. The effect may be seen by projecting all the delta function components of $R(u, v)$ onto a plane erected vertically above the u axis. Equivalently, the whole figure may be rotated by the angle θ, as illustrated in Figure 3.13.

The relationship between the spectrum of the image and the video spectrum, represented graphically in Figure 3.13, has a number of implications for video signal transmission. The image spectrum, as we have seen, typically has its energy concentrated at low spatial frequencies and decays to small values at high spatial frequencies. When sampled every $1/A$ in the u dimension and every $1/B$ in the v dimension, the sample magnitudes similarly decay with increasing

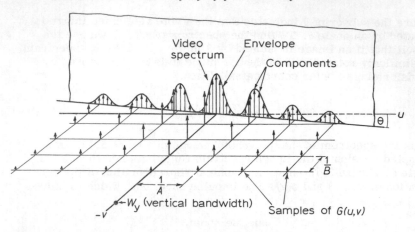

Figure 3.13 The video spectrum as a projection of the sampled spectrum of g(x, y) onto a vertical plane rotated through an angle θ from the u axis towards the −v axis.

values of u and v. Their projection onto the plane in Figure 3.13 produces a video spectrum with peaks of energy at frequencies $(1/A) \times \cos \theta = 1/T_L = f_L$, the line scanning frequency. These peaks gradually decay with increasing f. Around each peak there is a group of components spaced at the projection of the distance $1/B$ onto the video spectral plane. This distance is $(1/B) \times \sin \theta$. With reference to Figure 3.11, the distance travelled by the spot in scanning a complete frame is $B/\sin \theta$, hence the frame period is $T_F = B/\sin \theta$ and the frame frequency $f_F = (1/B) \sin \theta$. So the components in each of the line-frequency groups are spaced at intervals of the frame frequency, and their envelope is determined by the decay of the vertical spatial frequency spectrum. In a practical case θ is very small; for example in 625-line noninterlaced pictures with 575 active lines and 4/3 aspect ratio, $\theta = \arctan(0.75/575) = 0.075$ degree. Hence, depending on the vertical spatial-frequency energy in the image, there may be and typically are relatively large gaps in the video spectrum where there is little or no energy. This was pointed out by Mertz and Gray in their original paper.

Each component in the video spectrum is seen to convey a distinct piece of information about the image spectrum. The components occurring at exact harmonics of f_L, the line frequency, carry information about spatial frequencies with a zero vertical component. The components distant from harmonics of the line frequency carry information about the high vertical spatial frequencies. The information about the low horizontal spatial frequencies is carried in the low-frequency part of the video spectrum and the high horizontal spatial frequencies in the high-frequency part of the video spectrum. If during transmission, the properties of the channel cause any group of video frequency components to be lost, the effect on the image is calculable by excising the appropriate spatial-frequency components from the image spectrum and inverse Fourier transforming. From a knowledge of the properties of vision, it may be appreciated that video frequencies midway between the higher line harmonics in the spectrum are the ones most easily removed, added to or attenuated without serious impairment to the reconstructed image. A great deal of use is made of this in practice.

If the inclination θ of the scanning lines is large, corresponding to a coarse line spacing, there will be an increased spread of the frame-frequency components about each line harmonic. There may eventually come a point when the components of adjacent line harmonics overlap and add to or subtract frome one another. This is what Mertz and Gray termed 'confusion' in the video signal and corresponds to what we have termed aliasing. For if overlap is to be avoided, reference to the geometry of Figure 3.13 indicates that the projection of the vertical bandwidth W_y onto the video spectral plane must be less than $f_L/2 = (\cos \theta)/2A$. Hence

$$W_y \sin \theta < (\cos \theta)/2A$$

$$\therefore W_y < 1/(2A \tan \theta) = 1/2Y$$

This is the sampling theorem result previously derived

Aperture effect

It was noted previously that the effect of a spot aperture $h_0(x, y)$ was equivalent to convolution of the image with the rotated aperture function $h(x, y) = h_0(-x, -y)$, followed by ideal scanning. The effect on the image spectrum $G(u, v)$ is that of low-pass filtering by $H(u, v)$, the transform of $h(x, y)$. The video signal is modified in two ways: first, its overall or macro-envelope decay is steepened and the video bandwidth may be reduced: second, the micro-envelope of the line-harmonic groups is also modified. A spot profile which has a broader spread in the y direction than the x direction produces a sharper cut-off in the u, v plane for vertical spatial frequencies than for horizontal spatial frequencies; in turn this affects the micro-envelope decay of the line-harmonic groups more severely. An astigmatic spot profile of this type may be advantageous in systems with a tendency to produce vertical aliasing.

Influence of θ

The analysis of video spectra has been carried through under an assumption of sloping rather than purely horizontal scanning lines. The angle of inclination θ is about 0.1-0.2 degrees in the systems previously studied and the difference between this and horizontal scanning is for practical purposes negligible. An analysis of horizontal scanning may however be carried out by modifying Figure 3.11b such that the replications are not rotated but rather subject to successive vertical displacement. This can be produced by convolution of the basic image with a non-rectangular array of delta functions. This approach has been suggested by Huang.*

Effect of blanking and synchronising pulses

In practice the scanning spot takes a finite time for flyback, during which the spot is blanked to make it invisible (Figure 3.14).

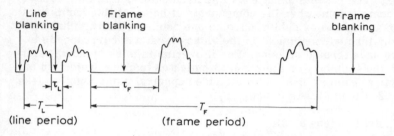

Figure 3.14 Blanking for a noninterlaced video signal.

In addition, synchronising pulses are inserted in the blanking interval to ensure that the receiver scan is locked to the transmitter scan.

We shall consider the effect of blanking only. The spectrum of the synchronising pulses may simply be added to that of the blanked video. To incorporate blanking we may suppose that it is imposed on the video signal $s(t)$ after zero flyback-time scanning, its effect being to reduce the size of the displayed image.

The blanking waveform in the temporal domain has both line and frame blanking. Let T_L and T_F be the line and frame periods respectively and τ_L and τ_F the respective blanking periods (Figure 3.14). To insert blanking in the video waveform, we multiply the video signal $s(t)$ by the blanking waveform

$$b(t) = b_L(t) \cdot b_F(t)$$

$$= \left[1 - \operatorname{rep}_{T_L}\left(\operatorname{rect}\frac{t}{\tau_L}\right)\right] \cdot \left[1 - \operatorname{rep}_{T_F}\left(\operatorname{rect}\frac{t}{\tau_F}\right)\right]$$

where the first term $b_L(t)$ describes the line blanking and the second term $b_F(t)$ the frame blanking. Both terms are rectangular waves

---

* T. S. Huang, private communication.

alternating between amplitudes of 0 and 1. The video signal with blanking is

$$s_1(t) = s(t) \cdot b(t)$$
$$= s(t) \cdot \left[1 - \mathrm{rep}_{T_L}\left(\mathrm{rect}\,\frac{t}{\tau_L}\right)\right] \cdot \left[1 - \mathrm{rep}_{T_F}\left(\mathrm{rect}\,\frac{t}{\tau_F}\right)\right]$$

Since $s_1(t)$ is the product of three separate components, its spectrum $s_1(f)$ is the convolution of their individual transforms. From Table 1.1,

$$S_1(f) = S(f) * B_L(f) * B_F(f)$$
$$= S(f) * \left[\delta(f) - \frac{1}{T_L}\,\mathrm{comb}_{1/T_L}\,\tau_L\,\mathrm{sinc}\,f\tau_L\right]$$
$$* \left[\delta(f) - \frac{1}{T_F}\,\mathrm{comb}_{1/T_F}\,(\tau_F\,\mathrm{sinc}\,f\tau_F)\right]$$

To appreciate the form of this spectrum, it is helpful to consider the simplest type of image, i.e. a uniform white or grey field.

Video spectrum of a uniform white field

The image of a uniform white field has a constant illuminance in the image plane, so that $g(x,y) = k_1$ (constant). Its two-dimensional transform (Table 1.2) is a delta function at the origin

$$G(u,v) = k_1\delta(u,v)$$

Replicating $g(x,y)$ throughout the x, y space and scanning, by the previous procedure, we get

$$s(t) = k_1$$

and

$$s(f) = k_1\delta(f)$$

This spectrum must be convolved with the blanking spectra to give the blanked video spectrum

$$S_1(f) = k_1\delta(f) * B_F(f) * B_F(f)$$

The three spectra are shown in Figure 3.15, together with the amplitude spectrum of their convolved product. Since the convolution of any function with a delta function reproduces the function at the location of that delta function, the convolution of $B_L(f)$ with $B_F(f)$ causes a replication of the latter about every line harmonic of the former. The second convolution with the image spectrum merely causes a multiplication by the constant k_1 and the form of the spectrum is determined solely by the blanking pulses in this case. The spectrum is seen to have a broad macro-envelope of the form sinc $(f\tau_L)$ decaying at 6 dB/octave within which the line harmonics occur every $f_L = 1/T_L$. About each line harmonic there is a group of frame harmonics every $f_F = 1/T_F$ with a micro-envelope of sinc $(f\tau_F)$ form. Since typically $T_F \gg T_L$ and $\tau_F \gg \tau_L$, the spectrum consists of clumps of energy every $f_L = 1/T_L$ with gaps in between.

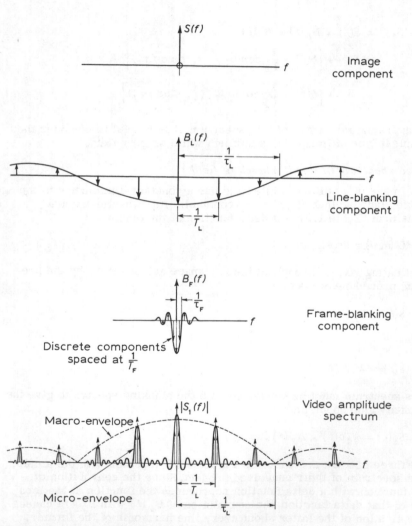

Figure 3.15 Compositional video spectra for a uniform white field.

Images with motion

The analysis of images with motion requires the use of three-dimensional Fourier transforms. If the image is $g(x, y, t)$, let it be replicated at $x = \pm A, \pm 2A, \pm 3A, \ldots, y = \pm B, \pm 2B, \pm 3B, \ldots$ (Figure 3.16). To scan the image the scanning spot locus is inclined at angle $\theta = $ arctan (Y/A) to the x, t plane and angle $\phi = $ arctan (T_F/A) to the x, y plane. This is equivalent to scanning along the x axis after a rotation of θ about the t axis, and ϕ about the y axis.

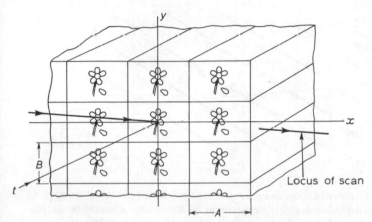

Figure 3.16 Analysis of the scanning process for an image with motion by replication in x, y, t space.

The three-dimensional spectrum $R_0(u, v, f)$ of the replicated image $r_0(x, y, t) = \mathrm{rep}_{x=A, y=B}[g(x, y, t)]$ is a line spectrum in the u and v dimensions but is continuous in the f dimension (Figure 3.17). With bandlimitation in the f dimension, $R_0(u, v, f)$ appears as a regular array of needles whose orientation is normal to the u, v plane. The video spectrum $S(f)$ is the projection of $R_0(u, v, f)$ onto a line with the same inclination as the scanning spot locus. This produces a continuous $S(f)$, since each of the needles projects as a finite-width pulse onto the line. In the special case when the image is stationary, the needles shrink to zero length and $S(f)$ becomes a line spectrum. In the practical case when $G(u, v, f)$ has very little high-frequency energy along the temporal-frequency axis, it can be seen that $S(f)$ will peak at harmonics of the frame frequency f_F and line frequency f_L.

As in the two-dimensional case, the video spectrum resulting from the scanning of an image with motion carries identifiable information about the image spectrum $G(u, v, f)$. The degree of spectral spread about any line or frame harmonic, corresponding to some spatial component in the image, indicates the amount of movement of that spatial component. If an image comprises high-resolution stationary objects and low-resolution moving objects, the video spectral components at low frequencies will be broader than at high frequencies. If $G(u, v, f)$ is not appropriately bandlimited in all three dimensions in relation to the scanning angles θ and ϕ, then aliasing occurs in the video signal and the image information cannot be recovered at the receiver.

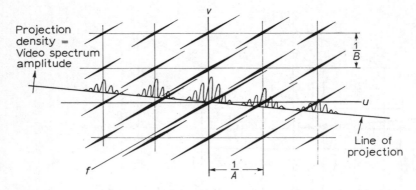

Figure 3.17   Needle spectrum $R_0(u, v, f)$ of the replicated image of Figure 3.16, showing the derivation of the video spectrum as the projection of the three-dimensional spectral components onto a single line.

Line-interlaced scanning

The procedure previously described for deriving video spectra by straight-line scanning through replications of the image $g(x, y)$ or $g(x, y, t)$ needs modification when the scanning is line-interlaced. In a rough analysis we might note that in an interlaced field the picture has not changed much from the previous field, because of the typical predominance of both slow movement and low spatial detail. In this case the spectrum is obtained approximately from the previous result by assuming an effective frame frequency equal to the field frequency.

Using a more exact analysis, the modification required for interlacing is to double the tangent of the angle θ which the scanning spot locus makes with the xt plane, while ensuring that each frame contains an *odd* number of lines. This means that at the end of the first field the spot completes only half a line before passing to the next replication. In the frequency domain the projection of $G(u, v, f)$ must be made onto a line at the increased angle ($\simeq 2\theta$).

The effect of this increased angle may be seen by reference to Figure 3.13 or 3.17 and is illustrated in Figure 3.18. What is produced is a video spectrum in which the peaks at field-frequency intervals centred about the nth line-frequency harmonic, interlace with the components of the adjacent $(n-1)$th and $(n+1)$th harmonics. The figure also shows the result previously derived—that aliasing occurs when there is movement of high vertical spatial-frequency image components; this broadens the interlaced components, producing overlap. In a practical case the interlace intrusion into neighbouring line harmonics might not be as severe as shown in Figure 3.18 because of the fall-off in the vertical spatial spectrum.

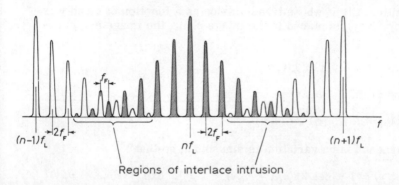

Regions of interlace intrusion

Figure 3.18 Video spectrum resulting from 2 : 1 line-interlaced scanning. The portion between the $(n-1)$th and $(n+1)$th line harmonics is shown. The spread of each component is determined by the degree of motion, and aliasing results when there is motion of high vertical spatial frequencies (f_L = line frequency; f_F = frame frequency; $2f_F$ = field frequency, n = a positive integer).

Effect of system nonlinearities

The relationship between image illuminance L and video signal amplitude s depends on the type of image sensor being used. The common form is a power law $s = kL^\gamma$ where k is a constant. For vidicons $\gamma \simeq 0.5$-0.6 but for image orthicons, plumbicons and silicon diode tubes $\gamma \simeq 1$. Prior to transmission the signal may also be corrected for the typically nonlinear characteristic of the display device and further modified to give an overall gamma appropriate to the viewing conditions at the display.

A nonlinearity in a communication circuit causes intermodulation distortion (Carlson, 1968). The effect on the spectrum is most easily analysed when γ is a positive integer; thus when $\gamma = 2$, the video signal amplitude is proportional to the square of the illuminance. Since self-multiplication in the time domain is equivalent to convolution in the frequency domain, the spectrum of the (linear) video signal is convolved with itself, doubling its bandwidth. The excess bandwidth is removed by the channel filter, such that even if an inverse gamma relationship exists at the receiver, the signal cannot be recovered. Normally, however, the transmitted video signal has, or is corrected to have, a gamma less than unity. It may be shown that certain types of signal have their bandwidth reduced rather than expanded when this type of nonlinearity is encountered. The effect on picture quality is not found to be serious, though the microstructure of the spectrum is modified.

3.7   Spatial Carrier Modulation

If an optical filter, whose transmission as a function of x and y is given by $h(x, y)$, is placed in the image plane, the image $g(x, y)$ becomes

$$g_1(x, y) = h(x, y) \cdot g(x, y)$$

with spectrum

$$G_1(u, v) = H(u, v) * G(u, v)$$

If the transmission variation is sinusoidal, so that

$$h(x, y) = 1 + \cos 2\pi(u_0 x + v_0 y) = 1 + \tfrac{1}{2} \exp\left[j 2\pi(u_0 x + v_0 y)\right]$$
$$+ \tfrac{1}{2} \exp\left[-j 2\pi(u_0 x + v_0 y)\right]$$

where u_0 and v_0 are the horizontal and vertical spatial frequencies respectively, we have, from Table 1.2,

$$H(u, v) = \delta(u, v) + \tfrac{1}{2}\,\delta(u - u_0, v - v_0) + \tfrac{1}{2}\,\delta(u + u_0, v + v_0)$$

and

$$G_1(u, v) = G(u, v) + \tfrac{1}{2}\,G(u - u_0, v - v_0) + \tfrac{1}{2}\,G(u + u_0, v + v_0)$$

The convolution of $G(u, v)$ with $H(u, v)$ in this case causes $G(u, v)$ to be shifted in frequency (Figure 3.19), the process being analogous to modulation of an electrical carrier $\cos 2\pi f t$ by a signal $g(t)$. For this reason $\cos 2\pi(u_0 x + v_0 y)$ can be regarded as a *spatial carrier* and the action of multiplication by $g(x, y)$ as *spatial carrier modulation*. A difference between spatial and temporal modulation is that the carrier cannot go negative in the spatial case. This means that $G(u, v)$ also appears in baseband form at the origin, as well as at the carrier position. Again, since $g(x, y)$ represents illuminance, $G(u, v)$ necessarily has a delta function at the origin. The modulation process produces a spatial carrier at $\pm u_0$, $\pm v_0$, so the process is not carrier-suppressing.

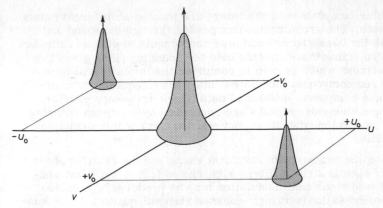

Figure 3.19 Spatial carrier modulation, showing G(u, v) shifted to

$$u = \pm u_0, v = \pm v_0.$$

Spatial carrier modulation is used in colour television cameras
having only one camera tube. In one version of this camera (Briel,
1970), two spatial carriers are utilised, one responding only to red
light (alternately neutral and cyan stripes) and the other to blue light
(neutral and yellow stripes). By using different spatial·frequencies
or different orientations of the filters (as shown in Figure 3.20) the

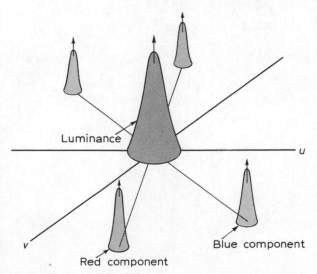

*Figure 3.20 Principal of the single-tube colour camera using spatial
carrier modulation of the red and blue components onto different
carriers.*

red and blue components of the image are located at different points in u, v space. The green component passes through baseband and sums with the baseband red and blue components to give a luminance signal. Projecting these spectra onto the scanning plane gives the video spectrum, which is seen to comprise the luminance at baseband, the red component modulated onto a low-frequency carrier and the blue component modulated onto a high-frequency carrier. The red and blue video signals are recovered by bandpass filtering followed by envelope detection. Several variants of this principle are possible.

By altering the number, the waveform shape and the relative phase of a set of optical striped filters $h_1(x, y), i = 1, 2, \ldots . n$, many analogues of unidimensional modulation may be produced, e.g. pulse amplitude modulation (with high-contrast stripes), quadrature modulation, frequency-division multiplex, etc. By the scanning process the two-dimensional case is converted to its unidimensional equivalent.

Chapter 4

RECEPTION AND DISPLAY OF MONOCHROME PICTURES

Displays take a variety of forms (Poole, 1966), but one of the most common is the cathode ray tube (CRT) display and this will be used by way of an example to illustrate certain principles. At the receiver the video signal must be demultiplexed and the samples rearranged in three-dimensional space-time in order to reconstruct the image. To accomplish this the CRT scanning beam is synchronised with that at the transmitter.

As the sampling density in practical systems is often less than the ideal, the sampling structure is visible to the viewer. He sees this in the form of discrete lines or dots in the spatial dimension and as flicker in the temporal dimension. In many cases no discrete structure in the horizontal spatial dimension is visible since the video signal is applied to the CRT cathode or grid in continuous form; whatever low-pass electrical filtering of the video signal has taken place results in proportional low-pass horizontal spatial filtering of the displayed image. In this instance the problem of sampling-structure visibility is confined to the vertical spatial and temporal dimensions.

It is possible to reduce the visibility of the scanning structure in the following ways.

4.1 Line Broadening

To minimise or eliminate line structure in the displayed image, the lines may be broadened. This is achieved if vertical astigmatism is introduced in the electron optics to distort the cross-section of the scanning spot. Alternatively, a low-amplitude high-frequency periodic signal can be added to the vertical deflection signal to cause the spot to be deflected rapidly up and down as it traverses the image. This method is known as *spot wobble* (Jesty, 1958). In a more complex arrangement, the spot wobble can be applied synchronously at scanner and display; this has the effect of scanning not in straight lines but in wavy lines, equivalent to a degree of spatial interlacing. However, we shall confine the discussion to straight-line scanning.

What is the ideal form of line broadening and what can be achieved practically? Line broadening is a method of interpolation between samples of the image in the vertical spatial dimension (Monteath, 1962) and has its equivalent in the Fourier transform domain as a form of low-pass filtering. The interpolation required depends on the spatio-temporal sampling pattern and the form of image bandlimitation used at the camera. In the simplest case the image spectrum $G(u,v,f)$ is bandlimited to a rectangular shape with bandwidths W_x, W_y and W_t in the u, v and f dimensions respectively, i.e. suppose this bandlimitation function is separable into a product of three rectangular functions and in particular, the v or vertical spatial frequency function is

$$H(v) = \text{rect}\left(\frac{v}{2W_y}\right)$$

Consider a vertical array of picture elements in the display (Figure 4.1). This array can be described as a train of samples of the image

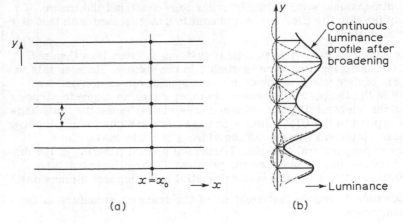

Figure 4.1 (a) Line structure and
(b) ideal line broadening with sinc functions.

$g(x, y, t)$ taken along a vertical line $x = x_0$ at $t = t_0$. Let $g_0(y) = g(x_0, y, t_0)$. Then the samples are describable as

$$s(y) = \text{comb}_Y[g_0(y)]$$

where Y is the vertical spacing between lines. If the image is infinite in extent in the vertical spatial direction, as it will be if it is strictly bandlimited to W_y, the sampling theorem tells us that $g_0(y)$ can be fully recovered from the samples $s(y)$ with an ideal low-pass spatial filter of bandwidth $1/2Y > W_y$. The equivalent operation in the vertical spatial domain is

$$g_0(y) = s(y) * \text{sinc}(y/Y)$$

Thus the ideal spot cross-section in this case is

$$\text{sinc}(y/Y) = \frac{\sin(\pi y/Y)}{(\pi y/Y)}$$

having zeros at $\pm Y, \pm 2Y, \pm 3Y, \ldots$, i.e. at each of the other lines. This spot cross-section gives a total elimination of line structure and an exact reproduction of the original image.

In the case of images bandlimited to non-rectangular shapes, a different form of line broadening may be required. For example, with line interlacing we saw that a circular shape in the v, f plane was a better one, to suppress frequencies which were high both in vertical space and time. The ideal type of display spot profile in this case is a circularly symmetrical $J_1(r)/r$ function (Table 1.2) in the y, t plane. In the general case therefore, for efficient scanning, the spot profile is not specifiable as a function of y only, but involves t and perhaps also x.

It is not possible to implement ideal spot cross-sections in CRT displays because of the negative values of luminance required. Practical spot design is a problem in low-pass filtering with the constraint that the impulse response may not have negative values. However, in comparison with electrical filters, which can only have a one-sided impulse response, spot cross-sections can be two-sided. More often than not, nothing is done about line broadening in scanned displays, reliance being placed on the eye to provide some filtering. With the observer seated far enough away from the screen this can be quite effective, since the eye's spatial frequency response cuts off fairly sharply. However, something could be gained by a better form of line broadening, allowing a reduction in the sampling frequency and a consequent lowering of the video bandwidth.

As a corollary, it may be noted that a rectangular spot (Figure 4.2), which gives a perfect interpolation between lines for a uniform white or grey field, is non-ideal for any informative image. It produces the equivalent of a sample-and-hold operation on $g_0(y)$ which, analysis shows (Cattermole, 1969), attenuates the spatial frequencies near W_y by 4 dB. This is because the aperture effect due to a rectangular spot is the equivalent of sinc function filtering. Other forms of practical line broadening also typically cause a loss in image resolution, and a balance must be found, by subjective experiment, between quality degradation due to resolution loss and quality improvement due to reduction in raster visibility.

Supersampled displays

A technique which it may be possible to use for producing complicated spot profiles is that of *supersampling* at the display. Instead of trying to produce a continuous display by electron-optical interpolation, the display is left in discrete, sample form in time and space. The

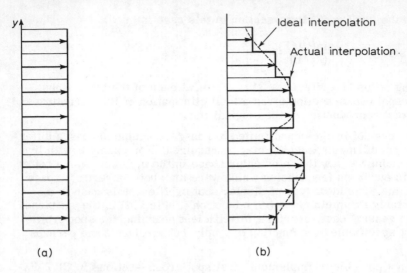

Figure 4.2 Effect of a rectangular spot
(a) uniform field (b) non-uniform field.

sampling frequency in each dimension is increased to several times normal so that it is comfortably about the eye's cut-off bandwidth. The spot profile is stored in sampled-data form and the convolution with the incoming, scanned image samples performed electronically, to give computed values for each of the samples in the supersampled display. This avoids the problem of negative light output but requires storage of the picture.

The storage problem could be alleviated if the picture were displayed in two-level form, as in Figure 2.9. Using solid-state displays such as arrays of light-emitting diodes, the display problem could also be made easier by this technique. The conversion to all-digital representation could be achieved at the camera by using a supersampled image sensor, the individual elements of which had a binary response with a dithered bias (Section 5.4). The bias, which could be either optically or electrically introduced, would be designed to allow progressively more binary response elements to be activated as the illuminance increased.

A lower-density pattern of transmitted multilevel samples could be derived from the high-density pattern by two- or three-dimensional digital filtering operations performed on the supersampled image elements, the operations being inverse to those used in the display.

4.2   Kell Factor

If a sine-wave grating is placed in front of the camera and turned so that its stripes are parallel to the scanning lines, an experiment can be carried out to determine the minimum number of lines needed to reproduce the grating. With ideal scanning and an ideal receiver having sinc function line broadening, the answer is given by the sampling theorem, namely two lines for every cycle of the grating. With the practical imperfections already discussed, it is found that rather more than two lines per cycle are required (Kell, Bedford and Trainer, 1934).

The ratio k_1 of the ideal to the experimentally determined number of lines per cycle is called the *Kell factor*. The numerical value obtained is influenced by the scanning parameters, line broadening, interlacing, the extent of involvement of the low-pass spatial filtering action of the eye (i.e. how near the observer is to the display) and the psychometric technique used for establishing the threshold; experimental results have been in the range 0.42-0.85, with interlaced scans giving lower figures than noninterlaced scans (Monteath, 1962). A mean figure of 0.7 is often used.

As defined above, the Kell factor is an indication of the imperfection of the vertical spatial sampling process in the transmission of the image. Better spot shapes or higher sampling densities could in principle raise the Kell factor. Some authors, however, have used a different definition of Kell factor (Lewis, 1962). In this alternative definition the factor is defined as the ratio k_2 of the vertical distance between scanning lines to the horizontal distance along a scanning line corresponding to a half-period of a sine wave at the upper video band edge. This definition does not involve any psychometrics, but it turns the Kell factor into a statement about the ratio of horizontal to vertical spatial sampling frequencies once the system has been designed, rather than a factor which could be used in arriving at a design for, say, equal horizontal and vertical sharpness. The numerical values obtained are also somewhat variable since the upper video band edge is subject to interpretation; however, Lewis has suggested ways of standardising the bandwidth measurement.

4.3   Phosphors

Phosphors serve, or should serve, the same purpose in the temporal domain as line broadening does in the spatial domain, i.e. to interpolate between image samples. If a given image is describable as $g(x, y, t)$, consider a series of samples in successive frames taken at the point $x = x_1, y = y_1$. Let $g_1(t) = g(x_1, y_1, t)$ and let the samples be

$$s_1(t) = \mathrm{comb}_T[g_1(t)]$$

where T is the frame period. As we have seen, the ideal form of interpolation depends on the sampling structure and pre-scan image bandlimitation. Taking the previous case where the image spectrum is separable, to recover $g_1(t)$ from its samples we convolve $s_1(t)$ with

$h(t)$, where

$$h(t) = \text{sinc } (t/T) = \frac{\sin (\pi t/T)}{(\pi t/T)}$$

An ideal phosphor would have this type of decay. This ideal character-istic is physically non-attainable, both because it has a response for negative values of t and because it has negative values corresponding to negative light output. Practical phosphors tend to have an approxi-mately exponential or power law decay. If the decay is exponential then the phosphor is equivalent to a one-stage RC filter (Figure 4.3).

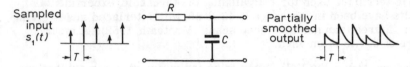

Figure 4.3 Equivalent circuit of an ex-ponentially decaying phosphor.

The frequency characteristic of this filter has a gentle roll-off with an asymptotic decay at 6 dB/ octave. Its filtering action is therefore very poor as regards the smoothing of $s_1(t)$. To appreciate this, consider Figure 4.4, which shows the replicated spectrum $S_1(f)$ filtered by (a) a practical phosphor having an exponential decay and (b) an ideal phosphor with a sinc function decay and rectangular frequency response. It can be seen that in the practical case a higher frame rate has to be used. The major problem in (a) is sampling frequency breakthrough; since there is a delta function at the centre of each replication of $G_1(f)$, a strong attenuation of the filter is required at the centre frequency of the first replication to avoid breakthrough. Breakthrough appears as flicker in the display.

The foregoing analysis assumes that the frame rate is low enough that the eye's temporal low-pass filtering action is not brought into play. However, the smoothing action of practical phosphors is so inadequate that for the avoidance of flicker it is usually necessary to raise the frame rate (or the field rate, for interlaced scanning) to near the cut-off frequency of the eye's characteristic. This, as we have seen, is about 70 Hz for bright displays. In broadcast television, the American 60 Hz field rate is not far short of this figure; the European 50 Hz field rate does not allow very bright flicker-free displays.

In Figure 4.5 are shown some of the phosphors used in CRT displays, classified according to their rate of decay. Since the smoothing effect of phosphors at practical field rates is small in comparison with the eye, the choice of phosphor is made primarily with respect to its

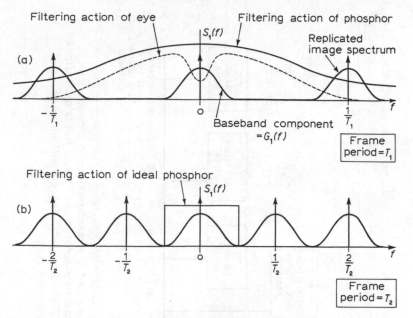

*Figure 4.4 (a) Temporal filtering action
of a practical phosphor. (b) Rectangular
filtering action of an ideal phosphor,
allowing a lower frame rate.*

luminous efficiency and colour, while ensuring that for adequate
rendition of motion there is decay to an insignificant value by the next
field. The eye's temporal cut-off characteristic approximates that of
a 6–9 stage RC filter, and the phosphor merely adds an additional
stage with, under the condition of no motion blurring, little effect in
reducing flicker (Sperling, 1971).

4.4 Visibility of Sine-wave Interference

During transmission the video signal may pick up interference or
noise, which appears as a spurious spatio-temporal pattern in the display. A study of this subject involves an appreciation of how video
frequencies convert to spatio-temporal frequencies. This is the
inverse process to that at the transmitter where, as we have seen,
video frequencies are generated as a projection of spatio-temporal
image frequencies onto the scanning plane. Provided the image is
appropriately bandlimited before scanning, the three-dimensional
spectrum of the image is fully reconstructable from the video
spectrum, and we can use Figures 3.13 and 3.17 to derive the effects
of sine-wave interference.

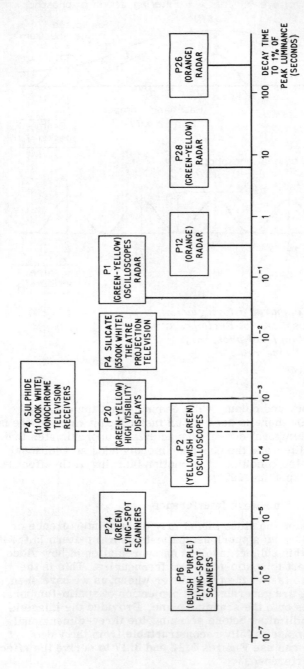

Figure 4.5 Some CRT phosphors having United States Electronic Industries Association registered P numbers, classified by approximate decay time to 1% of peak luminance (this is, however, affected by anode current). Also shown are approximate colours and typical fields of applications. Source: Optical Characteristics of Cathode Ray Tube Screens'. Jedec Publication No. 16–B (August, 1971). Electronic Industries Association, Washington, D.C.

Another method has been suggested by Brainard (1967). We first
examine the image pattern generated by a single interfering sinusoid
$\sin 2\pi f_0 t$. From this we can later generalise to other types of interference and noise. The appearance of the sinusoid on the display
screen may be derived with the aid of Figure 4.6. The figure shows
a set of orthogonal axes oriented in the x, y and t dimensions, with
strips of image samples along each axis. In terms of our established
convention, let the sample spacings be X, Y and T in the x, y and t
dimensions respectively. We proceed to determine the values of the
video frequency f_0 which produce high and low frequencies in each of
these strips.

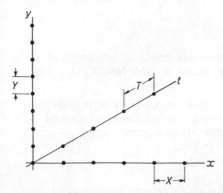

*Figure 4.6 Strips of picture elements in
the x, y and t dimensions.*

Horizontal spatial frequencies

For a horizontal direction of scan, there is a simple proportional
relationship between video frequencies and horizontal spatial frequencies. If the video bandwidth is W, then if $f_0 = W$, we must have
the horizontal spatial frequency

$$u = W_x$$

where W_x is the maximum reproducible horizontal spatial frequency.
For any other f_0

$$u = \frac{f_0}{W} \cdot W_x$$

We can therefore construct the following qualitative table

Table 4.1   Line-interlaced and noninterlaced pictures

Video signal frequency	high	low
Horizontal spatial frequency	high	low

The most visible video frequency, in so far as its horizontal spatial
component is concerned, occurs when

$$\frac{f_0}{W} \cdot W_x \simeq 3 \text{ cycles per degree}$$

or

$$f_0 \simeq \frac{3W}{W_x} \text{ hertz}$$

For example, if $W = 1$ MHz and $W_x = 12$ cycles per degree, then
$f_0 \simeq 250$ kHz.

Vertical spatial frequencies

For a noninterlaced picture, the picture elements in any vertical
strip are samples of the video signal taken at intervals T_L, the line
period.

These samples are spaced vertically at Y, so there is a proportion-
ality constant of Y/T_L between the temporal and vertical spatial
domains. If the video signal is $s(t)$, the strip samples are

$$\text{comb}_{T_L} [s(t)]$$

whose spectrum is a replicated version of $S(f)$, the spectrum of $s(t)$,
i.e.

$$(1/T_L) \text{ rep}_{1/T_L} [S(f)]$$

Consider now Figure 4.7a, in which the video signal $\sin 2\pi f_0 t$ lies
somewhere within a narrow band centred on $f = n/T_L = nf_L$, an
integral multiple of the line frequency f_L. In Figure 4.7b we have the
replication effect in the spatial domain caused by the sampling of $s(t)$.
The band of spatial frequencies centred around nY is repeated every
Y as shown. In particular, it is repeated about zero frequency.

Also shown in Figure 4.7b is the low-pass filtering action of the eye
(or of the eye in combination with the filtering effect of line broadening, if this is used). With an ideal system design there will be about
120 lines per degree, so that the eye will not see any of the replications in the figure except that at zero frequency. In practice, as we
have seen, this ideal is not achieved, but it is nevertheless the zero-
frequency replication which is of prime importance, the eye being
maximally sensitive to frequencies around 3 cycles/degree.

We see therefore that if $f_0 = nf_L$, the video sine wave appears at zero
spatial frequency in the vertical direction. If, however, $f_0 =
nf_L + f_L/2$, i.e. the video frequency is midway between line harmonics,

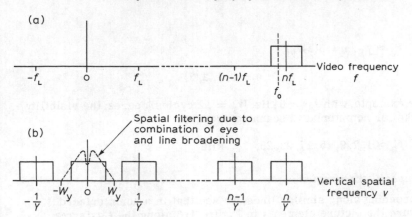

Figure 4.7 (a) Video input, comprising a narrow band about nf_L. (b) Vertical spatial output with superimposed spatial filter.

then this frequency is folded down to the maximum possible vertical spatial frequency, which we can call W_y. For any intermediate frequency, the vertical spatial frequency v is given by

$$v = \frac{2|f_0 - nf_L|}{f_L} \cdot W_y$$

n being adjusted to minimise $|f_0 - nf_L|$. This gives us the following table:

Table 4.2   Noninterlaced pictures

Video signal frequency	near $\dfrac{nf_L}{2}$	near $\dfrac{mf_L}{2}$
Vertical spatial frequency	low	high

$n = 0, 2, 4, 6, 8, \ldots$
$m = 1, 3, 5, 7, 9, \ldots$

The most visible video frequencies, in so far as their vertical spatial component is concerned, occur when

$$\frac{2|f_0 - nf_L|}{f_L} \cdot W_y \simeq 3 \text{ cycles per degree}$$

or

$$f_0 \simeq f_L \mid n \pm 3(2W_y)$$

$$n = 0, 1, 2, 3, \; \ldots$$

For example, with $f_L = 8\,\text{kHz}$, $W_y = 12$ cycles/degree, the visibility peaks for noninterlaced scanning occur at

$$f_0 \simeq 1, 7, 9, 15, 17, 23, 25, \; \ldots \text{ kHz}$$

Temporal frequencies

Proceeding along similar lines, we see that in a noninterlaced picture the picture elements in Figure 4.6 along the t axis are samples of the video signal taken at the frame period T_F. If the video frequency f_0 is close to a multiple of $f_F = 1/T_F$, then this is folded down to zero temporal (flicker) frequency in the image. On the other hand if $f_0 = nf_F + f_F/2, n = 0, 1, 2, 3, \ldots\ldots$, the temporal frequency has its maximum value $W_f = f_F/2$. For intermediate frequencies, the temporal frequency f is given by

$$f = |f_0 - nf_F|$$

with the integer n being adjusted to minimise $|f_0 - nf_F|$. Values of n which do not minimise $|f_0 - nf_F|$ give rise to higher temporal frequencies in the image. In an ideal system these higher temporal frequencies are above the eye's cut-off frequency. In practical systems, however, they may be visible; nevertheless the dominant component is the zero-frequency replication given by the above equation. Table 4.3 summarises the relationship.

Table 4.3   Noninterlaced pictures

Video signal frequency	near $\dfrac{nf_F}{2}$	near $\dfrac{mf_F}{2}$
Temporal frequency	low	high

$n = 0, 2, 4, 6, 8, \; \ldots$
$m = 1, 3, 5, 7, 9, \; \ldots$

The flicker caused by the video sine wave is at maximum visibility when the flicker frequency is about 8 Hz.* Therefore video frequencies

---

* This is a rough figure. In fact the peak visibility is interrelated with spatial frequency.

of peak visibility, in so far as their temporal component is concerned, occur at

$$f_0 = n f_F \pm 8 \text{ Hz}$$
$$n = 0, 1, 2, 3, \ldots$$

For example, if $f_F = 50$ Hz, the flicker maxima in a noninterlaced picture occur at

$$f_0 = 8, 42, 58, 92, 108, \ldots \text{Hz}$$

Interlaced pictures

In 2 : 1 line-interlaced pictures, the relationship between video frequencies and horizontal spatial frequencies set out in Table 4.1 still holds. However, the conversion to vertical spatial frequencies and temporal frequencies becomes more complex.

Along a vertical strip, as in Figure 4.6, every other picture sample is in a different field. *In any one field* the samples are spaced at T_L and therefore the rules of Table 4.2 apply. However, the two fields are spatially interleaved, and this produces a significant difference. As a specific example, a sinusoid at an integral multiple of f_L is folded down to zero spatial frequency (exactly) in each field. The two fields, when interleaved, still produce zero spatial frequency. But let the sinusoid drift by f_F, i.e. 25 or 30 Hz; then, although the rules tell us that each field will have a very low spatial frequency, there will be a 180° phase difference between the two fields. Interleaved, they produce the maximum possible spatial frequency. Large changes in vertical spatial frequency with small changes in video frequency in the vicinity of line harmonics are characteristic of interlaced pictures. This is because of the interlaced nature of the video spectrum (Figure 3.18). Sine-wave interference at video frequencies midway between line harmonics is more visible in interlaced than in noninterlaced pictures, since in interlaced pictures the vertical spatial frequency in each field, rather than in each frame, is maximised. Two such fields, when interleaved, do not increase the vertical spatial frequency so that it attains about half its maximum possible value, together with possible increased flicker due to poor spatial cancellation.

Visibility curve

As the frequency of the interfering video sinusoid is varied, its visibility varies, as shown in Figure 4.8 for a noninterlaced picture. Double peaks are obtained symmetrically disposed about every line and frame harmonic where the spatio-temporal frequencies set up in the displayed picture are maximally visible. Over the extent of a few line harmonics as shown, the horizontal spatial frequency in the image does not change very much; however with increasing orders of line harmonics the horizontal spatial frequency increases. This at first increases slightly and then progressively lowers the visibility of the overall pattern.

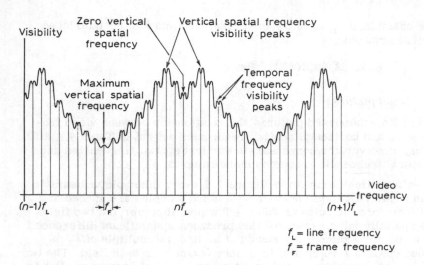

Figure 4.8 Microstructure of the visibility curve for video sine-wave interference as a function of frequency, noninterlaced pictures.

Although there are some differences, the shape of the visibility curve is seen to be roughly similar to that of the video signal spectrum itself. This is because the higher spatial and temporal frequencies in the transmitted image tend to have less energy than the lower frequencies, due in the main to their low frequency of occurrence in natural scenes. We may note that this indicates that the eye's spatio-temporal response is well matched to the Fourier content of natural scenes. Brainard (1972) has noted, however, that the visibility curve tends to fall off more slowly than the video spectrum.

In the case of interlaced pictures there is a similar correspondence between the visibility curve and the video signal spectrum. Referring to Figure 4.9, we see that the visibility minima now occur at $nf_L \pm f_F$ i.e. one frame harmonic removed from line harmonics. There is a rapid alternation of visibility as successive frame harmonics are encountered, the amplitude of the alternation diminishing as the midpoint between line harmonics is approached. Both Figures 4.8 and 4.9 are qualitative representations, since comprehensive data are lacking. In some spot measurements with 525-line 60 field per second pictures, Golding and Garlow (1971) have noted a 10-12 dB decreased sensitivity midway between line harmonics compared with the region near line harmonics. The variations are therefore quite large.

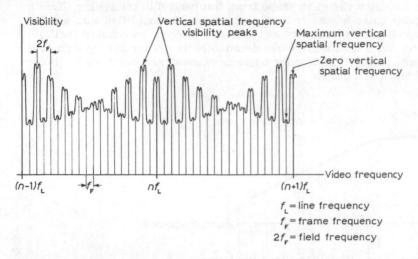

Figure 4.9 Microstructure of the sine-wave visibility curve for interlaced pictures.

The shape of the visibility curve is of importance not only in simple cases of sine-wave interference but also in such applications as the placement of colour subcarriers and chrominance information within the video band and the consideration of aliased energy which occurs in sampling the video signal.

4.5   Visibility of Random Noise

It may reasonably be supposed that the visibility curve for a narrow band of random noise as a function of the centre frequency of the band would look very much like Figure 4.8 or 4.9 with the exception that the fine structure would be smoothed to a degree dependent on the bandwidth of the noise. This has been qualitatively confirmed by Brainard (1967).

For noise extending over broad sections of the video band, the microstructure is completely smoothed and the visibility curve resembles that in Figure 4.10. Actual measurements of noise visibility have been made by several authors (Weaver, 1959; Barstow and Christopher, 1962; Prosser and Allnatt, 1965; Cavanaugh, 1970) and agreement on a standard visibility is being sought through the CCIR (CCIR Conclusions, 1970, Report 410-1). For broadcast television it appears from the measurements as if a simple weighting curve equivalent to passing the noise through a single-stage RC low-pass filter of time constant about 200 ns suffices to describe the overall visibility for the types of broadband random transmission noise typically encountered for both 525-line and 625-line pictures. The spectral power distribution of such noise varies in shape from flat (white) to triangular. Triangular noise is obtained when white noise is amplified with a gain proportional to frequency and is less visible on an equal overall power basis than white noise because of its predominantly high-frequency content. Triangular noise is encountered in FM radio links and equalised cables.

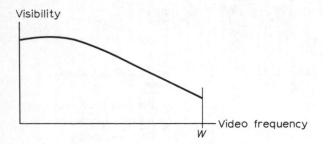

Figure 4.10 Visibility curve for broad-band noise as a function of centre-band frequency.

Suppose the noise power spectral density is $N(f)$ and the weighting function is

$$K(f) = \frac{1}{1 + (2\pi f T)^2}$$

whose 3dB point is at about 800 kHz for $T = 200$ ns. Then the weighted noise spectrum is $W(f)\,N(f)$ and the weighted noise power is

$$N = \int_0^W K(f)\,N(f)\ \mathrm{d}f$$

where W is the video bandwidth. This weighting, when applied to flat noise, reduces its power by 6.5 dB and to triangular noise by about 12.3 dB for 625-line broadcast television pictures (Prosser and Allnatt, 1965). Figures quoted by Cavanaugh (1970) for 525-line pictures give weightings of 6.2 dB for flat noise and 12.0 dB for A2A (high-frequency) noise.

It is of interest to consider the visual effect of variations in the shape of the noise power spectrum. By the sampling arguments pre-

viously considered, both the vertical spatial power spectrum and the
temporal power spectrum in the picture remain practically flat
(white) when the video noise spectrum changes from flat to triangular.
This is because the sampling process replicates and causes multiple
foldover of the video spectrum. Seen alternatively, noise samples
separated by a line or frame period are nearly statistically independent. The variation is therefore confined to the horizontal spatial
dimension, where the spatial power spectrum changes in direct proportion to the video noise spectrum. This variation is observed in a
situation where the vertical spatial and temporal components of the
noise are of constant visibility, so that the net change in visibility is
not great (about 6 dB from flat to triangular).

A more precise, analytical relationship between the video noise
power spectrum and the spatio-temporal picture noise spectrum
(Huang, 1965) may be obtained by referring to the scanning relationships in the previous chapter, as represented in Figures 3.13 and
3.17. The video noise can be imagined as having been generated by
scanning a random picture (moving or stationary, as the case may be).
In dealing with random pictures it is better to deal with their autocorrelation functions, which Fourier transform to power spectra. The
previously developed scanning relationships are therefore applied to
the scanning of the picture autocorrelation function in space and time,
rather than to the picture itself. It follows that, if the picture comprises three-dimensional bandlimited white noise, the video noise
power spectrum is bandlimited white, and vice versa, on the assumption that there is no aliasing in the system. Triangular video noise
can be generated from, and therefore converts into, a random picture
whose power spectrum is triangular in the horizontal spatial dimension and nearly flat in the horizontal spatial and temporal dimensions.

There is a small increase in the visibility of stationary noise, obtained
in the case of still photographs and facsimile, compared with that of
moving or scintillating noise of equal power, such as in television,
where every frame of noise is different. In the case of stationary
noise all the power is concentrated at harmonics of the frame frequency while for moving noise the power is spread over the continuum
between frame harmonics. The eye's temporal response rises over
the first 5—8 Hz and then falls. Thus part of the continuum of noise
(folded down to low temporal frequencies, as previously discussed) is
more visible than stationary noise while part is less visible. The net
effect was measured by Mounts and Pearson (1969) by freezing
frames of a 160-line picture. They obtained a roughly 4 dB decrease
in visibility for moving noise compared with stationary noise in 60
frames per second noninterlaced pictures and half this figure in 60
fields per second interlaced pictures.

The numerical values to be attached to the noise visibility curve
depend on the viewing conditions. If a given picture is viewed from a
short distance, a greater proportion of the spatial noise power may

fall in the low-frequency, sensitive region of the eye's characteristic, i.e. around 3 cycles/ degree, than when viewed from further away. Similarly, systems which have a low spatial bandwidth in cycles per degree, or which are viewed at a high display luminance, e.g. current visual telephone systems, convert transmission noise into spatial noise of relatively high visibility.

Signal-to-noise ratio

The signal-to-noise ratio S/N is commonly used as an indicator of picture quality, where S is usually the peak-white-to-black-level signal power and N the weighted noise power. For a high-quality picture, with the noise at or near the threshold of visibility, S/N is in the range 40-55 dB, the appropriate figure depending on system standards and viewing conditions (Prosser and Allnatt, 1965; Cavanaugh, 1970; Crater, 1971; Thompson, 1971). Objects can be recognised in noise down to about 0 dB S/N and detected in noise at —10 dB S/N or lower. These figures are again dependent on viewing conditions as well as scene content.

Schade (1971b) has suggested a method for rating systems according to their ability to resolve fine spatial detail in the present of noise. This is of particular interest in high-resolution aerial surveillance. Schade notes that a system with a high spatial bandwidth is of no use if the noise is high. A more relevant quantity than the spatial band-width is the 'resolving-power frequency', the spatial frequency at which it is just possible to resolve a grating target. This point is located at the crossover point of the system MTF curve, which falls with frequency, and the signal-to-noise ratio required for detection, which rises with frequency. The average resolving-power frequency evaluated over the grey scale of the picture provides the figure of merit for the resolving power of the system.

4.6   Grey Scale and Gamma

In Chapter 2 we saw that the relationship between subjective bright-ness B and luminance L in viewing a scene or a reproduction of the scene on a screen or in a photograph, was given approximately by $B = aL^{\gamma}$ where a is a constant; the exponent γ depended on the viewing conditions. In viewing a well-lit original scene or a reproduction with a bright surround, i.e. when adapted to a high level of luminance, $\gamma \simeq \frac{1}{2}$; in viewing an object or reproduction with a dark surround, $\gamma \simeq \frac{1}{3}$. These values may be affected by other viewing conditions and scene content.

If the system is to reproduce perceived brightness under conditions when the original scene is brightly lit and the display is viewed with a dark surround, the system gamma $\gamma_S = \log$ (display luminance)/log (original scene luminance) needs to be adjusted to compensate for this difference. In this case

$$\gamma_S = \frac{1/2}{1/3} = 1.5$$

For systems which usually have similar viewing conditions of illumination at camera and display (e.g. facsimile, visual telephone), γ_S can be made equal to unity. In broadcast television where brightly lit original scenes are typically viewed with a dim surround, an intermediate value of $\gamma_S \simeq 1.25$ is optimum (Bartleson and Breneman, 1967a; de Marsh, 1971). In bright surround conditions, room light reflected from the reproduction lowlights may lower the effective gamma of the system, necessitating an increase in the value of γ_S, if γ_S is based on measurements of reproduced luminance taken in a way which excludes this reflected light.

A picture reproduction system typically involves a number of non-linear elements, ranging from the camera through the gamma corrector to the display device. All can usually be approximated by a power law relationship relating output to input. If there are n cascaded system elements with gammas $\gamma_1, \gamma_2, \gamma_3, \dots \gamma_n$, the overall system gamma is equal to their product i.e.

$$\gamma_S = \gamma_1 \gamma_2 \gamma_3 \dots \gamma_n$$

The largest gamma in the chain is usually the display CRT, where it is usually between 2 and 3 (Heightman, 1971); in this case, gamma is the exponent in the power-law relationship $L = ke^\gamma$ relating screen luminance L to input signal voltage e on the grid of the CRT, k being a constant. If γ for the display is, say, 2.8 and the camera uses a vidicon with $\gamma = 0.5$, to obtain correct brightness transfer when viewing a picture of an outdoor scene in a dark room ($\gamma_S = 1.5$), we should have

$$\gamma_S = 1.5 = \gamma_1 \gamma_2 \gamma_3$$

$$= 0.5 . \gamma_2 . 2.8$$

$$\therefore \gamma_2 = 1.07$$

where γ_2 is the gamma of the gamma corrector in the system. The gamma corrector is therefore required to operate under the conditions $e_o = e_i^{1.07}$ where e_o and e_i are the output and input signal voltages respectively. Given the approximate nature of the gamma-law relationships, a gamma corrector might be felt to be an unnecessary expense in such a system.

4.7 Visibility of Noise over the Grey Scale

The various system nonlinearities affect the spectrum of the video signal and of the noise, and the visibility of the noise over the grey scale. In broadcast television, where gamma correction is carried out at the transmitter, noise added to the video signal in transmission is subjected to the gamma characteristic of the CRT display. Experimental observation in this case (Maurice, Gilbert, Newell and Spencer, 1955; Hacking, 1962; Newell and Geddes, 1963) indicates that there is a fairly gentle peak in the visibility in the dark grey areas of the picture. The gamma of the eye ($\frac{1}{3}$-$\frac{1}{2}$) and the gamma of the display CRT (2-3) approximately cancel each other out to give a near-unity gamma relating subjective brightness to input signal; however, the measurements indicate that the net curve is slightly S-shaped with its maximum slope in the dark greys. An additional factor is that in the darker parts of the picture the eye's bandwidth is reduced, both spatially and temporally, and only a fraction of the spatio-temporal noise power spectrum is seen. This contributes to the fall-off in noise visibility in the lowlights. Newell and Geddes have measured the visibility of interfering patterns which repeat every frame and found that their visibility increases relative to random noise in the dark grey areas, the noise power of such patterns being concentrated at zero frequency on the temporal axis. Quantising noise tends to be more visible than random noise for the same signal-to-noise ratio.

In conclusion, we note that the visibility of random noise can be related, at least qualitatively, to the known spatio-temporal frequency and brightness characteristics of the eye. The experimental evidence which we have at present has been obtained by a number of authors under many different viewing conditions and there exist gaps in the documentation which future research will no doubt fill. However, certain rough guidelines can be seen concerning the way in which visual information should be coded and transmitted so as to minimise the perceived distortion in the received picture. This is the topic we pursue in the next chapter.

Chapter 5

TRANSMISSION OF MONOCHROME
INFORMATION

5.1 Introduction

The material in this chapter comprises a survey of methods used to
transmit pictorial information in communications practice, together
with some mention of recent research into new transmission methods.
The approach is brief and introductory, since a full treatment would
necessitate a fair-sized book on its own; the interested reader is referred to the references cited for points which are cursorily treated.
The reference list is not a comprehensive one, since many more research workers have contributed to this field than it is practicable to
cite in a short chapter. It is hoped, however, that those which are
given provide a natural follow-on from the text for the specialist
reader and a starting point for a more detailed study.

The field of digital transmission is a particularly fast-moving one
and it is difficult to foresee with any certainty the way in which the
subject will develop. The treatment of this topic has again been kept
fairly short rather than expounded in the detail in which it is presently discussed, since in a few years' time some of the techniques
currently under scrutiny will doubtless have fallen by the wayside
and been replaced by others. The encoding and transmission of
colour signals are treated in Chapter 7.

5.2 Analogue Baseband Transmission

An ideal baseband transmission channel is able to pass all the Fourier components of the video signal, from zero frequency to the cut-
off bandwidth W, without amplitude or phase distortion. A practical
channel, however, might be as illustrated in Figure 5.1. The imperfections comprise a combination of low-frequency roll-off, high-
frequency roll-off, passband ripple and non-constant group delay,
together with random noise, sine-wave interference, crosstalk from
other channels, multipath transmission (echoes) and amplitude non-
linearities (Bell Laboratories Technical Staff, 1970; Crater, 1971).
The visual effect of these imperfections may be derived with a knowledge of the principles of scanning and display.

Low-frequency roll-off

The low frequencies in the video signal are generated by the spatial
frequencies in the image having a low horizontal component (Figure
3.13), irrespective of their vertical component. Attenuation or eli-

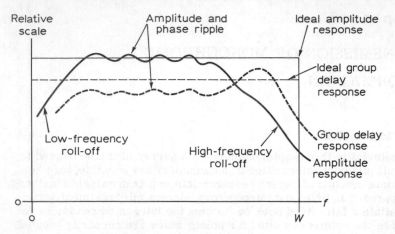

Figure 5.1 Defects in the transmission characteristics of video channels.

mination of the low video frequencies causes corresponding attenuation or elimination of these same spatial frequencies. Since the energy at any particular vertical spatial frequency is distributed throughout the video spectrum, while the energy at any horizontal spatial frequency is concentrated at a particular point in the video spectrum, low-frequency roll-off appears visually to attenuate the low horizontal spatial frequencies. However, in some circumstances loss or distortion of low vertical spatial frequencies may be evident.

Visually, attenuation *per se* of very low horizontal spatial frequencies in the picture is not serious, since the eye's sensitivity is low at these frequencies. However, attenuation may be accompanied by phase nonlinearity (non-constant group delay), giving rise to spatial phase errors, to which the eye is sensitive. A clamping circuit (Millman and Taub, 1965), acting on a reference level transmitted during line blanking, is commonly used to ease the transmission requirements for the low-frequency end of the band.

High-frequency roll-off

For similar reasons high-frequency roll-off attenuates picture components having a high horizontal spatial frequency (Figure 3.13). The effect on the image is mainly evident as a loss of horizontal resolution. Phase (or group delay) distortion at the high-frequency end of the channel causes phase shifts of corresponding spatial frequencies, to which the eye is sensitive. Therefore linear-phase filters are desirable. Controlled nonlinear amplitude distortion at edge transitions in the video signal with the effect of decreasing the rise time, can, however improve the sharpness of the picture (Goldmark and Hollywood, 1951). This technique is known as *crispening*. Picture sharpness can also be improved by subtracting the second derivative of the signal from the signal itself. Brown (1969) found the optimum amount of preshoot and overshoot to be about 12% for noiseless pictures, less for noisy pictures. These edge-improvement techniques require precise control and are therefore more in the line of post-reception options. As far as the transmission channel is concerned, a gradual high-frequency roll-off such as a Gaussian curve is aimed at to avoid any oscillatory transients at edges (ringing), the effects of which can be very noticeable.

Echoes

Echoes occur for a variety of reasons, such as multiple paths in radio transmission or impedance mismatches. Amplitude and phase ripples in the channel frequency response produce echoes in the time domain (Carlson, 1968). The visibility of echoes increases rapidly initially with the amount of delay followed by levelling off to a near-constant visibility at large delays (Allnatt and Prosser, 1965); short-delayed echoes tend to be masked by the signal. Again, the effect is perceived in the horizontal spatial direction in the image. A consequence is that passband ripple in video filter design has to be kept to low levels; however, acceptable echo levels are normally specified in the time domain (Lewis, 1954; Crater, 1971).

Noise and sine-wave interference

The visibility of narrowband noise or sine-wave interference in the video channel is markedly dependent on the (midband) frequency of the interference and its relation to line and field frequency harmonics. This relationship was discussed in some detail in the previous chapter, as was the procedure for frequency weighting wideband noise.

Crosstalk

Interference from an unwanted video signal is normally termed crosstalk, though it perhaps deserves to be called crossvision. Video crosstalk from a single source causes the superimposition of an interfering picture on the wanted picture. The interfering picture may be distorted by a sloping crosstalk gain versus frequency characteristic, but may be recognisable as a picture if its line and field frequencies are the same as the wanted picture. If not, it gives rise to an unstructured interfering pattern.

Typically, the interfering and wanted video signals have the same line and field synchronising frequencies, but are not phase-locked to one another. Since the most visible interference is in the medium-low spatial and temporal frequencies, to which the eye is maximally sensitive, the main practical problem results from the vertical and horizontal blanking and synchronising pulses of the interfering picture moving slowly across the wanted picture (Fowler, 1951; Brainard, 1967).

5.3   Transmission by Carrier Modulation

In the transmission of video signals at radio frequencies, double sideband (DSB) amplitude modulation of a carrier requires a transmission bandwidth of $2W$, where W is the video bandwidth; since W may be several megahertz, a large transmission bandwidth is required. Single sideband (SSB) transmission, which has a transmission bandwidth W, presents problems with the realisation of a sharp cutoff characteristic at the carrier frequency. It is not possible to find a realisation that does not introduce amplitude or phase distortion at the low video frequencies. While telephone speech signals can tolerate low-frequency distortion of this kind, video signals cannot; hence SSB is not an appropriate video modulation technique.

In broadcasting practice, vestigial sideband (VSB) transmission is used. A portion of one sideband is transmitted along with the whole of the other sideband. At the receiver the signal is filtered by a skew-symmetrical sideband filter with a slow roll-off and linear phase response. This procedure causes a small distortion in envelope-detected signals dependent on modulation depth, which has been analysed by Cherry (1942, 1943). In practice this distortion is not found to be serious, though the optimum skew-symmetrical roll-off characteristic and the possibility of pre-correction are being studied by the CCIR (CCIR Conclusions, 1970).

In conditions where the received signal-to-noise ratio is low (but not below threshold) and bandwidth is available, video signals may usefully be transmitted by frequency modulation (FM), as in terrestial and satellite microwave transmission. There is an increasing use here, however, of digital transmission methods.

5.4   Digital Transmission

With the trend towards digital transmission in national and international communication networks and the possibilities for digital processing of signals by computer, there is considerable interest at present in finding efficient methods for the digital coding and transmission of pictorial information. A general summary of the principles of picture coding has been given by Schreiber (1967), with specialised summaries by Connor, Brainard and Limb (1972) and by Haskell, Mounts and Candy (1972). The book edited by Huang and Tretiak (1972) has contributions from a number of persons active in the field.

Pulse Code Modulation (PCM)

In the conversion of a video signal to digital form, two operations are involved: sampling and quantizing. Efficiency demands a combined low sampling rate and a small number of quantising levels per sample. As we saw in Chapter 3, the sampling rate in samples per second is governed by picture size and the resolution requirements of the eye in space and time. An ideal system requires about 2×10^6 samples per second per square degree of picture with practical systems operating down to two orders of magnitude less than this.

The number of quantising levels required over the grey scale is governed by the spatio-temporal contrast sensitivity and brightness characteristic of the eye. As discussed previously, there is an approximately linear relationship between subjective picture brightness and voltage on the CRT grid, owing to the power-law characteristic of the CRT. Hence for CRT displays, equal steps of voltage in the quantised scale are appropriate (with perhaps, ideally, a small decrease in step size in the dark grey areas where the quantisation distortion is slightly more visible). In a system using gamma correction, notice that linear quantisation needs to be performed at a point where the signal voltage is proportional to subjective brightness, which is not necessarily at the output of the camera.

Experiment shows that the number of discrete voltage levels required to reduce impairment due to quantising distortion (which appears as contours of constant luminance in the slowly changing parts of the picture) to near or below threshold is between about 64 and 256 levels (6-8 bit) depending on the picture content and viewing conditions (Goodall, 1951). Taking the upper figure, we find that the digital channel capacity required to transmit a simply-encoded PCM signal is at most $8 \times 2 \times 10^6$ bit/s $= 16$ Mbit/s per square degree of picture. Attempts have been made to reduce this large figure using a variety of techniques. These rely on the fact that pictures contain redundant information, both from the statistical and perceptual points of view. The following is an account of some of these techniques; the quoted results are somewhat influenced by scan density, it being easier to code high-density scans because of high inter-sample correlation.

Subsampling

The sampling of any signal at an interval T produces replication of its spectrum at intervals $F = 1/T$ in the frequency domain. In the case of a signal strictly bandlimited to W hertz, the sampling interval would, by the sampling theorem, have to be $T < 1/2W$ or $F > 2W$ to avoid aliasing. Because of the comb-like structure of the video signal, however, sampling below the so called Nyquist rate of $2W$ samples is possible. This is known as *subsampling*.

The principle of subsampling is illustrated in Figure 5.2. In order to minimise the visibility of the aliased spectral components, these are arranged to fall in the gaps between the line harmonics. This demands an accurate control of the sampling frequency. The visibility of the aliased components may be further reduced by a comb filter; however, the added complication may not be justified for small amounts of aliasing. A reduction of the sampling frequency to about 70% of the Nyquist rate has been reported (Golding and Garlow, 1971).

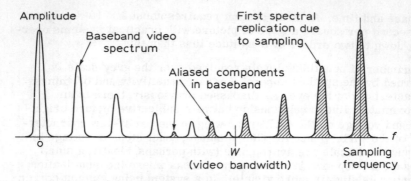

Figure 5.2 Principle of sampling below the Nyquist rate (subsampling).

Use of dither signals

It was noticed by Goodall (1951) in his initial experiments with PCM television, that the addition of random noise to the video signal prior to quantisation broke up the luminance contours resulting from quantisation and improved the picture quality. This technique has been further explored and improved by Roberts (1962), Limb (1969) and Thompson (1971), with the added signal being a controlled form of perturbation termed a *dither* signal. The principle is illustrated in Figure 5.3. The dither signal is a signal of about one quantal step in amplitude, which is arranged to have a good deal of high-frequency

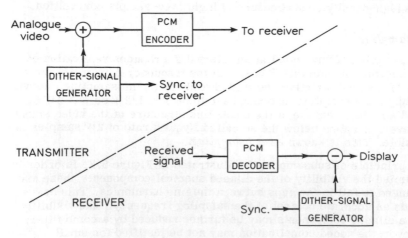

Figure 5.3 Addition and subtraction of dither signals.

energy. In slowly changing areas of the picture where coarse quantisation contours would normally be visible, dither causes frequent transitions between quantal steps. These frequent transitions markedly increase the proportion of high-frequency energy in the quantisation noise and can decrease its overall visibility. They also increase the overall noise power, but this can be alleviated by the subtraction of a synchronised dither signal at the receiver. However, with a well-designed dither signal the subjective advantage of subtraction has been found to be small.

Refinements to the basic system include pre-emphasis of the video signal before adding dither, with inverse de-emphasis after decoding at the receiver. An acceptable picture can be obtained with about 3 bits per sample. Dithered quantisation is found to be more useful in higher resolution systems where the dither noise is near the eye's spatial cut-off frequency; for lower resolution systems dither noise can be fairly visible.

Run-length coding

A characteristic of video signals is that they tend not to change very much from picture element to picture element; i.e. they are statistically correlated. This is, of course, the time-domain equivalent of the fact that the video spectrum has more energy in the lower frequencies than the upper frequencies, which again is linked to the predominance of low spatial frequencies in visual images.

One way in which this characteristic can be exploited is by specifying in the digital conversion only the amplitudes of video samples which are significantly different from preceding samples, together with their positions. This principle, known as *run-length coding* because the signal is broken up into runs of constant amplitude, produces two irregular streams of data relating respectively to the amplitude and lengths of the runs; in order to smooth the flow, buffer storage (elastic encoding) must be used. Run-length coding is being considered for the coding and transmission of newspapers and graphical information such as weather maps, whose structure, that of black lines separated by relatively large white spaces, is particularly appropriate for this type of coding (Cherry and Chitnis, 1972; Huang, 1972b). For half-tone pictures, i.e. pictures with a continuous grey scale, the data reduction is smaller and simpler schemes such as DPCM are more attractive.

With some graphical data, particularly that generated by computer, the video signal can be considered to be a two-level (black-and-white) signal which can therefore be encoded by normal PCM into 1 bit per sample; using run-length coding this can be reduced to an average of about 0.1-0.3 bit per sample or less, depending on the picture complexity. Not all graphical material, however, can be satisfactorily represented by two levels; added to this, practical problems can arise in scanning such as the non-uniform reflectivity of paper, non-uniform density of printing ink, non-uniform illumination of the paper or noise generated with the signal. Two-level quantisation of the video signal in these cases may impair the legibility of the data.

The run-coded signal is rendered more sensitive to transmission errors than a non-coded picture by the fact that an error in either the amplitude or position signal causes a spatially more widespread error in the received picture. Cherry and his co-workers have suggested means for alleviating this by using three or four standard run lengths only. Run-length coding can also be extended to two dimensions and other elaborations are possible.

Differential coding

Another way of exploiting the predominantly slow changes in video signal amplitude is by the use of differential coding schemes. These schemes, of which delta modulation (DM) (de Jager, 1952) and differential pulse code modulation (DPCM) (Cutler, 1952) are examples, code and transmit successive picture-element differences. An advantage of this technique over run-length coding is that no buffering is required. The principle is illustrated in Figure 5.4.

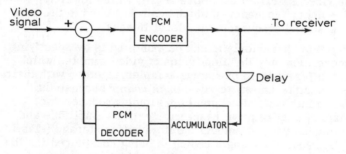

Figure 5.4 Principle of differential coding.

The loop comprises a PCM encoder, decoder and an accumulator, with a total loop delay of one sample interval. What is fed to the PCM encoder therefore is the analogue difference between the incoming video signal and its quantised value one picture element previously. This is encoded into digital form and transmitted over the channel. The digital difference signals are also added together in the accumulator, which is updated by each successive difference; at the receiver there is a similar accumulator and PCM decoder. Another way of looking at the process is to consider that the accumulator holds a *prediction* of the next sample, and the error between prediction and reality is transmitted (Graham, 1958; O'Neal, 1966).

In DPCM, the PCM encoder in the forward path is typically a 3- or 4-bit (8- or 16-level) companded-scale encoder (Abbott, 1971; Gerrard and Thompson, 1973), half the levels being used to specify positive changes and half negative changes relative to the previous sample. The smallest step is about 0.5-1% of the peak-to-peak video signal, whereas the largest step may be 30-35% of the peak-to-peak signal. Small inter-element differences, which occur frequently, are thus accurately represented. Large differences, occurring at edges in the picture, may be encoded with a substantial quantisation error. Edge information is known to be visually important and poor reproduction of edges cannot be justified purely on the basis of statistical infrequency; it is, however, a characteristic of the eye (spatial masking) that luminance errors in the vicinity of large edges are not very noticeable. Large-amplitude, high-frequency spatial sinusoids are reproduced at a somewhat reduced contrast, an acceptable distortion. A difficulty which is encountered with DPCM is that in successive frames of the picture, random noise accompanying the analogue signal can cause a different selection of step sizes in each frame, resulting in edge flicker.

In delta modulation the PCM encoder in Figure 5.4 is a 1-bit (2-level) encoder. This is attractive because of its instrumental simplicity and low cost. However, the advantage of fine steps for small differences and large steps for sudden changes, which DPCM possesses, is lost, since there is only one step size. With delta modulation the sampling rate is increased by a factor of n times that used in DPCM or PCM, where n is then the encoded number of bits per picture sample. For $n = 3$-4, i.e. the same bit rate as DPCM, the subjective picture quality for simple DM is inferior to DPCM. Adaptive schemes, in which the step size alters progressively according to picture content, show more promise (Abate, 1967; Candy, 1972).

Differential encoding has proved to be a successful method of encoding half-tone pictures, producing good-quality pictures at 3-4 bits per sample. Further improvements using two-dimensional spatial prediction (Connor, Pease and Scholes, 1971) and adaptive procedures are likely to result in further bit reductions, perhaps to 1-2 bits per sample.

Transform coding

In transform coding a block of picture elements in the picture is transformed via a linear transform computation to an equivalent group of coefficients to allow easier elimination of the statistical and visual redundancies in the data. Thus a block of correlated elements can be transformed into a set of relatively uncorrelated coefficients which are then individually quantised; a greater number of quantal levels can be associated with, say, those coefficients which have a large variance than those which have a small variance. Information is lost in this quantisation but the subjective effect in the picture obtained from the re-transformed coefficients can be made acceptable with appropriate choice of transform method and block size. The coefficients which are coarsely quantised tend to represent the high spatial frequencies in the picture, where the eye's sensitivity to contrast is low. Several authors have contributed to this field and a number of transforms—Hotelling, Fourier, Hadamard, Karhunen-Loeve, etc.—have been tried. A summary of this work has been given by Wintz (1972), who indicates that non-adaptive transform techniques can code to 2 bits per sample with a further reduction to 1 bit per sample possible with adaptive techniques. The instrumentation is generally more complex than for DPCM.

Coding schemes using frame storage

It has become possible in recent times to store pictures for long periods without noticeable degradation of quality. This can be accomplished by 8 bit parallel PCM encoding of the analogue video signal and storage of the bit sequences in eight separate circulating delay lines, with a delay equal to the frame period (Mounts, 1969). This facility has allowed the development of the earlier ideas of Kell (1929) and Seyler (1965), whereby the differences between successive frames are transmitted instead of the frames themselves. In videotelephone pictures, especially, there is relatively little movement and the difference information occurs at a considerably lower rate, on the average, than the full frame information. The cost of frame storage is large, but is decreasing quite rapidly.

Several methods of coding are possible using frame storage. One method is analogous to the element-differential or predictive coding principle illustrated in Figure 5.4, with the delay round the loop made equal to a frame period. Small differences between frames are quantised finely and large differences coarsely. However, the reduction in bit rate obtainable by this method without degradation of motion is modest, about the same order as with DPCM (Haskell, Mounts and Candy, 1972). Elaborations are possible, such as using a group of elements in one frame to predict a group in the next frame.

In a second method the picture is divided up into areas of motion or non-motion by a motion detector (Pease and Limb, 1971). The areas of motion may be classified into several categories, e.g. none, slow, fast, very fast. In areas with little or no movement, the elements in successive frames are essentially the same so that the temporal sampling rate in the picture may be reduced. In areas with substantial movement the eye's sensitivity to detail is reduced (i.e. for combined high spatio-temporal frequencies) and the spatial sampling density may be lowered. Hence this scheme trades spatial for temporal resolution and can operate at a constant but reduced sampling frequency—perhaps a quarter of the Nyquist rate.

Both the previous methods—and others are possible—produce output information at a constant rate and require little or no storage apart from the frame store. Larger reductions in bit rate have been obtained by introducing the added complexity of buffer storage. With buffer storage the sampling rate in the stationary areas may be reduced to zero, or to a low convenience level, and increased appropriately in areas of motion. At the receiver, where there is also a frame store, the stationary areas are repeated from frame to frame. The motion information, efficiently coded, is used to update the stored picture. In this method, termed conditional replenishment, the bit rate has been reduced to 1 bit per sample for videotelephone pictures (Candy *et al.*, 1971), with a modest buffer capacity.

The technology of frame storage has thus opened up the third dimension in picture processing, the temporal dimension, for utilisation in efficient coding procedures. The successful schemes which are emerging combine exploitation of both temporal and spatial redundancies; some are more complex and costly than others and some produce coded signals which are more sensitive to channel errors than others. The quest for a low-cost, error-insensitive, quality-preserving coding method which exploits the statistical and psychological redundancies in pictorial information to the fullest extent is likely to continue for some time, with, perhaps, increasing interaction with those researchers working in the fields of pattern recognition and feature extraction in machines and the visual systems of animals (Barlow *et al.*, 1972).

5.5   Image Restoration and Enhancement

If the nature of distortion, interference or noise suffered by the video signal during transmission is known or can be inferred, it is possible to process the image to correct for these effects. Simple examples would be equalising filters to compensate for say, high-frequency roll-off, notch filters to eliminate a particular frequency of sine-wave interference or multiple notch filters (comb filters) for the elimination of a colour subcarrier and sidebands. Sharp notches between line harmonics have little effect on the video signal as there is hardly any energy there. A notch near a line harmonic will distort or eliminate a particular horizontal spatial frequency, which may not be serious except when the picture has a strong component at this frequency.

More sophisticated processing is possible if the pictures can be input to a computer (Huang, Schreiber and Tretiak, 1971). This has been done very effectively, for example, in pictures obtained from space. A technique which can be used is two-dimensional spatial filtering, based on prior knowledge of the spectral characteristics of the interference. Thus, if the image is $g(x, y)$ with spectrum $G(u, v)$, the operation to produce an improved image $f(x, y)$ is

$$F(u, v) = H(u, v) \cdot G(u, v)$$

$H(u, v)$ being the inverse of the channel degradation function or some signal-to-noise optimising filter. On the digital computer the operation is equivalently carried out in the spatial domain as a (discrete) convolution

$$f(x, y) = h(x, y) * g(x, y)$$

Spatial filtering techniques of this sort are feasible if the interference has a distinctly different spectral characteristic from that of the picture and is known or can be estimated in some way.

5.6   Information Theory and Picture Coding

Shannon (1948) showed that for a discrete source which selects symbols probabilistically from a set of N possible symbols, the minimum number of bits per symbol into which the source can be coded is given by the entropy

$$H = -\sum_{i=i}^{N} P_i \log_2 P_i$$

where P_i is the probability of occurrence of the ith symbol.

The evaluation of this formula in the case of a picture source presents some difficulties. For sources generating symbols which are statistically dependent, computation of the entropy requires the source symbols to be considered in blocks over which the statistical dependency could be said to extend, and beyond which the dependency is zero or at least negligible. A picture source coded into 8 bit PCM selects successive elements from $2^8 = 256$ possible levels. However, statistical dependencies are known to extend over at least several seconds of picture material. Even in a single frame of a 500×500 element picture there are

$$N = 2^{8 \times 500 \times 500} = 2^{2\ 000\ 000} \simeq 10^{600\ 000}$$

different possible pictures. This astronomical number of possibilities precludes any computation of entropy based on experimental data giving estimates of the probabilities P_i. Further, even if the probabilities were known, the realisation of a data reduction approaching that given by H, by the usual procedure of assignment of unequal code-word lengths to the N possible picture sequences (Huffman, 1952), would require speed and storage capacity beyond present capabilities.

Thus the approach to picture coding via information theory has to be a very limited one based on small blocks of elements. With this restriction, it is possible to compute upper bounds on performance; thus in the literature on picture coding there is reference to entropy and Huffman codes in connection with specific coders such as DPCM coders where the output symbols may be found to occur with non-equal probability, suggesting additional bit rate reduction by the assignment of unequal-length code words. Again, practical consider-ations involving the provision of additional buffer storage and in-creased sensitivity to channel errors may turn the scales against such schemes.

What information theory has done is to provide research workers in the field with a good deal of insight and inspiration. Much of the im-petus for the work on bandwidth compression in the 1950s and early 1960s derived from the qualitative knowledge that only a minute fraction of the astronomical number of possible picture sequences were ever generated or seen in any picture transmission system. Information theory did not prescribe, however, how to realise the bandwidth compression which appeared possible and exaggerated claims for some of the early, unrealistic schemes caused a scepti-cism for the subject to develop in some quarters. The exploitation of picture redundancy in the form of cost-saving, quality-preserving coding schemes has not proved easy, though some of the successes have been cited. These successes are modest when seen in relation to earlier expectations, but are useful enough, given the high channel capacity required for digital picture signals.

Rate-distortion theory

In comparison with some of the earlier attempts, latter-day efforts at picture coding have paid more attention to the subjective quality of the picture in the presence of realistic levels of transmission noise. Coding not only introduces distortion during the quantisation process but may also render the transmitted signal more sensitive to noise. Source noise generated with the video signal may make coding diffi-cult and require special techniques to discriminate signal from noise (Kubba, 1963). The task therefore is to ensure that subjective picture quality is maintained in the coding and transmission process.

In line with this increased awareness of the need for appropriate subjective assessment, there has been a shift in information-theoretic descriptions towards rate-distortion theory. Rate-distortion theory is a development from simple information theory which Shannon suggested in his 1948 paper and elaborated in a later paper (Shannon, 1960). It deals with the case where it is required to transmit infor-mation over a noisy channel with a finite rate of error. The theory examines the way in which the average distortion or cost of the errors can be minimised, given that a distortion or fidelity criterion for a single error can be specified. It also evaluates the minimum rate at which information needs to be transmitted over the channel in order to ensure that the average distortion is less than or equal to some value D. The function specifying this minimum rate is de-noted $R(D)$, the rate-distortion function; its general form is illustrated in Figure 5.5. As the allowable distortion D is increased, so the

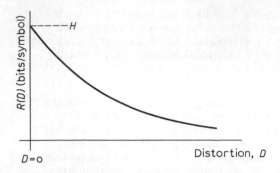

Figure 5.5 Typical form for the rate-distortion function R(D).

transmission rate in bits per symbol or bits per second can be decreased. For zero distortion the function has a value equal to the entropy of the source *H*.

Rate-distortion theory thus accords more realistically with practical efforts to obtain channel capacity reduction, where there is a trade-off between bit rate and subjective quality, and for which the $R(D)$ function, in principle, provides the lower bound. Its deficiencies as a theory are that it does not explicitly indicate the avenues to be followed in obtaining the compression, nor the way in which the quantity *D* can be evaluated in relation to the properties of human vision. Progress in this field has not yet reached a point where it is possible to predict the subjective costs of all forms of coding and transmission distortion. Frequency-weighted mean square error is a useful measure when the distortion looks like random thermal noise, but for other types of distortion it is an unreliable measure. The bounds given by rate-distortion theory can in practice therefore only be evaluated for specific forms of coder such as run-length or differential coders where the subjective costs are known or can be measured (Pearson, 1967; Limb, 1967; Budrikis, 1972). The development of a sound general visual distortion or fidelity measure may be contingent upon an increase in our knowledge of the higher-order processes in human vision.

Chapter 6

DISPLAYS IN COLOUR

6.1 Introduction

In the design of coloured displays, the designer is concerned to produce, at any given point in the display, radiant power in the visible
range with a spectral distribution which elicits a given sensation of
colour when viewed by an observer. In colour reproduction systems,
such as colour television, the aim is to make the colour sensation
correspond in some way with the sensation the viewer would have if
he were present at the original scene. In other instances, such as
computer-generated visual displays, the reproduction requirement
may be absent but the aim is also to create some particular colour
sensation associated with a given spatio-temporal location in the display. To proceed to a particular design, we need, firstly, to have some
method of specifying the desired colour sensation or, as it is often
called, the *perceived colour;* secondly, to be able to calculate the perceived colour corresponding to any given spectral distribution of
radiant power, taking into account any other relevant stimulus parameters in the display and its surround. We shall attempt, in this
chapter, to examine these requirements in more detail.

As in the monochrome case, an important consideration is the econo-
mical representation of the colour information, so as to reduce transmission or storage costs. Any properties of vision which permit
such economy are therefore of interest. The chief of these is the tri-
chromatic nature of colour vision (Le Grand, 1968), i.e. that colours
can be specified as a mixture of three *primary colours* or *primaries*.
Any three colours can be used as primaries, provided that one of the
primaries is not simply a mixture of the other two. Red, green and
blue are commonly used in practical displays for reasons which it is
hoped will be apparent in due course; however, other sets of primaries
are also used, as for example in colour transmission. The fact that a
colour can be specified in terms of only three primaries is thought
to be due to the retina possessing three different types of colour
receptor which sample the incident radiation in three overlapping
areas of the visible spectrum (for an introductory account, see Hunt,
1967). To produce a particular colour sensation it is sufficient to
stimulate each of the colour receptors by some given amount; many
different spectral distributions of radiant power are equivalent in this
respect. Thus practical display design devolves into procedures for
choosing the primary colours (in CRT displays this amounts to
choosing phosphors) and arranging to mix them in the right proportions. The body of knowledge which had accumulated in this field is
known as *colorimetry* (Wyszecki and Stiles, 1967) of which we shall

recount the essential principles. More detail is available in the references cited.

It is as well to appreciate at the start that the basic, formalised knowledge in the field of colorimetry, much of which has been standardised by international agreement through the Commission Internationale de l'Eclairage (CIE), falls short of providing all the information necessary for the design of a colour display or reproduction system. Standard CIE colorimetry is concerned with mixing primaries so that they *match* (have the same perceived colour as) a given test colour when viewed under the same viewing conditions as the test colour. But standard colorimetry does not attempt to describe perceived colour *per se*. To describe our own colour perceptions we use, in ordinary English, phrases like 'dark red' or 'light yellow' or 'sky blue'; it is possible, as we shall see, to specify perceived colour more accurately than this, but it is not the function of basic CIE colorimetry, which we introduce in the next section, to give this kind of information. After examining the principles of CIE colorimetry, we turn to the relationship between perceived colour and CIE-specified colour in Section 6.3.

6.2   The CIE System of Colour Measurement

The CIE system of colour measurement centres round the concept of *colour matching*. Colour matching is by convention related to the experimental situation portrayed in Figure 6.1, in which the test

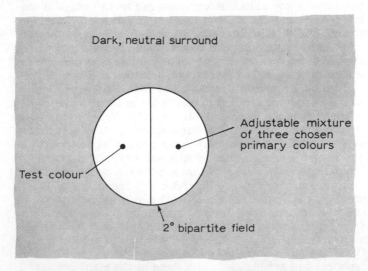

Figure 6.1 The basic experiment in colour matching.

colour and the primary mixture are presented side by side in a *colori-meter*, having a bipartite or split field, usually subtending 2° at the eye, with a dark surround. It is found experimentally that a colour-normal observer can match any test colour using a physical set of three primaries, such as red, green and blue, subject, however, to a slight arithmetic complexity which arises in the matching of some saturated colours. This is that one of the primary colours must be present in a *negative* amount to effect the match. Physically interpreted, this means that the primary in question has to be added to the test colour, rather than to the other two primaries.

In the CIE system of colour measurement, transfer of one of the primaries to the other half of the bipartite field to effect the match is avoided. This is made possible by specifying three non-physical primaries X, Y and Z, roughly corresponding to supersaturated red, green and blue respectively. *Saturation* is a term we discuss more fully in Section 6.3; it is used here in an attempt to described the nature of the CIE primaries. Thus an unsaturated colour is a pastel colour, while a saturated colour approximates a pure spectral colour. The use of the term 'supersaturated' is meant to indicate that the colour is more saturated than the purest spectral colour. Although these supersaturated primaries cannot be created in the laboratory, they suffice for colour representation since measurements with practical primaries can be transformed to the CIE primaries.

Transformation of primaries

The procedure for transforming a colour representation from one set of primaries R, G and B to another set X, Y and Z, may be appreciated by reference to Figure 6.2, which is a geometrical or vector representation of the colour-matching experiment in Figure 6.1. In the figure the amounts of each primary required to effect a match to some test colour C are marked off along three axes R, G and B in three-dimensional space. The axes are not necessarily orthogonal; however, they must specify three unique directions in the space. The characteristics of the space are of course determined by the initial directions chosen for the axes. The test colour C is specified as the point whose projections onto each axis correspond to the measured amounts of each primary.

It is possible to write down the relationship between C and its constituent primaries as a vector equation, based on Figure 6.2. Thus if R, G and B are unit vectors along the three axes, and R, G and B the scalar multipliers corresponding to the measured amounts of each primary (termed *tristimulus values* in the language of colorimetry), then

$$CC = RR + GG + BB$$

indicates that C units of the test colour C are matched by the additive combination of R units of R, G units of G and B units of B. It is poss-

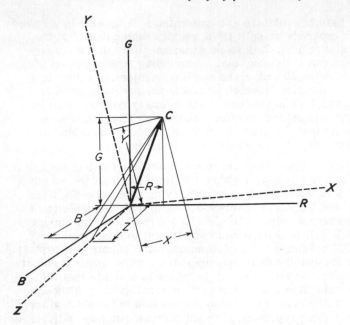

*Figure 6.2 Geometrical representation
of a colour C in colour space, based on the
matching experiment of Figure 6.1. The
coordinate axes are R, G and B, corresponding to the experimental primaries, but
three alternative axes X, Y and Z may be
used instead; this is said to constitute a
transformation of the primaries R, G and B
to X, Y and Z.*

ible for either R, G or B to be negative, which is the equivalent of addition to the left-hand side of the equation and to the left-hand half of the field in Figure 6.1.

Suppose now we match the same C units of **C** using the primaries **X**, **Y** and **Z**. Then

$$CC = XX + YY + ZZ$$

where the tristimulus values of the new primaries required for the match are X, Y and Z. The representation of this equation in colour space is shown in Figure 6.2, where **X**, **Y** and **Z** specify three new directions. Knowing R, G and B, how can we find X, Y and Z? This is possible by resolving the unit vectors **R**, **G** and **B** into components along the **X**, **Y** and **Z** axes, which is the equivalent of finding a colour match for one unit each of **R**, **G** and **B** in terms of **X**, **Y** and **Z**. Suppose the match to one unit of the red primary is given by

$$1\mathbf{R} = X_R\mathbf{X} + Y_R\mathbf{Y} + Z_R\mathbf{Z}$$

where X_R, Y_R and Z_R are the tristimulus values of unit amount of the red primary in terms of the **X**, **Y** and **Z** primaries. Similarly, suppose the matches to unit amounts of the green and blue primaries are given by

$$1\mathbf{G} = X_G\mathbf{X} + Y_G\mathbf{Y} + Z_G\mathbf{Z}$$

$$1\mathbf{B} = X_B\mathbf{X} + Y_B\mathbf{Y} + Z_B\mathbf{Z}$$

Then since $C\mathbf{C} = R\mathbf{R} + G\mathbf{G} + B\mathbf{B}$, by substitution

$$C\mathbf{C} = RX_R\mathbf{X} + RY_R\mathbf{Y} + RZ_R\mathbf{Z}$$

$$+ GX_G\mathbf{X} + GY_G\mathbf{Y} + GZ_G\mathbf{Z}$$

$$+ BX_B\mathbf{X} + BY_B\mathbf{Y} + BZ_B\mathbf{Z}$$

It follows that the tristimulus values of the new primaries required for the match are

$$X = X_R R + X_G G + X_B B$$

$$Y = Y_R R + Y_G G + Y_B B$$

$$Z = Z_R R + Z_G G + Z_B B$$

which can be written in matrix form as

$$\begin{bmatrix} X \\ Y \\ Z \end{bmatrix} = \begin{bmatrix} X_R & X_G & X_B \\ Y_R & Y_G & Y_B \\ Z_R & Z_G & Z_B \end{bmatrix} \begin{bmatrix} R \\ G \\ B \end{bmatrix}$$

The matrix

$$\mathbf{T}_{RGB \rightarrow XYZ} = \begin{bmatrix} X_R & X_G & X_B \\ Y_R & Y_G & Y_B \\ Z_R & Z_G & Z_B \end{bmatrix}$$

is termed the *transformation matrix* converting the old tristimulus values to the new tristimulus values. The columns of the transformation matrix are the tristimulus values of the new primaries **X**, **Y** and

Z required to match unit values of the old primaries **R, G** and **B**. Note that the transposition (interchange of rows and columns) of the matrix $\mathbf{T}_{RGB\to XYZ}$ gives the appropriate matrix for transforming the *primaries themselves* (considered as vectors), since we can write the initial colour matching equations as

$$\begin{bmatrix} \mathbf{R} \\ \mathbf{G} \\ \mathbf{B} \end{bmatrix} = \begin{bmatrix} X_R & Y_R & Z_R \\ X_G & Y_G & Z_G \\ X_B & Y_B & Z_B \end{bmatrix} \begin{bmatrix} \mathbf{X} \\ \mathbf{Y} \\ \mathbf{Z} \end{bmatrix}$$

Indicating transposition by a superscript T, we have therefore

$$\mathbf{T}^T_{RGB\to XYZ} = \mathbf{T}_{XYZ\to RGB}$$

To transform from XYZ to RGB tristimulus values we have to invert the matrix $\mathbf{T}_{RGB\to XYZ}$ and to transform from **RGB** to **XYZ** primaries we invert the matrix $\mathbf{T}^T_{RGB\to XYZ}$.

By convention, the units in which tristimulus values are expressed are derived from a preliminary experiment. Prior to matching the test colour, the left-hand half of the bipartite field (Figure 6.1) is made to emit radiation which is constant as a function of wavelength; this appears as a white, the so-called *equal-energy white* or *standard source E* of CIE colorimetry. The subject then adjusts the primaries for a match. By definition, the amount of each primary required for the match is one unit. In order to give absolute values to the units, the reference white may be adjusted to have unit luminance. In colour television applications, a match to a reference white approximating daylight rather than to equal-energy white is usual.

A plot of the results of experimental matches to a variety of test colours using physical primaries **R, G** and **B**, is found to be confined within some solid angle. At the limits of this solid angle are the spectral colours together with colours comprised of mixtures of the extreme spectral colours, red and violet. All other colours lie within these limits. Since a coordinate system based on some specified laboratory primaries **R, G** and **B** as fundamental primaries means that saturated colours have negative coordinates, in 1931 the CIE proposed a new coordinate system based on non-physical primaries **X, Y** and **Z**, whose directions in colour space were chosen to have certain properties (Le Grand, 1968). The first of these was that all physical colours were to have positive coordinates. Another property was that **Y** was to contain all the luminance information, **X** and **Z** having a zero luminance contribution to any mixture of the three.

The concept of a zero-luminance, non-physical primary is at first strange; but given that it is mathematically possible to choose primaries corresponding to any direction in colour space, then a direction **X** can be found which has, as its components along the **R, G** and **B** axes, a positive value of primary **R** and negative values of both **G** and **B**. We saw in Chapter 2 how the luminance of any spectral distribution of radiance is calculated by weighting the distribution using the V_λ curve. Hence it is possible that the luminance of the **R** primary can exactly equal the sum of the luminances of the **G** and **B** primaries. Under this condition, the effect of adding an amount of **X** primary to the right-hand side of the bipartite field in Figure 6.1 is equivalent to adding a certain amount of **R** and at the same time *subtracting* certain amounts of **G** and **B**, leaving the luminance of the right-hand side unchanged, but altering its colour appearance. Zero-luminance primaries are used in the transmission of colour information in broadcast colour television, as we shall see in the next chapter.

Colour-matching functions

Following the agreement on the primaries **X, Y** and **Z**, the CIE made available averaged experimental data pertaining to the way in which subjects match pure spectral colours. Obtained in the laboratory with real primaries, the results were transformed to the **X, Y, Z** system and tabulated as the response of the so-called *standard observer*. The tristimulus values of the **X, Y** and **Z** primaries for a match to a spectral colour of wavelength λ were termed respectively $\bar{x}_\lambda, \bar{y}_\lambda$ and $\bar{z}_\lambda$ and are plotted as a function of λ in Figure 6.3. They have been

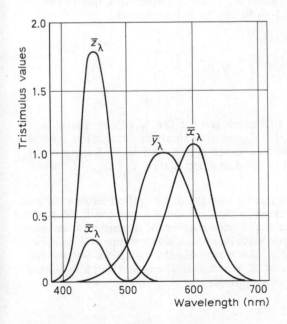

Figure 6.3 The CIE colour-matching functions $\bar{x}_\lambda, \bar{y}_\lambda$ and $\bar{z}_\lambda$.

given the name of *colour-matching functions*. The 1931 colour-matching functions are for a 2° field; subsequently, in 1964, the CIE published functions $\bar{x}_{10\lambda}, \bar{y}_{10\lambda}, \bar{z}_{10\lambda}$ for a 10° field (Wyszecki and Stiles, 1967). We shall, in what follows, use the 2° functions since individual patches of colour in a display are more likely to be of this size; for large areas of colour the 10° functions may, however, be more appropriate.

The significance of the CIE colour-matching functions lies in the fact that they make possible the specification of the colour of a source from a knowledge of the spectral distribution of radiant flux from the source, without recourse to a laboratory experiment. Thus a first and important step in relating perceived colour to spectral power distribution is achieved with, furthermore, a reduction in the information content of the specification, from a continuous function to three numbers.

Given, say, some spectral distribution of radiance $L_{e\lambda}$ in the left-hand half of the bipartite field in Figure 6.1, we may regard this distribution as the sum of an infinite number of spectral components, the magnitude of each being specified by the function $L_{e\lambda}$. Using the colour-matching functions of Figure 6.3, we can find out how much of each primary is required to match each component wavelength. Then, from the experimentally verified fact of the eye's linearity of response, the tristimulus values X, Y and Z required to match the colour of the left-hand half-field can be calculated as

$$X = k \int_0^\infty L_{e\lambda} \bar{x}_\lambda \, d\lambda$$

$$Y = k \int_0^\infty L_{e\lambda} \bar{y}_\lambda \, d\lambda = k \int_0^\infty L_{e\lambda} V_\lambda d\lambda$$

$$Z = k \int_0^\infty L_{e\lambda} \bar{z}_\lambda \, d\lambda$$

Since for convenience the CIE arranged for the $\bar{y}_\lambda$ colour-matching function to be identical to the V_λ relative luminosity function for the standard observer, Y is the *luminance* of the source; by letting $k = k_m$ = 680 lm/W, Y is obtained in candelas per metre (for $L_{e\lambda}$ in watts/(m^3 sr) and λ in metres).

The $\bar{x}_\lambda$, $\bar{y}_\lambda$ and $\bar{z}_\lambda$ functions can be thought of as optical filters through which the radiant power passes, with X, Y and Z being their total power outputs. It can be seen that if the power spectral distribution is concentrated, say, in the shorter wavelengths, a large value of Z will be produced relative to X and Y. As Z represents the amount of super-saturated blue, the mixture of X, Y and Z in the bipartite half-field of Figure 6.1 will be bluish, as required.

The 1931 CIE chromaticity diagram

As a further convenience, colours are often specified in terms of their chromaticity. Chromaticity is expressed in terms of *chromaticity coordinates* x and y which are derived from the tristimulus values by the equations

$$x = \frac{X}{X + Y + Z}$$

$$y = \frac{Y}{X + Y + Z}$$

$$z = \frac{Z}{X + Y + Z} = 1 - x - y$$

Thus x, y and z represent the *proportions* of the **X** primary, **Y** primary and **Z** primary respectively in a given mixture. If x is a fairly large proportion, say greater than 0.6, it indicates that the mixture contains a good deal of (supersaturated) red light and will appear under the conditions of Figure 6.1 as orange, red or reddish-purple. If y is fairly large the **Y** primary is dominant in the mixture, which will appear yellowish-green, green, bluish-green or green. Also, since **Y** contains all the luminance, a high value of y indicates that a colour has a relatively high luminance. If both x and y are small, the primary **Z** is dominant and the mixture will appear blue, violet or purple.

Figure 6.4, termed the 1931 CIE chromaticity diagram, represents chromaticity graphically, with x plotted horizontally and y vertically. All physical colours lie within the triangle formed by the origin and the points $x = 1$ and $y = 1$, since no physical colour can have a proportion of any of the primaries **X, Y** and **Z** which is greater than unity or less than zero. The boundary of physical colours is given more precisely by plotting the locus of spectral colours obtained from the colour-matching functions of Figure 6.3, the coordinates of which are

$$x = \frac{\bar{x}_\lambda}{\bar{x}_\lambda + \bar{y}_\lambda + \bar{z}_\lambda}$$

$$y = \frac{\bar{y}_\lambda}{\bar{x}_\lambda + \bar{y}_\lambda + \bar{z}_\lambda}$$

This locus is a curve as shown in Figure 6.4, the boundary of physical colours being completed by a straight-line section joining the ends of the curve (the line of purples).

The 1931 CIE chromaticity diagram is a useful, concise way to represent the chromatic quality of a given spectral power distribution. This distribution may be measured and subsequently converted first to X, Y, Z tristimulus values and then to chromaticity coordinates by the procedures indicated. Using modern techniques such procedures can be automated and the chromaticity coordinates made available in a digital display. Shown plotted in Figure 6.4 and listed in Table 6.1 are the chromaticities of the red, green and blue colour television phosphors recommended as primaries for the PAL System I and NTSC systems (Wood and Sproson, 1971; CCIR Conclusions, 1970, Report 407-1). Also shown in the table are the coordinates u, v on the 1960 CIE-UCS diagram, which will be discussed presently.

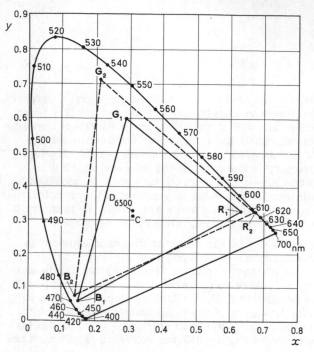

Figure 6.4 The 1931 CIE chromaticity diagram, showing the location of the red, green and blue colour television primaries for PAL System I (R_1, G_1, B_1) *and for the NTSC system* (R_2, G_2, B_2).

Table 6.1   Chromaticity coordinates of colour television phosphors for the United Kingdom PAL System I and the United States NTSC system.

	PAL System I				NTSC			
	x	y	u	v	x	y	u	v
Red (**R**)	0.64	0.33	0.451	0.349	0.67	0.33	0.477	0.352
Green (**G**)	0.29	0.60	0.121	0.374	0.21	0.71	0.076	0.384
Blue (**B**)	0.15	0.06	0.175	0.105	0.14	0.08	0.152	0.130

We shall presently see that the chromaticity of any mixture of two primaries lies on a straight line joining the primaries on a chromaticity diagram. Hence the chromaticity of a mixture of three primaries is bounded by the triangle whose apices are the primaries. The triangles $R_1 G_1 B_1$ and $R_2 G_2 B_2$ in Figure 6.4 therefore indicate the limits to the reproducible chromaticities in colour television displays.

The 1960 CIE-UCS chromaticity diagram

The 1931 CIE diagram, though still widely used, has a deficiency in so far as some practical applications are concerned. This is that colours on the diagram which are an equal distance from one another are not equally different in appearance. It is therefore difficult to judge the significance of differences between reproduced chromaticities and original chromaticities or the range of reproducible chromaticities in a colour reproduction system.

The 1960 CIE Uniform Chromaticity Scale (UCS) diagram is derived from the 1931 CIE diagram by stretching it unevenly over its surface in an attempt to make linear distances correspond more closely to perceptible differences. This is done by transforming the x and y chromaticity coordinates to new coordinates u and v, with

$$u = \frac{4x}{-2x + 12y + 3}$$

$$v = \frac{6y}{-2x + 12y + 3}$$

The inverse transformations are

$$x = \frac{\tfrac{3}{2}u}{u - 4v + 2}$$

$$y = \frac{v}{u - 4v + 2}$$

These transformations may be arrived at more fundamentally by transforming the X, Y, Z tristimulus values to new tristimulus values U, V, W with

$$U = \tfrac{2}{3}X \qquad\qquad X = \tfrac{3}{2}U$$

$$V = Y \qquad\qquad Y = V$$

$$W = -\tfrac{1}{2}X + \tfrac{3}{2}Y + \tfrac{1}{2}Z \qquad Z = \tfrac{3}{2}U - 3V + 2W$$

The chromaticity coordinates may then be calculated as $u = U/(U + V + W)$, $v = V/(U + V + W)$ and $w = W/(U + V + W) = 1 - u - v$, giving the same results above.

It is not in fact possible by transformations of this kind to make the diagram exactly uniform, but it is a considerable improvement on the 1931 CIE diagram. Figure 6.5 shows the transformed diagram with the red, green and blue colour television primaries of Figure 6.4 and Table 6.1.

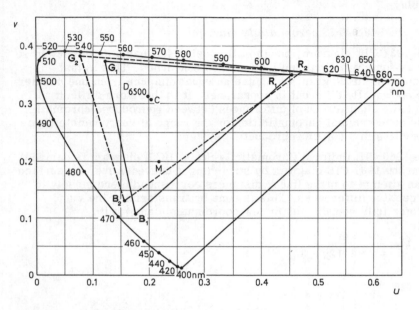

Figure 6.5 The 1960 CIE—UCS diagram showing the chromaticities of PAL System I (R_1, G_1, B_1) *and NTSC phosphors* (R_2, G_2, B_2).

It can be seen that in comparison with the 1931 diagram the green (left-hand, top) area of the diagram is compressed and the blue and magenta (bottom and lower right-hand) areas are expanded. The colour television primaries are now seen to be capable of reproducing less than half of the area of visible colours. As we shall see, however, this is not the only consideration in selecting display primaries.

Colour mixture on the 1960 CIE-UCS diagram

Suppose we are given three primaries R, G and B which are mixed in some proportion. How do we find the chromaticity of the mixture? In a typical colour CRT display problem we might know the chromaticity of the phosphors from the manufacturer's specification. We might also know, or could measure, the relationship between input signal voltage and the luminance for each phosphor colour. Suppose for three given signal inputs, the luminances and chromaticity coordinates are

Primary	*Luminance (cd/m²)*	*Chromaticity coordinates*
R	L_R	u_R v_R
G	L_G	u_G v_G
B	L_B	u_B v_B

To calculate the chromaticity coordinates of the mixture we first find the sum of the tristimulus values for each primary. If the V tristimulus value is made numerically equal to the luminance in candelas per square metre, this fixes the magnitude of unit tristimulus value. Thus, let $V_R = L_R$, $V_G = L_G$ and $V_B = L_B$. Then, since for any primary the sum of the tristimulus values $S = U + V + W$ and since $S = V/v$, we have

$$S_R = U_R + V_R + W_R = V_R/v_R = L_R/v_R$$

$$S_G = U_G + V_G + W_G = V_G/v_G = L_G/v_G$$

$$S_B = U_B + V_B + W_B = V_B/v_B = L_B/v_B$$

with the subscripts R, G and B denoting the three primaries. Thus the sum of the tristimulus values for each primary is calculable from the given data. Since $u = U/S$ and $w = 1-u-v = W/S$, we can calculate the U and (if necessary) the W tristimulus values for each primary

$$U_R = u_R \, S_R \qquad W_R = w_R \, S_R = (1-u_R-v_R)S_R$$

$$U_G = u_G \, S_G \qquad W_G = w_G \, S_G = (1-u_G-v_G)S_G$$

$$U_B = u_B \, S_B \qquad W_B = w_B \, S_B = (1-u_B-v_B)S_B$$

If **R**, **G** and **B** are now mixed together, the mixture can be regarded as a vector addition in three-dimensional colour space. To find the resultant, the components of each primary along the **U**, **V** and **W** axes can be separately added to give the tristimulus values of the mixture **M**. The chromaticity coordinates of the mixture u_M, v_M are then given by

$$u_M = \frac{U_R + U_G + U_B}{S_M} = \frac{u_R \, L_R/v_R + u_G \, L_G/v_G + u_B \, L_B/v_B}{L_R/v_R + L_G/v_G + L_B/v_B}$$

$$v_M = \frac{V_R + V_G + V_B}{S_M} = \frac{L_R + L_G + L_B}{L_R/v_R + L_G/v_G + L_B/v_B}$$

where

$$S_M = U_R + V_R + W_R + U_G + V_B + W_G + U_B + V_B + W_B$$
$$= S_R + S_G + S_B$$

As a numerical example, consider the PAL System I colour television primaries in Table 6.1. Suppose the measured luminances of each phosphor, separately stimulated, are the same and equal to 1 cd/m². Then we can calculate the following

$$S_R = 1/0.349 = 2.86 \qquad S_G = 1/0.374 = 2.67 \qquad S_B = 1/0.105 = 9.52$$

$$U_R = 0.451 \times 2.86 = 1.29 \qquad U_G = 0.121 \times 2.67 = 0.32 \qquad U_B = 0.175 \times 9.52 = 1.67$$

$$V_R = 1 \qquad\qquad V_G = 1 \qquad\qquad V_B = 1$$

$$S_M = 2.86 + 2.67 + 9.52 = 15.05$$

$$u_M = \frac{1.29 + 0.32 + 1.67}{15.05} = 0.22 \qquad v_M = \frac{1 + 1 + 1}{15.05} = 0.20$$

The result is plotted as the point M in Figure 6.5. It is interesting to note that it falls not far from the blue primary, from which we deduce that the blue primary has a more powerful effect on the mixture than the other two primaries. Inspection of Figure 6.5 reveals the reason: the blue primary has a low value of v and therefore unit tristimulus value has a relatively low luminance. By specifying equal luminances in the example, we assign a relatively large number of tristimulus units to the blue primary. This has a practical implication, namely that in typical colour displays the blue primary operates at an average luminance lower than the red and green primaries and the blue phosphor can have a lower luminous efficiency in converting electron beam current to luminous flux. However, because of the low value of the V_λ curve in the blue region, a low luminous flux output may require a relatively high radiant power output.

In the case of mixing two primaries only, say **R** and **G**, the chromaticity coordinates of the mixture are

$$u_M = \frac{u_R \; L_R/v_R + u_G \; L_G/v_G}{L_R/v_R + L_G/v_G} = \frac{u_R \; m_R + u_G \; m_G}{m_R + m_G}$$

$$v_M = \frac{v_R \; L_R/v_R + v_G \; L_G/v_G}{L_R/v_R + L_G/v_G} = \frac{v_R \; m_R + v_G \; m_G}{m_R + m_G}$$

Thus both the u and v coordinates of the mixture are weighted averages of the u and v coordinates respectively of the primaries, the weights being $m_R = L_R/v_R$ for the primary **R** and $m_G = L_G/v_G$ for the primary **G**. It follows therefore, that the point (u_M, v_M) lies on a straight line joining the points (u_R, v_R) and (u_G, v_G) on the chromaticity diagram. By extension of this argument, the point representing the mixture of all three primaries **R, G** and **B**, is confined to the triangle whose apices are $(u_R, v_R), (u_G, v_G)$ and (u_B, v_B).

Colour temperature and standard illuminants

An alternative way in which the chromaticities of some colours can be expressed is in terms of their *colour temperatures*. This stems from the fact that, as the temperature of a blackbody radiator is increased, its spectral power distribution, initially skewed towards the red end of the spectrum, becomes gradually richer in the shorter wavelengths. Its chromaticity coordinates follow the locus shown in Figure 6.6, where the figures are temperatures in kelvins (K).

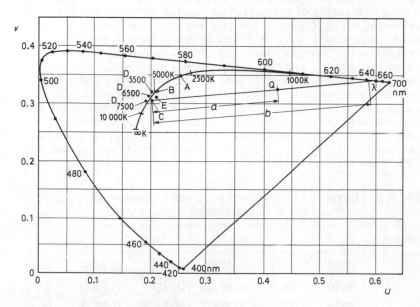

Figure 6.6 CIE standard illuminants and the locus of blackbody radiation shown plotted on the 1960 CIE–UCS chromaticity diagram. Also shown is the way a colour **Q** *can be specified in terms of its dominant wavelength* λ *and excitation purity a/b with respect to a reference white (illuminant C in the figure).*

It turns out that a large number of radiant sources, whose colour we would describe as roughly white, have chromaticity coordinates close to the colour temperature locus. Thus average daylight has a colour temperature of about 6500 K and incandescent light about 3000 K. Phosphors used in monochrome television CRTs often have quite a high colour temperature, perhaps 11 000 K.

When the chromaticity of the radiant source is not near enough to the colour temperature locus to be able to determine its colour temperature precisely, the *correlated colour temperature* is used. This is the colour temperature which most closely resembles the source, in a way which has been defined by Judd. Correlated colour temperature may be read from a diagram once the x and y or u and v coordinates are known (see Judd and Wyszecki, 1967).

For convenience the CIE defined in 1931 three standard sources A, B and C representing incandescent light, sunlight and average daylight respectively, together with source E, representing equal-energy white. In 1965 a new series of spectral distributions was defined which represented daylight more accurately, especially in the shorter wavelengths. This series is the D series, with a subscript denoting correlated colour temperature. Thus D_{6500} represents average daylight, while D_{5500} and D_{7500} represent a sunnier daylight and a cloudier daylight respectively. Some standard sources and their chromaticity coordinates are given in Table 6.2. It can be seen that D_{6500} and standard source C (which has a correlated colour temperature of 6740 K) are very similar. Colour television engineers nowadays tend to use D_{6500} (sometimes abbreviated to D_{65}) in preference to standard source C, but in practical terms there is not a great deal of difference between them.

Table 6.2   Correlated colour temperature and chromaticity coordinates of CIE standard illuminants.

Standard	*K*	*x*	*y*	*u*	*v*
A	2854	0.4476	0.4075	0.2560	0.3495
B	4870	0.3484	0.3516	0.2137	0.3235
C	6740	0.3101	0.3162	0.2009	0.3073
D_{5500}	5500	0.3324	0.3475	0.2043	0.3205
D_{6500}	6500	0.3127	0.3291	0.1977	0.3122
D_{7500}	7500	0.2991	0.3150	0.1935	0.3057
E	5500	0.3333	0.3333	0.2105	0.3158

Yet another way of representing the chromaticity of a colour is by polar coordinates, with some chosen reference white, say illuminant C, as origin. This is shown for a colour Q in Figure 6.6. The angular orientation is expressed in terms of the *dominant wavelength,* this being the point at which the line CQ, when projected, cuts the spectral locus. For colours in the lower right-hand section of the diagram, the projection fails to intercept the spectral locus and the line is therefore projected backwards from C, the wavelength being expressed as that of the complementary colour, e.g. 540 c, where the c indicates a complementary wavelength. *Complementary colours,* which are a function of the chosen reference white, are such that a mixture of positive amounts of a colour and its complement can be found which produces the reference white. The radius of the colour measured from the reference white is the *excitation purity,* which is equal numerically to a/b in Figure 6.6. A unity or 100% excitation purity corresponds to a spectral colour. In the case of colours in the lower right-hand section of the diagram, the distance b is measured from C to the line of purples. In either case, from elementary geometry it follows that

$$\text{Excitation purity} = \frac{u_Q - u_C}{u_\lambda - u_C} = \frac{v_Q - v_C}{v_\lambda - v_C}$$

where the subscripts Q, C and λ refer to the colour Q, the reference white C and the spectral colour λ.

Since a straight line on the 1960 CIE diagram has the equation $v = au + b$, a and b being constants, it becomes by substitution $6y/(-2x + 12y + 3) = 4ax/(-2x + 12y + 3) + b$ or $y = cx + d$ on the 1931 diagram, where $c = (2a - b)/(3 - 6b)$ and $d = b/(2 - 4b)$. Thus dominant wavelength is the same on both 1960 and 1931 diagrams; however, owing to the area stretching and compression, excitation purity may be different.

6.3 Perceived Colour

The CIE system of colour measurement enables us to proceed from a known spectral power distribution or known mixture of certain primaries to a specification of colour (u, v, L), where u and v are chromaticity coordinates on the 1960 CIE-UCS diagram and L is the luminance. In describing this system it has been difficult to avoid using words such as 'red' or 'green' in referring to colours, since this is the way we normally refer to them, but the whole of the necessary measurement and computation could be carried out by an automaton without any sense of colour. We may ask therefore: what does (u, v, L) look like?

Seen in the viewing situation of Figure 6.1, that is, as a 2° patch of colour with a dark surround, there is a well-documented relationship between chromaticity and perceived colour. Colours on the spectrum locus range through red, orange, yellow, green and blue to violet, with colours in the interior part of the diagram becoming progressively desaturated as the distance from the spectrum locus increases, culminating in white somewhere near the upper middle part of the diagram.

However, colours seen in coloured displays (or in everyday life) are rarely seen in this way. They are surrounded by other colours and, because of temporal changes in the display and movement by the eye, they are preceded by and followed by other colours in time. The juxta-position of other colours can have a marked influence on the perceived colour of a given patch of light, the spatial and temporal effects being known as *simultaneous* and *successive colour contrast* respectively. If light which appears white against a neutral background is sur-rounded by a bright, saturated blue, the light appears yellow; the same is true if the eye fixates such a blue before looking at the white.

A general term which is used to describe these modifications to our colour vision is *chromatic adaptation*. A number of theories have been advanced to account for the facts (for a summary see Wyszecki and Stiles, 1967). The term itself can be misleading since, unlike dark adaptation, it can take place very quickly. It can also take place selectively so that an observer can have one adaptation state in rela-tion to a display and another in relation to the room surround, seen simultaneously. Thus chromatic adaptation is in general a complex phenomenon, probably involving higher-order processes in the brain. In coloured displays it can produce remarkable effects, as for example in the pictures of Land (1959). Land, and others before him, noted the extraordinary variety of colours—amongst them orange, green, purple and blue—in pictures reproduced with only two primaries, red and white. Despite this general complexity, chromatic adaptation is amenable to approximate numerical treatment, sufficient for some purposes in display engineering and colour television, using the 1960 CIE-UCS diagram.

Characterisation and measurement of perceived colour

An accumulation of evidence, from both colour scientists and artists, indicates that any colour we perceive has three attributes: *hue, brightness* (or, if it is non-self-luminous, *lightness*) and *saturation. Brightness* is that same characteristic we discussed in Chapter 2, being our subjective impression of how bright or dim an object or area in a display appears. *Hue* is that attribute we commonly des-cribe as red, yellow, orange, green, etc. *Saturation* is our impression of how different the colour is from an *achromatic* (white or grey) colour; thus pastel colours are of low saturation and spectral colours of high saturation.

The measurement of perceived colour involves some attempt to record the sensory impressions of hue, brightness and saturation occurring inside an observer's head. The techniques which are used are similar to those previously discussed in connection with bright-ness alone. The difference is that in the case of colour the subjective response space has three dimensions as opposed to one. We shall proceed to describe two methods which have been found to be useful; the first uses binocular matching and the second associative colour memory.

Binocular matching method

In the binocular matching method (Wright, 1934; Hunt, 1965; Bartleson, 1966) a subject records his sensory impression of a test colour by directly relating it to another colour seen under standard viewing conditions. The test colour is viewed with one eye, and a reference colour, comprised of adjustable amounts of three suitable primaries with a fixed neutral surround, is viewed with the other eye. This allows the adaptation state to be different for each eye, the viewing conditions for the test colour being typically quite different from the reference, e.g. the test colour may be of lower luminance and have a different colour surround. The outcome of the experiment is an expression of the perceived test colour in terms of the tristimulus values or (u, v, L) of the reference colour.

Memory method

The memory method of recording perceived colour (Judd, 1940; Rubinstein, Pearson and Spivack, 1969) is really a refinement of the process we use in everyday life. Thus 'lemon yellow' is one of many phrases commonly employed to describe a colour by reference to our memory of a previously perceived colour. Since, however, the associative learning procedure has been different for each of us, the use of everyday colour names is unlikely to yield maximum precision. Instead, in about five or six hours of training, it is possible to teach subjects to classify their colour perceptions in a more precise language by allowing them to look at and later to guess at standard colours labelled in a suitable language. The colours are viewed under standard viewing conditions, e.g. 2° with a neutral surround. For this purpose an ordered collection of paint chips such as that in the *Munsell Book of Color* may be used, illuminated by a standard illuminant, e.g. illuminant C.

In the Munsell Renotation System (the current revised version) the chips are calssified by *hue, value* (corresponding to lightness) and *chroma* (corresponding to saturation). There are ten hues: R, YR, Y, GY, G, BG, B, PB, P, RP with ten subdivisions of each, of which four are commonly used: 2.5R, 5R, 7.5R, 10R; nine steps of value, 1 being at the dark end and 9 at the light end of the scale; and up to about 20 steps of chroma for reproducible paint colours, 0 being for a neutral colour and 20 being for a high-saturation colour. Thus a subject learns to substitute for 'lemon yellow' a response of say, 7.5Y 8/10, meaning that he sees the hue as 7.5Y, the value as 8 and the chroma as 10. The relation between common colour names and the Munsell system has been studied and documented in the *ISCC–NBS Method of Designating Colors and Dictionary of Color Names* (Kelly and Judd, 1955).

The Munsell designation hue value/chroma may be converted to a (u, v, V) specification using tables of the CIE equivalents of the Munsell Renotation System (Newhall, Nickerson and Judd, 1943; Wyszecki and Stiles, 1967). Thus 7.5Y 8/10 converts to ($u = 0.2197$ $v = 0.3626$ $V = 0.5910$) when illuminated by standard source C, with the V figure being proportional to luminance on a scale ranging from 0 to 1. The equivalence is illustrated graphically in Figures 6.7-6.15 (by courtesy of the Munsell Color Co., Baltimore, Md.) These diagrams provide sufficient precision for the conversion in many cases.

Representation of perceived colour on the 1960 CIE–UCS chromaticity diagram

Although both the binocular matching method and the memory method have defects which can cause problems in some situations, it is nevertheless true that by one or other or both we can obtain a fairly accurate measurement of the perceived colour of an area in a complex pattern of colours, such as a display. The result can conveniently be plotted on the 1960 CIE–UCS chromaticity diagram as a *vector of perceived hue and saturation* (Figure 6.16). The origin n of the vector is the chromaticity of the reference neutral colour which the observer views with one eye in the binocular matching method, or which he was taught to recognise as neutral in the memory method. In the figure this point has the coordinates of illuminant C. The arrowhead a of the vector represents the *apparent chromaticity* of the test colour, meaning that a colour of this chromaticity, seen under the reference viewing conditions, has the same perceived colour as the test colour when the perceived brightnesses of the two are equal.

Although Figure 6.16 is similar in appearance to the previously discussed specification of chromaticity in terms of dominant wavelength and excitation purity, it is significantly different in that the vector is derived from a subjective experiment rather than an objective measurement. The objective measurement of the chromaticity of colours corresponding to n and a typically yields two other points and some other vector $n_0 a_0$ (Figure 6.17). The interest lies in the relationship between these two vectors.

It should be noted that the representation of saturation as the length of a vector on the 1960 CIE–UCS diagram is valid for a particular value of brightness only. A different scaling factor relating saturation to length is necessary for each brightness step (Munsell value step). For a given length of vector, the saturation is much higher for the higher brightnesses (see Figures 6.7-6.15). Thus a spectral yellow has a chroma (saturation) on the Munsell scale of about 20 at a Munsell value of 9, whereas the same spectral yellow has a chroma of only 3 when seen as a dark area of Munsell value 1.

Relationship between chromaticity and perceived colour

It is possible to find the perceived hue and saturation of an area in a display by first finding the chromaticity of the *achromatic point*, representing the state of chromatic adaptation of the observer in looking at the display. The achromatic point is the chromaticity of a

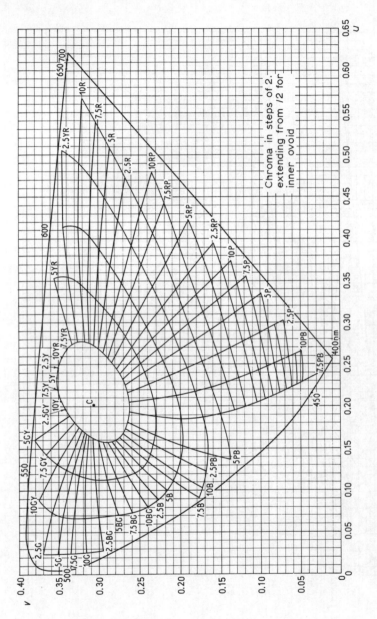

Figure 6.7 Munsell Renotation System for illuminant C, Value 1/.

146

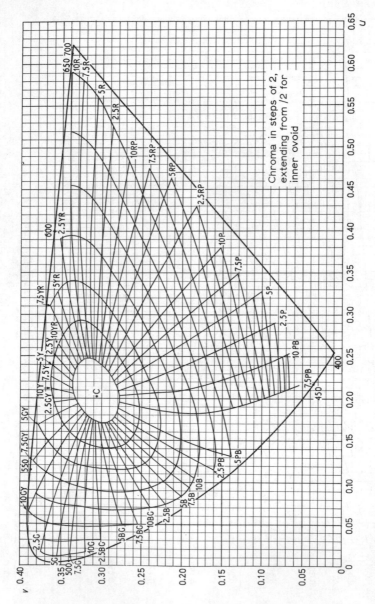

Figure 6.8 *Munsell Renotation System for illuminant C, Value 2/.*

147

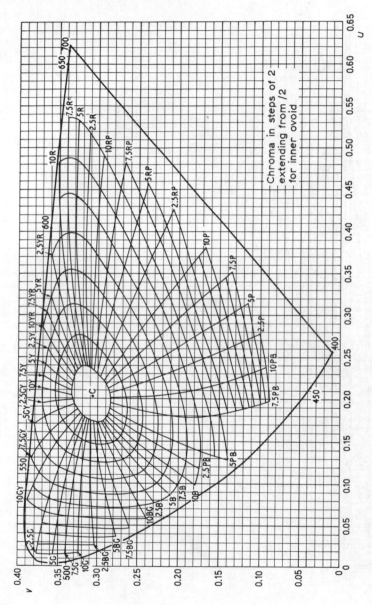

Figure 6.9 Munsell Renotation System for illuminant C, Value 3/.

148

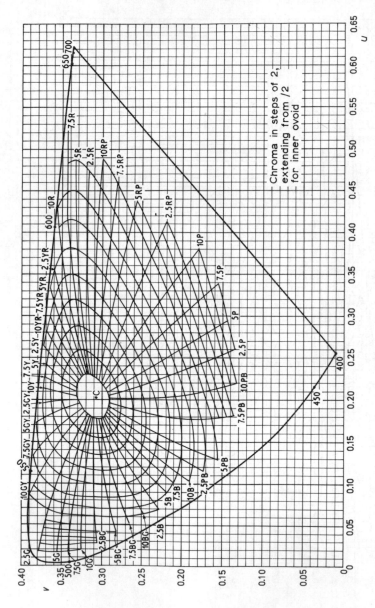

Figure 6.10 Munsell Renotation System for illuminant C, Value 4/.

149

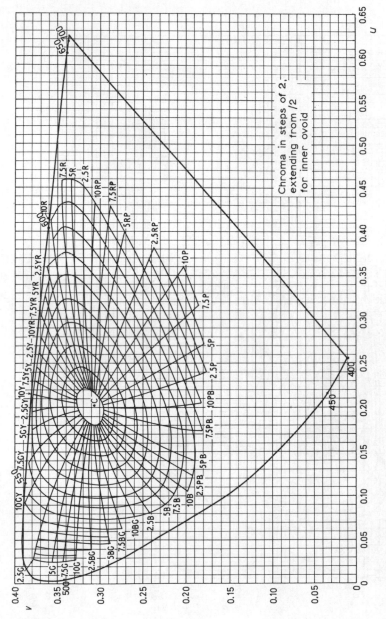

Figure 6.11 Munsell Renotation System for illuminant C, Value 5/.

150

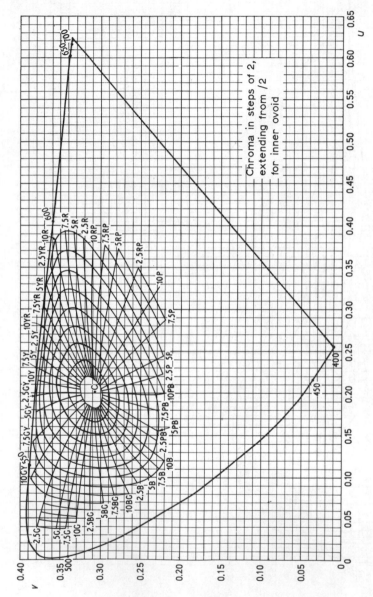

Figure 6.12 Munsell Renotation System for illuminant C, Value 6/.

151

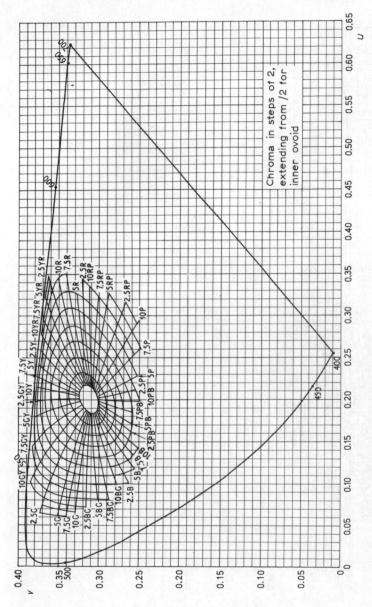

Figure 6.13 Munsell Renotation System for illuminant C, Value 7/.

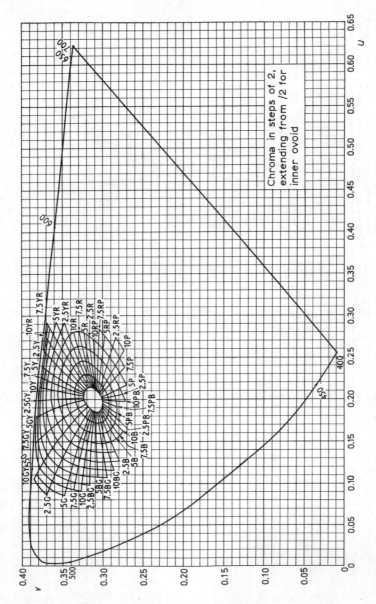

Figure 6.14 Munsell Renotation System for illuminant C, Value 8/.

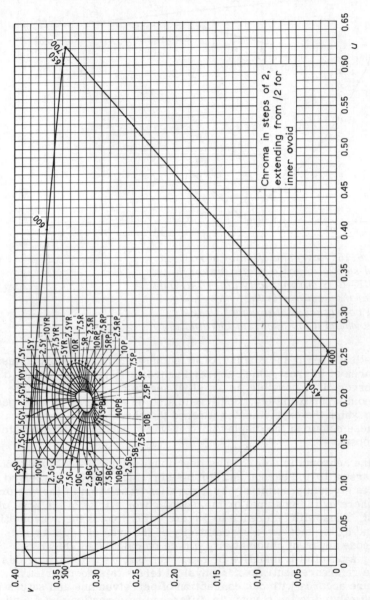

Figure 6.15 Munsell Renotation System for illuminant C, Value 9/.

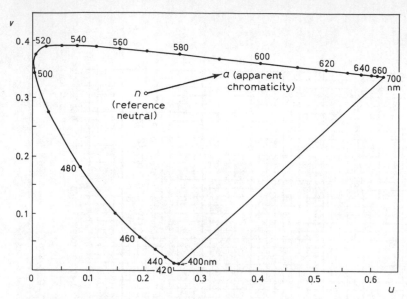

*Figure 6.16 Representation of perceived
hue and saturation as a vector **na** on the
1960 CIE—UCS chromaticity diagram. The
origin of the vector **n** is the reference
neutral colour (here illuminant C) and
the arrowhead **a** the apparent chromaticity.*

hypothetical area in the display, of brightness equal to the brightness
of the area of interest, which appears achromatic (grey or white) to
an observer. It is possible, as we shall see, to calculate the achromatic point approximately, but it could also be estimated by an experiment in which the experimenter altered the chromaticity of an equal-
brightness colour in the display until it was reported as achromatic
by the observer.

Given the achromatic point, it has been found (Judd, 1940; Rubinstein
and Pearson, 1970; Pearson and Rubinstein, 1971) that the perceived
colour is given approximately by a parallel translation of the vector
$n_0 a_0$, where a_0 is the actual or measured chromaticity of the area of
interest. Thus, with reference to Figure 6.17, if n_0 is the achromatic
point and a_0 the measured chromaticity of the area of equal brightness whose apparent chromaticity a is to be calculated, then a is
given by a parallel translation of $n_0 a_0$ such that its origin coincides
with the reference neutral n. In physical terms this geometrical
procedure accords with our conception of perceived hue and saturation
as being related to the chromatic difference, in direction and magnitude, between the test colour and an achromatic-appearing colour of
the same brightness.

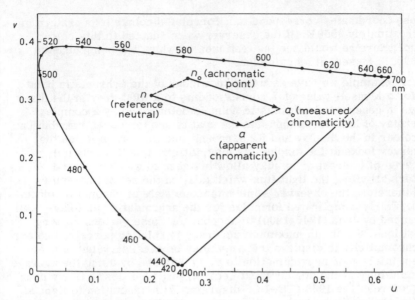

*Figure 6.17 Approximate calculation of
perceived colour as the parallel shift of
the vector representing measured quantities
$n_0 a_0$ to na, n being the reference neutral.*

As a numerical example, consider the inverse problem of creating a
desired colour sensation at a given point in a display. Suppose this
colour is a pale blue whose Munsell specification is 10B 7/4 when
viewed under illuminant C with a neutral surround. Suppose the eye's
chromatic adaptation in viewing the display is to a colour temperature
of 3000 K ($u = 0.25, v = 0.35$). By reference to Figure 6.13 we obtain

	u	v
Achromatic point n_0	0.25	0.35
Reference neutral n	0.20	0.31
Apparent chromaticity of test colour a	0.18	0.29

To calculate the u and v coordinates of point a_0, we take the difference
in both u and v coordinates of n_0 and n and add these differences to
the coordinates of a, since na and $n_0 a_0$ are parallel and of equal
length. This gives

$$u_{a_0} = u_a + (u_{n_0} - u_n) = 0.18 + (0.25 - 0.20) = 0.23$$

$$v_{a_0} = v_a + (v_{n_0} - v_n) = 0.29 + (0.35 - 0.31) = 0.33$$

These coordinates correspond to a correlated colour temperature of approximately 3900 K. If the observer were adapted to this colour temperature he would see the test area as white, but being adapted to 3000 K, he sees it as pale blue.

In this example we have assumed knowledge of the achromatic point n_0 for a Munsell value of 7, corresponding to a light grey in the display. In general the achromatic point is determined by a complex interplay of factors, comprising the spatial and temporal distribution of colour in the display and its surround, and the way in which the observer looks at the display—he may, for example, look steadily at the area of interest or he may allow his gaze to wander. These factors all affect the light flux which falls on the retinal receptors and therefore the observer's instantaneous state of chromatic adaptation. Fairly complicated formulae for the achromatic point have been advanced by Judd (1940, 1960) to account for these various viewing conditions. To obtain maximum accuracy in relating perceived colour to chromaticity in displays their use may be necessary, but in practice a fairly good approximation to n_0 is obtained by using the average chromaticity of the display (next section) provided this is fairly near the centre of the 1960 CIE–UCS diagram. With adaptation to light of a high chromatic content, represented by points towards the extremities of the diagram, the main additional complication is the necessity to compute an achromatic point for each level of brightness in the display. The reader interested in further details of the theory underlying these procedures is referred to the papers already cited, and to the explanations of Richards (Richards and Parks, 1971; Richards, 1972) based on a nonlinear von Kries formulation.

Colour balance

In the case of a display using three primaries, **R**, **G** and **B**, the average chromaticity of the display can be calculated from a knowledge of the luminance of each primary for each picture element in the display. Suppose the display consists of $M \times N$ picture elements; then the average luminance of each primary is

$$L_R = \frac{1}{MN} \sum_{i=1}^{M} \sum_{j=1}^{N} L_{R_{ij}}$$

$$L_G = \frac{1}{MN} \sum_{i=1}^{M} \sum_{j=1}^{N} L_{G_{ij}}$$

$$L_B = \frac{1}{MN} \sum_{i=1}^{M} \sum_{j=1}^{N} L_{B_{ij}}$$

where $L_{R_{ij}}$, $L_{G_{ij}}$ and $L_{B_{ij}}$ are the luminance contributions of the **R**, **G** and **B** primaries respectively to the ijth picture element and

L_R, L_G and L_B the respective average luminances. The average chromaticity coordinates of the display $\bar{u}, \bar{v}$ are

$$\bar{u} = \frac{u_R\, L_R/v_R + u_G\, L_G/v_G + u_B\, L_B/v_B}{L_R/v_R + L_G/v_G + L_B/v_B}$$

$$\bar{v} = \frac{L_R + L_G + L_B}{L_R/v_R + L_G/v_G + L_B/v_B}$$

where the chromaticities of the **R, G** and **B** primaries are (u_R, v_R), (u_G, v_G) and (u_B, v_B) respectively.

The point $(\bar{u}, \bar{v})$ can be said to represent the *colour balance* of the display. It is the centre of gravity on the 1960 CIE–UCS chromaticity diagram of all the colours in the display, appropriately weighted. The colour balance point is frequently the dominant factor in determining the achromatic point, and in many viewing situations the coordinates of n_0 may be taken as approximately equal to $(\bar{u}, \bar{v})$. This is often true of displays using red, green and blue primaries, as in Figure 6.5, when mainly desaturated colours are being displayed or when there is a balanced use of saturated colours. The colour balance point in this case is near the centre of the 1960 CIE–UCS diagram.

If, in particular, the colour balance point corresponds with the reference neutral, there is a convenient simplification in the calculation of perceived colour. Suppose, for example, that the colour balance point has coordinates equal to or near to illuminant C; then in this case the apparent chromaticity referred to illuminant C is approximately equal to the actual chromaticity. In this case Figures 6.7–6.15 can be used directly for the design of the system, without recourse to the additional construction of Figure 6.17.

When there is not a balanced use of the red, green and blue primaries, or when some other set of primaries are employed, conversion from CIE measured chromaticity to perceived colour requires the calculation of the achromatic point. Figure 6.18 illustrates some experimental results (Pearson and Rubinstein, 1971) for two-primary displays of the type demonstrated by Land (1959). The method has also been tested extensively on three-primary displays (Rubinstein and Pearson, 1970). The primaries used in the two-primary case were a red (R) of high excitation purity and a white (W) of 3375 K. The colour balance point is at a point intermediate between W and R and is fairly near the edge of the diagram. The irregular line shows the range of apparent chromaticities recorded by subjects, with reference to a neutral of illuminant C, using the memory method. These were well predicted using the principle of Figure 6.17, with the neutral point being calculated by the more complicated formulae of Judd (1940). Using the approximation of an achromatic point equal to the colour balance point, a straight line parallel to WR and passing through C is obtained.

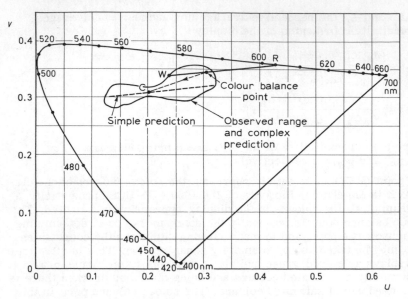

*Figure 6.18 Experimentally determined
range of apparent chromaticities (irregular
outline) in a two-primary red (R) and
white (W) display of the Land type, highlight luminance 500 cd/m² (after Pearson
and Rubinstein, 1971).*

Influence of the surround

Under conditions where the display is viewed in a dark room or in
low-level ambient illumination, the chromatic adaptation of the
observer has been found experimentally to be close to the colour
balance point of the display. What, however, is the state of chromatic
adaptation of the observer when the display is seen in fairly bright
room lighting?

A procedure whereby the observer's adaptation is determined by a
weighted average of room light and display light, according to the
angular subtense and average chromatic content and luminance of
each, falls short of explaining what is observed. For example, the two-
primary pictures of Figure 6.18 can be surrounded by bright incandescent light and the apparent chromaticities are found to be little
altered. Using a simple weighting procedure, we would expect all the
colours to become much redder and for there to be hue reversals, for
example of low-saturation greens. This is not observed.

Again, in the literature on colour television and colour photography
there have been a number of studies of the preferred colour temper-

ature of whites in the display for various surround conditions (e.g. Townsend, 1962; Bartleson and Witzel, 1967). These show fairly broad preference curves over a range of colour temperatures and no recorded hue reversals; the displays merely vary from warm to cool in appearance as the colour temperature of the whites is increased.

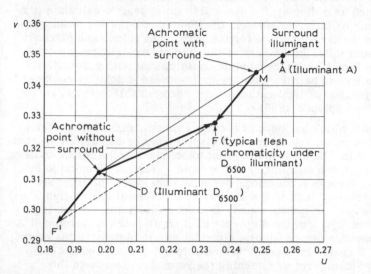

Figure 6.19 Hypothesis regarding the influence of incandescent surround illumination (A) on perceived colour in a display having a colour balance point at D_{6500}. On the assumption of a shift of the achromatic point from D to M, flesh tones F turn from pink to blue.

Figure 6.19 illustrates this situation graphically. The colour balance point of the display is taken as D_{6500} and the bright surround illumination as equal to illuminant A. If the achromatic point is assumed to be point D in the absence of the surround illumination, colours such as flesh tones F would be seen to have a hue and saturation given by the vector DF. If when the surround illumination is switched on the achromatic point shifts to M, representing an average of surround and display chromaticities, the perceived colour of the flesh tones changes to the vector MF, or if it is parallel shifted, to DF'. In this case the direction of the vector corresponds approximately to a hue of blue.

In practice this is not observed. While flesh tones and other colours in the display may take on a bluish *cast* in relation to colours in the room surround, the flesh tones still appear to be flesh tones. Furthermore, the colours in the room seem satisfactory too and there are no

hue reversals there. So we are led to the conclusion that there may
be different achromatic points for display and surround. This much
was pointed out by Land (1959) who, however, invoked his own theories
to explain it. In his appraisal of Land's work, Judd (1960) used a
description of Helmholtz's in describing chromatic adaptation, namely
that the eye *discounts the illuminant colour*. In a complex viewing
situation such as a display, the eye and brain appear to calculate perceived colour by different rules in the display and the surround, per-
ceiving each to have its own effective illuminant colour and discount-
ing each separately. In the case of the display, experiment indicates
that the eye forms an impression of an illuminant with chromaticity
close to the colour balance point, even though the display is composed
of random patches of light rather than a recognisable scene (Pearson,
Rubinstein and Spivack, 1969).

This analysis, which has need of further experimental confirmation,
indicates that perceived colour in a display may be calculated approximately by taking the achromatic point to be equal to the colour balance
point. However, the complexity of the topic is further illustrated by
the fact that, through a conscious decision, observers can compare
selected patches of light in the display with other patches of light,
regarded as such, in the surround. In colour television, comparing a
white patch at D_{6500} in the display, with a white patch at illuminant A
in the surround, gives the impression that one is bluish and the other
yellowish. It is this impression which colour television engineers
may attempt to correct by matching the reproduced white to the
surround illuminant.

The U^* V^* W^* system

The U^* V^* W^* system is a CIE-recommended uniform perceptual
colour space in three dimensions related to the Munsell system. It
can be viewed as an extension of the 1960 CIE–UCS diagram to include the brightness dimension. The quantities U^*, V^* and W^* describe the three coordinates of a colour in the space and are defined†
as

$$U^* = 13\ W^*\ (u-u_0)$$

$$V^* = 13\ W^*\ (v-v_0)$$

$$W^* = 25\ Y^{1/3} - 17$$

where Y is the relative luminance of the colour on a scale of 1 to 100,

---

† At the time of writing, a modification of the space has been proposed
for study by the CIE, with new coordinates $U' = U^*$, $V' = 1.5V^*$, W'
$= W^* - 1$. The main effect of the modification, if adopted, will be to
scale up chromaticity differences in the v dimension of the 1960
CIE–UCS diagram.

u and v its measured 1960 CIE–UCS chromaticity coordinates and u_0, v_0 the chromaticity of the perceived achromatic colour. The formulae are often applied to reflecting colour samples to calculate a measure ΔE of the perceived colour difference between two samples viewed in close proximity, u_0 and v_0 being taken as the colour of the illuminant. ΔE is then the geometrical distance in three-dimensional space given by

$$\Delta E = [(U_1^* - U_2^*)^2 + (V_1^* - V_2^*)^2 + (W_1^* - W_2^*)^2]^{1/2}$$

where U_1^*, V_1^*, W_1^* and U_2^*, V_2^*, W_2^* are the coordinates of the two samples in the space.

Applied to displays, the coordinates u_0, v_0 can be taken as the achromatic point, or approximately equal to the colour balance point. The quantities U^* and V^* then specify the departure from the achromatic point along axes corresponding approximately to the hue directions 10PB − 2.5GY and 2.5BG − 10RP respectively in Munsell space. W^* represents brightness; we saw in Chapters 2 and 4 that brightness is approximately proportional to the cube root of luminance for dark surrounds; hence W^* satisfactorily represents brightness for a relatively dark surround to the display.

In the formulae for U^* and V^*, the coordinate differences $(u - u_0)$ and $(v - v_0)$ are multiplied by 13 W^*. With reference to Figures 6.7–6.15, we see that this is necessary to increase the perceptual colour difference for brighter (higher Munsell value) colours. W^* is approximately equal to $10 \times$ Munsell value, so that for a value of 5, $W^* \simeq 50$. The numerical values of U^* and V^* make 1 CIE unit of colour difference ($\Delta E = 1$) equal to about 0.1 Munsell value steps or 0.15 chroma steps or 2.5 hue steps at chroma/1 (Judd and Wyszecki, 1963), which is at or near the threshold of perceptibility.

If the chromaticity is held constant and only the brightness is changed, the colour difference formula becomes $\Delta E = W_1^* - W_2^*$, so that $\Delta E = 1$ corresponds to unity change in W^*, or about 1% of the total range of W^*. We have previously noted that in quantised pictures the number of quantal levels of brightness is typically between 64 and 256 (6–8 bits), so the CIE unit falls in this range.

If the brightness is held constant and the chromaticity is varied, say in the u direction, the colour difference formula becomes $\Delta E = U_1^* - U_2^* = 13 \, W^* \, (u_1 - u_2)$. For a bright colour, with $W^* = 90$, 1 CIE unit corresponds to a chromaticity difference $u_1 - u_2 = 1/(13 \times 90) = 0.00085$, whereas for a dark colour with $W^* = 20$, 1 CIE unit corresponds to $u_1 - u_2 = 1/(13 \times 20) = 0.0038$. For comparison, we may note that in the BBC Research Department a chromaticity error of 0.00384 on the 1960 CIE–UCS diagram is considered to be significant under average television viewing conditions, although errors of one-tenth of this size (0.0004) may be perceptible under good viewing conditions (Wood and Sproson, 1971).

Chapter 7

TRANSMISSION OF COLOUR INFORMATION

7.1 Principles of Colour Reproduction

Display primaries

The colorimetric analysis of the coding and transmission of colour information begins at the receiver, with the choice of the display primaries. The **X, Y** and **Z** primaries of the CIE system cannot be realised in practice, so that, for three-primary reproduction, a set of three non-colinear points lying within the area of physical colours on a chromaticity diagram must be chosen.

It is, as we have seen, a property of both the 1931 and 1960 CIE diagrams that a mixture of any two primaries has chromaticity coordinates lying on a straight line joining the chromaticity coordinates of the primaries, and that a mixture of any n primaries has chromaticity coordinates lying within the polygon whose vertices are the chromaticity coordinates of the (outermost) primaries. Inspection of the 1960 CIE-UCS diagram (Figure 6.5) reveals that almost all physically realisable chromaticities can be reproduced with three primaries located at the extremities of the diagram in the red, green and blue spectral regions. It is for this reason that three, rather than any other number of primaries are used in practical colour reproduction systems and that they are usually chosen to be red, green and blue rather than any other triad.

Practical considerations make it necessary to reduce by some considerable amount the range of reproducible chromaticities obtainable with spectral primaries. It is not possible to manufacture CRT phosphors with high excitation purities which, at the same time, have luminous efficiencies sufficient to produce reasonably bright displays. The National Television Systems Committee in the United States acknowledged this fact in the early 1950s in drawing up specifications for colour television receiver primaries. The chromaticities of these primaries are given in Table 6.1, and are further illustrated in Figure 6.5 as R_2, G_2 and B_2. They correspond approximately to the silicate phosphors available at that time. Later developments have involved the introduction of the sulphide phosphors, with a higher luminous efficiency but more restricted reproduction gamut, followed by a further improvement through the use of the rare earth phosphor europium yttrium vanadate for the red primary, which has both a higher excitation purity and a better luminous efficiency (Hunt, 1967). The chromaticities of the primaries in PAL System I, the version of PAL used in the United Kingdom, accord more closely with phosphors now being used (Wood and Sproson, 1971) and are also shown in Table 6.1 and in Figure 6.5 as R_1, G_1 and B_1.

As can be seen from Figure 6.5, more than half of the area of the diagram lies outside the triangle of reproducible chromaticities using practical phosphors. Saturated magentas, purples and cyans cannot be reproduced. The situation, however, is not as catastrophic as the diagram appears to indicate. The colours of everyday scenes are generally rather unsaturated and have chromaticities lying near the centre of the chromaticity diagram. Figure 7.1 summarises some

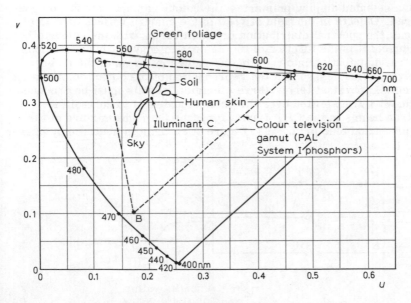

Figure 7.1 The chromaticities of common objects with daylight illumination (after Hendley and Hecht, 1949; MacAdam, 1954).

measurements made by Hendley and Hecht (1949) and MacAdam (1954). MacAdam's measurements showed that human skin tones of very different ethnic groups all lie in a small area quite near to the neutral centre of the diagram. Thus colour television phosphors handle the frequently occurring colours satisfactorily and it is only the occasional saturated hue that suffers. By sacrificing some chromaticity range, a greater range in the third dimension of colour—luminance—is obtained. Increased luminance, besides alleviating desaturation due to reflection of white room light from the screen, provides a subjective increase in saturation (Hunt, 1965; Bartleson and Witzel, 1967). Thus the choice of phosphors must be considered in three-dimensional rather than two-dimensional colour space. Indeed there is a case, where good reproduction of low-saturation colours in bright room lighting is of especial importance, for further reducing the excitation purity of the reproduction primaries (Pearson and Rubinstein, 1971). One example could be the colour videotelephone, where pleasing and stable flesh tone reproduction might be found to be more important than accurate reproduction of high-saturation hues.

Criteria for colour reproduction

Having selected display primaries, the colour camera can now be considered. Objects in the field of view of the camera reflect light into its lens, the spectral distribution of which varies with the colour of the object. It is the function of the camera to convert this continuous spectral distribution into tristimulus values in terms of the three receiver primaries, so that the reproduction of the object colour is correct. In physical terms, three electrical signals must be produced which, when transmitted over the channel and used to control the electron beams in the CRT display, produce the right mixture of the red, green and blue primaries (Figure 7. 2). This is achieved by pass-

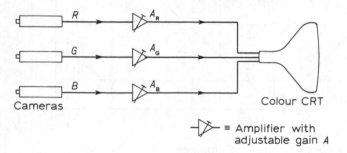

Figure 7.2 Principle of three-primary colour reproduction, as in colour television. Signals from the red (R), green (G) and blue (B) cameras are fed to the red, green and blue guns of a colour CRT. The channel gains A_R, A_G and A_B are used to control the colour balance of the display.

ing the light from the scene through broadband red, green and blue filters whose spectral sensitivities are designed to produce the requisite output signals.

It may at first be supposed that the correct criterion for reproduction is to make the chromaticity coordinates of the reproduction the same

as those of the original. However, this is not necessarily desirable.
Viewing conditions are often widely different at camera and display;
the display may have a different luminance from that of the original
scene, it may have a greater or lesser contrast, it probably has a
lower spatial bandwidth and it is two-dimensional. When the scene
illuminant changes, it may be desirable to alter the gains A_R, A_G and
A_B (Figure 7.2) to ensure constancy of the colour temperature of
white in the display. Broadcast colour television cameras incorporate
such controls (Heightman, 1972).

The correct criterion for colour reproduction in displays is a complex one which is the subject of current investigation and research.
This criterion is thought to be more nearly that of making the
perceived colour at the receiver the same as that of the perceived
colour at the camera. This does not necessarily mean reproduction
of chromaticity. However, in the absence of a complete understanding
of these processes, reproduction of chromaticity is often used as an
approximate goal, while bearing in mind its limitations. Indeed, it can
be argued that, since the camera embodies colour filters whose
characteristics cannot easily be adapted to changing conditions of
illumination, etc., the criterion of reproduction of chromaticity is the
right one for the design of these filters, with corrections and em-
bellishments being carried out subsequently on the red, green and
blue camera signals.

Since it is rarely possible to ensure exact reproduction of chromaticity, we may note the types of error which are more acceptable than
others, on the assumption that it is perceived colour which should be
reproduced correctly. These errors are illustrated in Figure 7.3.
In Figure 7.3a the original chromaticities are shifted in parallel
straight lines in the reproduction; within limits this is an acceptable
form of error because the relative chromatic spacing of the colours
is maintained and the colour balance point (average chromaticity)
shifts along with the colours, preserving hue and saturation, by the
arguments previously advanced. As we shall see, small changes in the
gains A_R, A_G and A_B in Figure 7.2 have approximately this effect on
desaturated colours.

In Figure 7.3b the excitation purity of all the colours is proportion-
ately reduced. This in turn reduces the saturation, but the change is
one we commonly experience when, for example, the amount of
natural daylight falling on a scene is reduced or the scene is seen
through haze (Hunt, 1967).

The effect is therefore not as serious as in Figure 7.3c, where the
errors occur in random directions and give rise to random errors in
perceived colour. In some cases errors of the form illustrated in
Figure 7.3c may be resolvable into parallel components of the type
shown in Figure 7.3a together with smaller random components; in
this case the parallel components may be discounted.

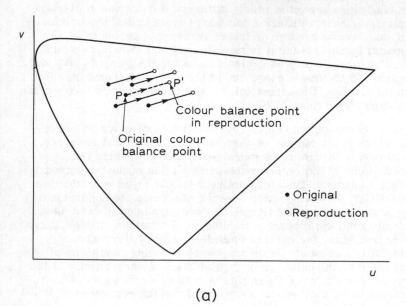

(a)

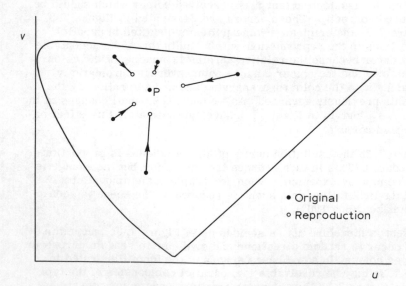

(b)

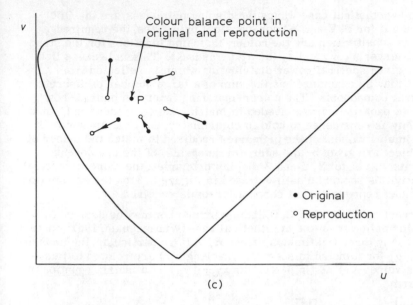

*Figure 7.3 (a) Acceptable form of chroma-
ticity error, involving the parallel translation of all chromaticities. Since the
colour balance point P is likewise trans-
lated to P', the hue and saturation of the
colours are (approximately) preserved.
(b) The perceived saturation of the colours
is reduced, their hue remaining unchanged,
by the reduction is excitation purity in
the reproduction. However, this type of
change is one encountered frequently in
everyday life when the magnitude of the
overall scene illuminance changes.
(c) Least acceptable form of error in
which the colour balance point remains
unchanged with the errors being in random
directions.*

Spectral sensitivities of the camera channels

In the hypothetical case where the display primaries are the CIE **X, Y** and **Z** (or **U, V** and **W**) non-physical primaries, the required camera sensitivities are the colour-matching functions for the standard observer, $\bar{x}_\lambda, \bar{y}_\lambda$ and $\bar{z}_\lambda$ (or $\bar{u}_\lambda, \bar{v}_\lambda$ and $\bar{w}_\lambda$). This is because light of any given spectral power distribution which is reflected from an object may be considered as the sum of a large number of discrete spectral components. The colour-matching functions indicate how much of each primary is needed to match each component and, since linearity is considered to hold in colorimetry, the total amounts (tristimulus values) of the primaries required to match the colour of the object are given by the sums (or integrals) of the component amounts. Thus, for **X, Y** and **Z** display primaries, the camera spectral sensitivities should be as illustrated in Figure 6.3, on the assumption that exact reproduction of chromaticities is required.

The practical case of **R, G, B** display primaries may be derived by transformation from the hypothetical case (Wintringham, 1951; Epstein, 1953). Any three tristimulus values R, G, B (in particular, the amounts $\bar{r}_\lambda, \bar{g}_\lambda, \bar{b}_\lambda$ for a match to spectral wavelength λ) are related to tristimulus values X, Y, Z (in particular $\bar{x}_\lambda, \bar{y}_\lambda, \bar{z}_\lambda$) by a matrix equation of the form

$$\begin{bmatrix} R \\ G \\ B \end{bmatrix} = \begin{bmatrix} a_1 & a_2 & a_3 \\ a_4 & a_5 & a_6 \\ a_7 & a_8 & a_9 \end{bmatrix} \begin{bmatrix} X \\ Y \\ Z \end{bmatrix}$$

where the transformation matrix

$$\mathbf{T}_{XYZ \rightarrow RGB} = \begin{bmatrix} a_1 & a_2 & a_3 \\ a_4 & a_5 & a_6 \\ a_7 & a_8 & a_9 \end{bmatrix}$$

transforms the tristimulus values for the **X, Y** and **Z** primaries to equivalent tristimulus values for the **R, G** and **B** primaries. We can calculate the element values of this matrix by inverting the matrix $\mathbf{T}_{RGB \rightarrow XYZ}$, whose columns are the tristimulus values of **X, Y** and **Z** needed to match unit amounts of **R, G** and **B** (Section 6.2). In terms of the chromaticity coordinates of the primaries, which are known,

$$\mathbf{T}_{RGB \rightarrow XYZ} = \begin{bmatrix} k_1 x_R & k_2 x_G & k_3 x_B \\ k_1 y_R & k_2 y_G & k_3 y_B \\ k_1 z_R & k_2 z_G & k_3 z_B \end{bmatrix}$$

where k_1, k_2 and k_3 are constants and where x_R, y_R and z_R are the chromaticity coordinates of the red primary, x_G, y_G and z_G those for the green primary and x_B, y_B and z_B those for the blue primary. Since the chromaticity coordinates specify the proportion of each primary in any match, the tristimulus values for that match are simply the chromaticity coordinates multiplied by a constant. The numerical values of the constants k_1, k_2 and k_3 are adjusted to the size of the unit chosen for each of the **R, G** and **B** primaries. In colour television it is usual to define unit amounts (voltages) of **R, G** and **B** as those which produce the system reference white; by inversion of the matrix $\mathbf{T}_{RGB \rightarrow XYZ}$ we can discover their appropriate values. By the usual formula for matric inversion (Judd and Wyszecki, 1963) we have

$$
\mathbf{T}_{XYZ \rightarrow RGB} =
\begin{bmatrix}
\dfrac{y_G z_B - y_B z_G}{k_1 \Delta} & \dfrac{x_B z_G - x_G z_B}{k_1 \Delta} & \dfrac{x_G y_B - x_B y_G}{k_1 \Delta} \\[2ex]
\dfrac{y_B z_R - y_R z_B}{k_2 \Delta} & \dfrac{x_R z_B - x_B z_R}{k_2 \Delta} & \dfrac{x_B y_R - x_R y_B}{k_2 \Delta} \\[2ex]
\dfrac{y_R z_G - y_G z_R}{k_3 \Delta} & \dfrac{x_G z_R - x_R z_G}{k_3 \Delta} & \dfrac{x_R y_G - x_G y_R}{k_3 \Delta}
\end{bmatrix}
$$

where $\Delta = x_R(y_G z_B - y_B z_G) + x_G(y_B z_R - y_R z_B) + x_B(y_R z_G - y_G z_R)$ is numerically equal to the determinant of the matrix $\mathbf{T}_{RGB \rightarrow XYZ}$ with $k_1 = k_2 = k_3 = 1$. From this expression it may be seen that the column multipliers k_1, k_2 and k_3 become row dividers in the inverted matrix. Substituting the appropriate values for the chromaticity co-ordinates for PAL System I and NTSC primaries from Table 6.1, we obtain

PAL System I

$$
\mathbf{T}_{XYZ \rightarrow RGB} =
\begin{bmatrix}
\dfrac{2.0609}{k_1} & \dfrac{-0.9374}{k_1} & \dfrac{-0.3201}{k_1} \\[2ex]
\dfrac{-1.1415}{k_2} & \dfrac{2.2094}{k_2} & \dfrac{0.0489}{k_2} \\[2ex]
\dfrac{0.0807}{k_3} & \dfrac{-0.2720}{k_3} & \dfrac{1.2712}{k_3}
\end{bmatrix}
$$

NTSC

$$
\mathbf{T}_{XYZ \rightarrow RGB} =
\begin{bmatrix}
\dfrac{1.7301}{k_1} & \dfrac{-0.4823}{k_1} & \dfrac{-0.2611}{k_1} \\[2ex]
\dfrac{-0.8135}{k_2} & \dfrac{1.6517}{k_2} & \dfrac{-0.0234}{k_2} \\[2ex]
\dfrac{0.0834}{k_3} & \dfrac{-0.1694}{k_3} & \dfrac{1.2845}{k_3}
\end{bmatrix}
$$

The values of k_1, k_2 and k_3 are now chosen such that when the system is reproducing reference white, the tristimulus values R, G and B are equal. Taking reference white for PAL System I as D_{6500} $(x = 0.3127, y = 0.3291, z = 0.3582)$ and for NTSC as illuminant C $(x = 0.3101\ y = 0.3162\ z = 0.3737)$ and normalising the X, Y, Z tristimulus values such that the reference white has unity luminance $(Y = 1)$, we obtain the equations

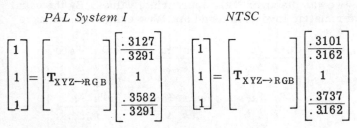

       PAL System I   *NTSC*

which gives the values for k_1, k_2 and k_3 as

PAL System I	*NTSC*
$k_1 = 0.6724$	$k_1 = 0.9059$
$k_2 = 1.1781$	$k_2 = 0.8262$
$k_3 = 1.1882$	$k_3 = 1.4305$

Using these values, the elements of the transformation matrices $T_{RGB \rightarrow XYZ}$ and $T_{XYZ \rightarrow RGB}$ can be evaluated and are given in Table 7.1, together with the chromaticity coordinates of the primaries and the reference white. Also shown in the table are the results of similar calculations made in terms of the U, V and W primaries from the u, v chromaticity coordinates.

It is of interest to note that from the $RGB \rightarrow XYZ$ or $RGB \rightarrow UVW$ relations, we have the fact that the luminance Y (or V) is given by

      PAL System I   *NTSC*

$$Y = 0.222R + 0.707G + 0.071B \qquad Y = 0.299R + 0.587G + 0.114B$$

The major proportion of the luminance of the picture is carried in the green camera signal in both systems, this proportion being significantly higher in PAL System I, its green primary having a lower excitation purity than in the NTSC system.

Using $XYZ \rightarrow RGB$ transformations for a D_{6500} white we obtain from Figure 6.3 the transformed colour-matching functions appropriate to RGB primaries. These are illustrated in Figure 7.4. Because the primaries are real and lie inside the spectral locus on the CIE chromaticity diagram, negative amounts are required to match some spectral colours. This is apparent in Figure 7.4 as negative lobes in the required camera sensitivities. Since optical filters can only be

Table 7.1 Relationships between RGB, XYZ and UVW tristimulus values in PAL System I and NTSC colour television systems with linear transfer characteristics.

PAL System I

Display primaries

	x	y	u	v
R	0.64	0.33	0.451	0.349
G	0.29	0.60	0.121	0.374
B	0.15	0.06	0.175	0.105

NTSC

Display primaries

	x	y	u	v
R	0.67	0.33	0.477	0.352
G	0.21	0.71	0.076	0.384
B	0.14	0.08	0.152	0.130

Reference white

Illuminant D_{6500} 0.3127 0.3291 0.1978 0.3122

Illuminant C 0.3101 0.3162 0.2009 0.3073

Transformation of tristimulus values

$$\begin{bmatrix} R \\ G \\ B \end{bmatrix} = \begin{bmatrix} 3.065 & -1.394 & -0.476 \\ -0.969 & 1.875 & 0.042 \\ 0.068 & -0.229 & 1.070 \end{bmatrix} \begin{bmatrix} X \\ Y \\ Z \end{bmatrix}$$

$$\begin{bmatrix} X \\ Y \\ Z \end{bmatrix} = \begin{bmatrix} 0.430 & 0.342 & 0.178 \\ 0.222 & 0.707 & 0.071 \\ 0.020 & 0.130 & 0.939 \end{bmatrix} \begin{bmatrix} R \\ G \\ B \end{bmatrix}$$

$$\begin{bmatrix} R \\ G \\ B \end{bmatrix} = \begin{bmatrix} 3.884 & 0.034 & -0.952 \\ -1.391 & 1.751 & 0.083 \\ 1.707 & -3.439 & 2.140 \end{bmatrix} \begin{bmatrix} U \\ V \\ W \end{bmatrix}$$

$$\begin{bmatrix} U \\ V \\ W \end{bmatrix} = \begin{bmatrix} 0.287 & 0.228 & 0.119 \\ 0.222 & 0.707 & 0.071 \\ 0.128 & 0.954 & 0.487 \end{bmatrix} \begin{bmatrix} R \\ G \\ B \end{bmatrix}$$

Transformation of tristimulus values

$$\begin{bmatrix} R \\ G \\ B \end{bmatrix} = \begin{bmatrix} 1.910 & -0.532 & -0.288 \\ -0.985 & 1.999 & -0.028 \\ 0.058 & -0.118 & 0.898 \end{bmatrix} \begin{bmatrix} X \\ Y \\ Z \end{bmatrix}$$

$$\begin{bmatrix} X \\ Y \\ Z \end{bmatrix} = \begin{bmatrix} 0.607 & 0.174 & 0.200 \\ 0.299 & 0.587 & 0.114 \\ 0 & 0.066 & 1.116 \end{bmatrix} \begin{bmatrix} R \\ G \\ B \end{bmatrix}$$

$$\begin{bmatrix} R \\ G \\ B \end{bmatrix} = \begin{bmatrix} 2.432 & 0.332 & -0.576 \\ -1.519 & 2.084 & -0.057 \\ 1.434 & -2.812 & 1.796 \end{bmatrix} \begin{bmatrix} U \\ V \\ W \end{bmatrix}$$

$$\begin{bmatrix} U \\ V \\ W \end{bmatrix} = \begin{bmatrix} 0.405 & 0.116 & 0.134 \\ 0.299 & 0.587 & 0.114 \\ 0.145 & 0.826 & 0.629 \end{bmatrix} \begin{bmatrix} R \\ G \\ B \end{bmatrix}$$

built with a positive or zero transmission at any wavelength, we are faced, in a three-tube camera, with the impossibility of manufacturing the required sensitivities. Ironically, the use of physical display primaries produces the requirement for non-physical optical filters at the camera.

In modern television cameras this problem is overcome by the use of an electrical matrix following the camera (Heightman, 1972; Underhill 1972) as shown in Figure 7.5. The gains A_1-A_9 determine the elements of the transformation matrix converting the colour representation from non-physical camera primaries R_0, G_0, B_0 to the display primaries R, G, B. Thus

$$\begin{bmatrix} R \\ G \\ B \end{bmatrix} = \begin{bmatrix} A_1 & A_2 & A_3 \\ A_4 & A_5 & A_6 \\ A_7 & A_8 & A_9 \end{bmatrix} \begin{bmatrix} R_0 \\ G_0 \\ B_0 \end{bmatrix}$$

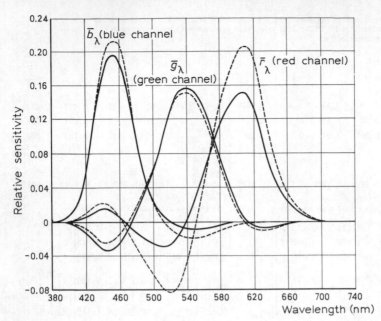

Figure 7.4 Spectral sensitivities required in the red, green and blue camera channels, obtained by transforming the colour-matching functions for the standard observer, $\bar{x}_\lambda, \bar{y}_\lambda, \bar{z}_\lambda$. The solid lines show the sensitivities appropriate to the NTSC primaries and the dotted lines the PAL System I primaries, both using a D_{6500} reference white (after Wood and Sproson, 1971).

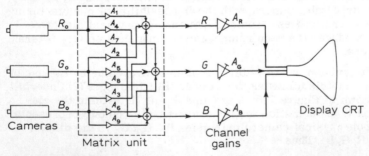

Figure 7.5 Principle of matrixing the output signals R_0, G_0, B_0 from an all-positive lobe camera to give the required R, G, B signals appropriate to the display phosphors.

To arrive at an exact solution for the element values A_1-A_9 the camera sensitivities must be linear combinations of $\bar{r}_\lambda, \bar{g}_\lambda, \bar{b}_\lambda$ (Figure 7.4); the red channel sensitivity $\bar{r}_{0\lambda}$, for example is given by $\bar{r}_{0\lambda} = a_1\bar{r}_\lambda + a_2\bar{g}_\lambda + a_3\bar{b}_\lambda$ where $a_1 - a_3$ are elements of the inverse matrix $\mathbf{T}_{RGB \to R_0 G_0 B_0}$. Since $r_\lambda, g_\lambda, b_\lambda$, in turn are linear combinations of the $\bar{x}_\lambda, \bar{y}_\lambda, \bar{z}_\lambda$ functions, it follows that the $\bar{r}_{0\lambda}, \bar{g}_{0\lambda}, \bar{b}_{0\lambda}$ camera sensitivities must be linear combinations of the $\bar{x}_\lambda, \bar{y}_\lambda, \bar{z}_\lambda$ functions.

Practical combined filter-camera sensitivities do not fulfil this condition exactly, so that it is not possible, strictly, to speak of camera primaries $\mathbf{R}_0, \mathbf{G}_0, \mathbf{B}_0$, except as a function of wavelength. However, element values A_1-A_9 can be chosen which optimise the colour reproduction while admitting chromaticity errors. The procedure described by Jones (1968) utilises a set of test colours whose spectral characteristics and R, G, B tristimulus values are known. A computer program calculates the values of A_1-A_9 which minimise the subjective error, based on a criterion similar to that in the $U^* V^* W^*$ system.

In colour CRTs it may be difficult, as a practical matter, to produce pure reds, greens and blues with a chromaticity equal to the manufacturer's specification for the phosphors being used in the CRT. One reason is that the electron beam spreads out to excite phosphors other than the desired one, especially at high brightness; another is that ambient room light is reflected from the screen. The net result may be a loss of excitation purity of each of the three primaries.

The subjective effect is not serious, however. Colours in the picture suffer a loss of saturation as in Figure 7.3b, but the effect is common to all colours and the eye is very tolerant of it. In the so-called *Ives-Abney-Yule* compromise (Hunt, 1967) the eye's tolerance in this regard is exploited by designing the camera spectral sensitivities to match non-physical receiver primaries lying outside the spectral locus. The camera spectral sensitivities may then be all-positive. If subsequently a display is used with real phosphors having the same dominant wavelength as the non-physical primaries, the uniform desaturation in the picture may be quite acceptable. Even if one of the primaries loses considerably more purity than the other two in this process, the result may still be acceptable (Pearson and Rubinstein, 1971).

Effect of channel gains on colour reproduction

With reference to Figure 7.2 or Figure 7.5, suppose that the channel gains A_R, A_G and A_B have initially been set up to reproduce reference white (say D_{6500}) when the camera is looking at the same reference white. Suppose also that the internal gains and biases in the camera and the display are such that under this condition $A_R = A_G = A_B = 1$ and $R = G = B = 1$.

In broadcast television it is the practice to try to maintain reproduced white in the display at a fixed colour temperature equal to the reference, even though the colour temperature of the illuminant at the camera is quite different. The scene illuminant reflected from a white card may be 3000 K incandescent light but the system is required to reproduce this as 6500 K. This is arranged by altering the gains A_R, A_G and A_B; it can be carried out semi-automatically by pointing the camera at a white card and adjusting the gains until the three camera voltages are each equal to unity (Heightman, 1972). Another method is to sense the illuminant colour by three independent sensors (Taylor and Chambers, 1971) and thereby to adjust the gains appropriately; a third is to integrate to grey over part or all of the picture, as in colour photography (Hunt, 1967).

The effect of gain alterations may be derived by using the $RGB \rightarrow XYZ$ or $RGB \rightarrow UVW$ transformations in Table 7.1 to recalculate the reproduced chromaticity coordinates. Figure 7.6a illustrates the form of the changes occasioned by increasing the gain A_B of the blue channel and Figure 7.6b the effect of increasing both A_G and A_B in such amounts as to change the colour temperature of white from illuminant A to illuminant D_{6500}. In Figure 7.6a the reproduced chromaticities tend to move towards the blue primary **B**. This may be appreciated by considering any colour Q as some mixture of the primary **B** and a supposed primary **M**, with **M** being some mixture of **G** and **R**. Increasing **B**, by the straight-line rule of colour mixture, causes Q to move to Q' along the line MB. If the blue gain is increased indefinitely, **Q'** approaches **B**. In Figure 7.6b the movement towards the blue primary is supplemented by a movement towards the green primary, the total movement being the resultant of the two. Colours with a high green-primary contribution are most affected by the green channel gain increase.

If we suppose that the colour balance point of the display is approximately equal to the reproduced white W_2 in Figure 7.6b and if, by the arguments previously considered, the eye adapts to or discounts the illuminant represented by W_2, the change in *perceived* colour is smaller than that indicated by the size of the arrows in Figure 7.6b For, by the approximate method of calculation represented in Figure 6.17, perceived colour is given by the vector difference between the achromatic point, here assumed to be W_2, and the reproduced chromaticities. For colours of low saturation, which are the more critical ones, there is a near-parallel shift in chromaticity caused by the gain adjustments. The chromatic spacing of such colours relative to the achromatic point is virtually unchanged by modest changes in the colour temperature of the reference white and therefore they are satisfactorily reproduced. With excessive alteration of the channel gains this spacing may be impaired and the quality of the reproduction will suffer.

It may be noted that by such chromatic shifts as are illustrated in Figure 7.6b, the system cannot hope to reproduce exactly the changes in the chromaticities of the original objects which would occur if the original scene illuminant were changed from A to D_{6500}, since this depends on the spectral reflectance of the objects as a function of

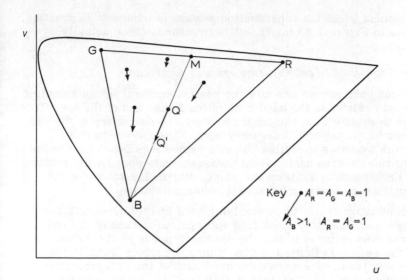

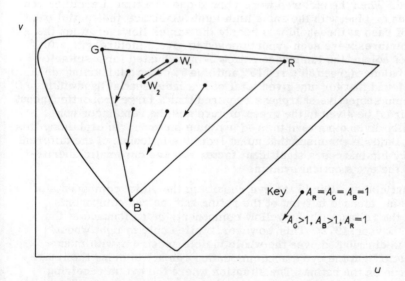

*Fig 7.6 Effect on the reproduced
chromaticity of changes in the channel
gains. In (a) the blue channel gain only is
increased and in (b) both blue and green
gains are increased to change the system
white (W₁) from 2854 K (illuminant A) to
6500 K (illuminant D₆₅₀₀), represented
by W₂.*

wavelength, of which the reproduction system is ignorant. In practice, the shifts in Figure 7.6b might well approximate those actually occurring.

Sampling densities in colour scanners and displays

In previous chapters we saw how the spatio-temporal image sampling density was related to the bandwidth of the image and of the eye. This leads us to inquire what sampling densities are necessary in the red, green and blue images in a colour system. The answer to this question is available in outline but with rather less detail than in the monochrome case, as basic visual measurements specifically relating to this problem have not been extensive. Particular solutions have been obtained, however, in broadcast colour television.

The complicating factor in determining what spatial bandwidth, and therefore what sampling density, is appropriate in each of the red, green and blue pictures is that the answer depends on the colour content of the scene. In Baldwin's experiments (Baldwin, 1951; Baldwin and Nielsen, 1956), observers defocused each of the red, green and blue pictures until the threshold of detectability of blurring was reached. When the pictures were viewed one at a time, i.e. either red or green or blue, with the same high light luminance, the spatial bandwidth of each at threshold was nearly the same. However, when the three pictures were seen superimposed to give a picture with a full range of colour, the luminance ratios being adjusted for a suitable colour balance (green 80%, red 15% and blue 5% of the total luminance), it was found that for any given total of available spatial bandwidth, maximum subjective sharpness required that a large proportion (about two-thirds) be given to the green picture and the remainder non-critically divided between the red and blue pictures. In explaining this result, Baldwin surmised that apart from the influence of the different primary luminances, a significant factor was the chromatic aberration of the eye's optical system.

Chromatic aberration in the eye results in the violet components of light being focused in front of the retina and the red components behind the retina, with the yellow components being focused at the retina (Davson, 1972). This, however, applies only to light whose power is distributed over the whole visible spectrum; with monochromatic light the eye's accommodation can act to bring the image into focus on the retina. The situation where the eye is receiving light of several wavelengths is the one relevant to coloured displays. With the change in focal length being about 2 dioptres over the range of the visible spectrum, it is possible to reduce the spatial bandwidth of the red and blue images in a colour display to some considerable extent without affecting overall quality, on the assumption that large areas of one colour in the display occur infrequently.

Baldwin's results suggest that, in scanning the three images, the spatial sampling densities in the red and blue images can be lower than in the green image. In broadcast colour television systems this is not done, each image being scanned with the same number of lines and at the same number of frames per second. However, in the subsequent coding of the signal for transmission, the eye's acuity limitations are exploited.

7.2 Analogue Transmission

Transmission by luminance and chrominance signals

Since colour information can be represented in terms of any three independent primaries, it is possible, for transmission purposes, to transform the tristimulus representation in terms of **R, G** and **B** receiver primaries to new primaries. The hope in doing this is that the transformed signals will not only require less transmission bandwidth than R, G and B signals but that they will also be less sensitive to channel noise.

In the NTSC system of broadcast colour television (Fink, 1955) and in variants such as PAL (Bruch, 1966; Townsend, 1970), the R, G and B signals are transformed into a *luminance* signal Y_t and two *chrominance* or *colour-difference* signals C_1 and C_2 (Figure 7.7). The word *chrominance* is an engineering term referring to the chromaticity difference between a colour and the system reference white, i.e. to dominant wavelength and excitation purity with respect to this white. *Colour-difference* refers to the way the chrominance signals are generated in the transformation.

While it is not yet established that this form of transformation is optimum in all circumstances, it is probably fairly near optimum and has been very successful in its particular field of application. The philosophy of the transformation is one of choosing new axes in three-dimensional colour space (as in Figure 6.2) such that one, the luminance axis, corresponds to luminance changes at constant chromaticity and the other two, the chrominance axes, correspond to chromaticity changes at constant luminance.

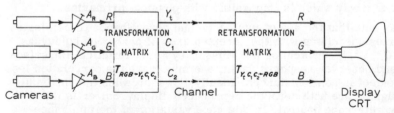

Cameras   Channel   Display CRT

Figure 7.7 Principle of transmission of colour information by transformation of the R, G and B signals to luminance (Y_t) and chrominance signals (C_1 and C_2) with retransformation at the receiver.

Because variation of the chrominance signals does not affect the luminance of the display, the transmission of the colour information is said to obey the *constant-luminance principle* (Bailey, 1954).

The transformation of the R, G, B tristimulus values to Y_t, C_1, C_2 tristimulus values can be viewed as a transformation of the representation of colour at a particular point in the display from **R, G** and **B** phosphor primaries to new primaries Y_t, C_1 and C_2, whose chromaticities we shall compute presently. These new primaries, known as *transmission primaries* (Howells, 1954), are the means whereby the luminance and chromaticity of the display colour are represented and controlled during transmission. Because of the interposition of the receiver matrix $T_{Y_tC_1C_2 \to RGB}$ (Figure 7.7) with appropriately chosen matrix elements, any variation in Y_t acts to stimulate the red, green and blue phosphors in such proportions as to constitute a completely new primary. The chromaticity of this primary lies, as we shall see, at the system reference white point and for this reason could be called a *white* rather than a luminance transmission primary. Since, however, the magnitude of the luminance primary Y_t is always equal to the actual luminance Y, it has come to be known by its present name. We have here used the subscript t to indicate the transmission primary as distinct from the CIE non-physical primary **Y**, whose chromaticity is $u = 0, v = 1$.

By calculating the chromaticities of the two chrominance primaries C_1 and C_2 we shall find that, for a constant-luminance system, they are non-physical primaries lying on the $v = 0$ axis in the 1960 CIE-UCS diagram. Alteration of their magnitude does not therefore affect luminance in the display but does affect chromaticity. Thus the receiver retransformation matrix $T_{Y_tC_1C_2 \to RGB}$ has the effect of producing primaries lying outside the RGB triangle of reproducible colours on the 1960 CIE-UCS diagram and indeed outside the area of physically reproducible colours. This does not mean, of course, that colours outside the RGB triangle can be produced by this means (this would require negative light output from at least one of the phosphors), but rather that the chrominance primaries control the display colour in a way which is impossible with physical primaries.

We may note that the use of luminance and chrominance transmission primaries correlates with the accepted axes of *perceived* colour, as in the U^*, V^*, W^* system or the Munsell system. Practical imperfections and observer response variations may make the correlation less than perfect in some instances. Ideally, however, when the chrominance signals are both zero, the reproduced display colour is the system reference neutral. In this case variation of the luminance signal Y_t causes a variation along the W^* axis of perceived colour space. If the luminance signal is held constant and the chrominance signals C_1 and C_2 are varied, the hue and saturation of the colour change in the U^*, V^* plane. Thus consideration of the effects of band-limitation and noise on luminance and chrominance signals amounts to consideration of the relative sensitivity of the eye to brightness and chromaticness hue and saturation changes.

A detailed argument in favour of luminance and chrominance representation for transmission purposes is a complex one. Since we do not possess a comprehensive set of visual data in the six-dimensional space of brightness, hue, saturation, horizontal and vertical space, and time, it is difficult to justify its optimality. Indeed research may eventually show more promising transformations. It is interesting to note, however, that a fairly widely accepted theory of colour vision, the *opponent-colour* theory (Hurvich and Jameson, 1957; summary in Judd and Wyszecki, 1963) holds that retinal responses from the red, green and blue cones are coded into white—black, yellow—blue and red—green responses for neural transmission. It is not entirely unexpected therefore that a system transmitting information to the eye should be found to be optimised by a similar form of coding.

Transmission primaries

The conversion of R, G and B signals to Y_t, C_1 and C_2 signals is accomplished by a standard transformation of the form

$$\begin{bmatrix} Y_t \\ C_1 \\ C_2 \end{bmatrix} = \begin{bmatrix} a_1 & a_2 & a_3 \\ a_4 & a_5 & a_6 \\ a_7 & a_8 & a_9 \end{bmatrix} \begin{bmatrix} R \\ G \\ B \end{bmatrix}$$

For Y_t to be equal to the luminance, we have from Table 7.1, for the CIE **Y** (or **V**) primary, that $Y = 0.222R + 0.707G + 0.071B$ in PAL System I or $Y = 0.299R + 0.587G + 0.114B$ in the NTSC system. These then are the required element values for a_1, a_2 and a_3 in the two systems.

In broadcast television practice the R, G and B signals are gamma-corrected before matrixing to compensate for the gamma of the red, green and blue guns in the display CRT. This considerably complicates the colorimetry of the system, invalidating the assumed linear transformation and making the transmission primaries dependent on the transmitted colour (Hacking, 1966). The constant-luminance principle then operates only as an approximation for colours of low excitation purity. The argument for gamma-correction at the transmitter rather than just prior to the display is one involving the cost of producing stable, close-tracking correction in the three channels, a feat which presently requires care and temperature control (Heightman, 1972). In broadcast television it is economically more justifiable to include one such corrector at the camera output rather than in millions of receivers. In other systems where there is only one display per camera this may not be necessary, although the effect of the gamma correction on noise visibility is one which, depending on the levels of noise, may be influential. Thus present broadcast television practice can be regarded as only an approximation to the ideal, linear case which we here consider. Further, in the case of PAL System I, the present radiated luminance signal is, for historical reasons, the NTSC luminance signal $Y_t = 0.299R + 0.587G + 0.114B$ rather than the true luminance signal (CCIR Conclusions, 1970). In the following, however, we shall assume an idealised PAL signal.

In both the NTSC and PAL systems, the chrominance or colour-difference signals are formed by first subtracting the luminance signal Y_t from the blue and red camera signals to give $B - Y_t$ and $R - Y_t$ signals. As the Y_t signal is itself a combination of R, G and B signals, this operation merely produces a given linear combination of R, G and B signals in each case. In order to moderate the chrominance signal excursions, it is conventional to reduce the chrominance signal amplitudes by division by constant factors of 2.03 and 1.14 (Carnt and Townsend, 1961), giving $U_t = (B - Y_t)/2.03$ and $V_t = (R - Y_t)/1.14$. The two signals U_t and V_t (which are more usually termed simply U and V but which we have subscripted to distinguish them from the CIE-UCS primaries $\mathbf{U}$ and $\mathbf{V}$) are those which are used as chromin-ance signals in PAL System I (CCIR Conclusions, 1970). In the NTSC system, however, the chrominance signals I and Q are formed as com-binations of U_t and V_t; the effect of this is, as we shall see, to alter the direction of the chrominance axes in colour space.

The equations for the formation of the luminance and chrominance signals in ideal, linear cases of the two systems are

PAL System I (true luminance)

$$Y_t = 0.222R + 0.707G + 0.071B$$

$$C_1 = U_t = \frac{B - Y_t}{2.03} = 0.493\,(B - Y_t)$$

$$C_2 = V_t = \frac{R - Y_t}{1.14} = 0.877\,(R - Y_t)$$

NTSC

$$Y_t = 0.299R + 0.587G + 0.114B$$
$$C_1 = I = 0.736\,(R - Y_t) - 0.268\,(B - Y_t)$$
$$C_2 = Q = 0.478\,(R - Y_t) + 0.413\,(B - Y_t)$$

In the NTSC system the proportions of the $R - Y_t$ and $B - Y_t$ signals used in the formation of the I and Q signals are obtained as

$$I = \frac{R - Y_t}{1.14}\cos 33° - \frac{B - Y_t}{2.03}\sin 33° = 0.736\,(R - Y_t)$$
$$- 0.268\,(B - Y_t)$$

$$Q = \frac{R - Y_t}{1.14} \sin 33° + \frac{B - Y_t}{2.03} \cos 33° = 0.478 (R - Y_t$$

$$+ 0.413 (B - Y_t)$$

The I and Q chrominance axes correspond therefore to a 33° rotation from orthogonal $R - Y_t$ and $B - Y_t$ axes. The factors of 1.14 and 2.03 were chosen to limit the transmitted signal amplitude (Figure 7.14) to an arbitrary 1.33 times the monochrome case under conditions of signal restriction R ⩽ 1, G ⩽ 1, B ⩽ 1.

By substituting for Y_t in the chrominance signal equations and expressing the results in matrix form, we obtain the equations

PAL System I *(true luminance)*

$$\begin{bmatrix} Y_t \\ U_t \\ V_t \end{bmatrix} = \begin{bmatrix} 0.222 & 0.707 & 0.071 \\ -0.109 & -0.348 & 0.458 \\ 0.682 & -0.620 & -0.062 \end{bmatrix} \begin{bmatrix} R \\ G \\ B \end{bmatrix}$$

NTSC

$$\begin{bmatrix} Y_t \\ I \\ Q \end{bmatrix} = \begin{bmatrix} 0.299 & 0.587 & 0.114 \\ 0.596 & -0.275 & -0.321 \\ 0.212 & -0.523 & 0.311 \end{bmatrix} \begin{bmatrix} R \\ G \\ B \end{bmatrix}$$

At the receiver the R, G, B signals are reformed by the inverse matrix relationships

PAL System I *(true luminance)*

$$\begin{bmatrix} R \\ G \\ B \end{bmatrix} = \begin{bmatrix} 1 & 0 & 1.14 \\ 1 & -0.202 & -0.357 \\ 1 & 2.03 & 0 \end{bmatrix} \begin{bmatrix} Y_t \\ U_t \\ V_t \end{bmatrix}$$

NTSC

$$\begin{bmatrix} R \\ G \\ B \end{bmatrix} = \begin{bmatrix} 1 & 0.956 & 0.620 \\ 1 & -0.272 & -0.647 \\ 1 & -1.108 & 1.705 \end{bmatrix} \begin{bmatrix} Y_t \\ I \\ Q \end{bmatrix}$$

Where the matrix coefficients are found by inverting the matrices for the $RGB{\rightarrow}Y_t U_t V_t$ and $RGB{\rightarrow}Y_t I Q$ transformations.

To find the 1960 CIE-UCS chromaticities of the transmission primaries $\mathbf{Y_t, U_t, V_t}$ and $\mathbf{Y, I, Q}$ we transform the R, G, B tristimulus values to U, V, W tristimulus values using the relationships in Table 7.1. Thus for PAL System I we have

$$
\begin{bmatrix} U \\ V \\ W \end{bmatrix} = \begin{bmatrix} \mathbf{T}_{RGB \to UVW} \end{bmatrix} \begin{bmatrix} \mathbf{T}_{Y_t U_t V_t \to RGB} \end{bmatrix} \begin{bmatrix} Y_t \\ U_t \\ V_t \end{bmatrix}
$$

$$
= \begin{bmatrix} 0.287 & 0.228 & 0.119 \\ 0.222 & 0.707 & 0.071 \\ 0.128 & 0.954 & 0.487 \end{bmatrix} \begin{bmatrix} 1 & 0 & 1.140 \\ 1 & -0.202 & -0.357 \\ 1 & 2.03 & 0 \end{bmatrix} \begin{bmatrix} Y_t \\ U_t \\ V_t \end{bmatrix}
$$

$$
= \begin{bmatrix} 0.634 & 0.196 & 0.246 \\ 1 & 0 & 0 \\ 1.569 & 0.796 & -0.195 \end{bmatrix} \begin{bmatrix} Y_t \\ U_t \\ V_t \end{bmatrix}
$$

and for the NTSC system, similarly

$$
\begin{bmatrix} U \\ V \\ W \end{bmatrix} = \begin{bmatrix} 0.655 & 0.207 & 0.405 \\ 1 & 0 & 0 \\ 1.600 & -0.783 & 0.628 \end{bmatrix} \begin{bmatrix} Y_t \\ I \\ Q \end{bmatrix}
$$

The U, V, W tristimulus values can now be evaluated for the luminance and chrominance primaries in turn; for example, the I primary in the NTSC system is obtained by letting $Y_t = 0, I = 1$ and $Q = 0$, giving $U = 0.207, V = 0, W = -0.783$ and $u = U/(U + V + W) = -0.359$, $v = V/(U + V + W) = 0$. Evaluating all the primary chromaticity coordinates in this way, we obtain

PAL Systen I (true luminance)   NTSC

	u	v		u	v
Y_t	0.198	0.312	Y_t	0.201	0.307
U_t	0.198	0	I	−0.359	0
V_t	4.81	0	Q	0.392	0

These primaries are plotted in Figure 7.8. It may be seen that if, in either system, both chrominance signals are zero, the reproduced colour is a white or grey with chromaticity equal to the system reference white. The location of the chrominance primaries is, in both systems, on the zero-luminance or $v = 0$ axis. This result follows from the choice of a true luminance signal used for Y_t. If, for example, the calculation is carried through with $Y_t = 0.299R + 0.587G + 0.114B$ in the PAL case, all other parameters being the

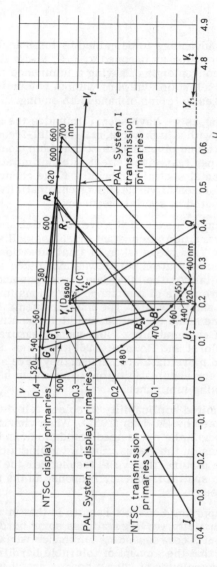

Figure 7.8 Location of the luminance and chrominance transmission primaries for a linear NTSC system ($\mathbf{Y}_{t_2}$, $\mathbf{I}$ and $\mathbf{Q}$) and idealised, linear PAL System I ($\mathbf{Y}'_{t_1}$, $\mathbf{U}_t$, $\mathbf{V}_t$) on the 1960 CIE–UCS diagram, together with their respective display primaries $\mathbf{R}_2$, $\mathbf{G}_2$, $\mathbf{B}_2$ (NTSC) and $\mathbf{R}_1$, $\mathbf{G}_1$, $\mathbf{B}_1$ (PAL System I). The colour gamut is limited by the display primaries only, since the chrominance primaries can be present in negative amounts.

same, U_t and V_t will be found to lie well away from the $v = 0$ axis. In this case the system will not be a constant-luminance system and fluctuations in the values of U_t and V_t will cause fluctuations in luminance as well as chromaticity.

Bandwidth limitation

We may now consider the advantage to be gained by luminance and chrominance signal transmission as opposed to R, G, B signal transmission. Apart from the convenience of having a luminance signal immediately available for television viewers without colour receivers, there are certain advantages in terms of bandwidth saving.

Video bandwidth restriction, as we have seen, eliminates the spatial frequencies in the picture with a high horizontal-spatial-frequency component. With red, green and blue images scanned horizontally at the same number of lines per frame, the effect of bandlimitation is noticed as a loss of horizontal spatial bandwidth. If the chrominance signals are bandlimited, horizontal variations of chromaticity at constant luminance are restricted in spatial frequency.

Schade (1958) measured the response of the eye to spatial sine wave patterns of chromaticity variation at constant brightness. His results, reproduced here in Figure 7.9a, were taken in axial directions from the reference white; i.e. the excitation purity was modulated sinusoidally. The results are similar for the three hue directions and similar in turn to Schade's measurements of luminance variations for the red, green and blue primaries and for white. The measurements indicate that the eye has roughly the same spatial bandwidth for contrast modulation of brightness and of chromaticity. Subsequent measurements, such as those of van der Horst and Bouman (1969), have not agreed with Schade's in detail and more data are needed; they have also shown that the spatial bandwidth for chromaticity-only variations increases fairly rapidly with increasing luminance.

Schade's results are of limited applicability in colour television systems for the reason noted by Baldwin (1951). When viewing light of predominantly one wavelength, the eye's accommodation can bring spatial variations into focus on the retina. But in viewing a complex scene such as a television picture, the eye is focused for the yellow-green wavelengths and the spatial frequency response in the reds and blues is materially affected.

Another complication in applying Schade's results is that in a colour television picture a chromaticity variation across some border is seldom encountered without a corresponding luminance variation. Hacking (1957) has shown that the amount of tolerable bandlimitation depends on whether the two colours at such a border are of unequal luminance. If they are unequal by a ratio of more than about 3 : 1, the luminance transition should be sharp, i.e. high bandwidth, and the chrominance signals, which affect the rate of change of chromaticity

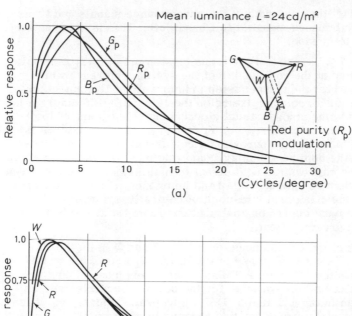

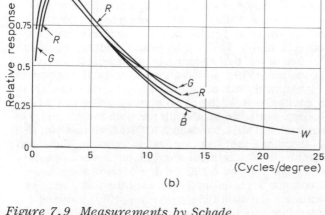

*Figure 7.9 Measurements by Schade
(1958) of the spatial frequency response
of the eye (a) to chromaticity variations
at constant brightness and (b) to luminance
variations at constant chromaticity. W =
white and R, G, B are the three colour
CRT phosphor primaries used by Schade.*

across the border, may be blurred, i.e. low bandwidth. With low-contrast borders where the luminance change is less than 3 : 1, it is better to blur the luminance signal and make the chromaticity transition sharp. If a picture contains many more high-contrast borders than low-contrast borders, as is often the case, then, at the cost of some blurring at the relatively few low-contrast borders, it is pos-

sible to restrict the bandwidth of the chrominance signals and transmit only the luminance signal at full bandwidth. This is the practice
in broadcast television.

From Figure 7. 8 we see that the transmission primary Y_t is a white
primary located at the coordinates of the system reference white.
Since we may treat the transmission primaries just like any other
primaries as far as colour mixture on the 1960 CIE-UCS diagram is
concerned, and since most naturally occurring colours are of low
excitation purity, the proportion of Y_t primary in most mixtures is
near unity. Placed at the approximate colour-balance point of most
scenes, Y_t is the dominant primary, carrying most of the information.
This is not the case with R, G, B signal transmission, where the green
primary G, carries only 60-70% of the luminance information, is not
located near the statistical mid-point of naturally occurring colours
and therefore must depend on contributions from the R and B primaries to a much greater extent.

The locations of the chrominance primaries I and Q in the NTSC
system are different from those of the U_t and V_t primaries in PAL
System I. With the 525-line, 4. 2 MHz American standard there is less
transmission bandwidth available for the colour subcarrier and its
sidebands than in the 625-line 5. 5 MHz European standard, and it is
desirable to restrict one of the two chrominance signals to a fairly
small bandwidth (Townsend, 1970). In the NTSC system, the specification calls for an I signal bandwidth of nominally 1. 3 MHz and a Q
signal bandwidth of nominally 0. 4 MHz (2 dB points), while in PAL
System I there is enough available bandwidth for both the U_t and V_t
signals to have a nominal 1. 3 MHz bandwidth (CCIR Conclusions, 1970).
In the NTSC system therefore there is interest in choosing the I and
Q axes so that the picture has maximum sharpness. Several experimental studies have shown that the NTSC choice of an orange—cyan
direction for the I axis and a green—magenta axis for the Q axis is
optimum or near-optimum (Brown, 1954; de Vrijer, 1957; Hacking
1957). It may be noted that this choice is influenced by the statistical
distribution of colours in a scene; if the majority of colour transitions
lie along the orange—cyan axis, it is better, from a purely statistical
argument, to place the higher-bandwidth chrominance axis in this
direction. We may note that flesh tones, whose proper rendition in
colour television is important, lie roughly along the I axis (Figure 7. 1).

Effects of noise

If the chrominance signals are perturbed by noise there is, in a constant-luminance system, a perturbation of the reproduced chromaticity
but not the luminance. Perturbation of the amount of the white
luminance primary Y_t in general causes a perturbation of both luminance and chromaticity; however, in the special case of neutral or low
excitation-purity colours, the chromaticity variation is zero or small
in comparison with the luminance variation.

How sensitive is the eye to luminance variations compared with chromaticity variations? The visual situation as it affects system design is a complex one, since, for example, chromaticity noise may be masked by a relatively noiseless luminance variation, and the relative visibility of each is affected by brightness level in the picture. We do not possess a comprehensive set of visual data relating to this problem, although specific solutions have been obtained (Bailey 1954; Hacking, 1966). For 625-line, 5.5 MHz broadcast-standard pictures, Allnatt and Prosser (1966) found that for equal subjective effect the signal/weighted-noise ratio for noise in the chrominance channel alone was about 6 dB lower than for noise in the luminance channel alone.

Some insight into the relative visibility of luminance and chrominance errors can be obtained from the U^*, V^*, W^* uniform colour system. If the luminance, but not the chromaticity, of a colour changes in this space by 1 CIE unit, the change in brightness $\Delta W^* = 1$. If the chromaticity changes in the direction of the u axis on the 1960 CIE-UCS diagram by one unit, we have $\Delta U^* = 1$. Using the formula for U^*, we obtain

$$\Delta U^* = 1 = U^*_1 - U^*_2 = [13W^*(u_1 - u_0)] - [13W^*(u_2 - u_0)]$$

$$= 13W^*(u_1 - u_2)$$

$$= 13W^* \, \Delta u$$

or $$\Delta u = \frac{1}{13W^*}$$

There are roughly 100 CIE units of brightness in a black-to-white transition in a picture. From Figure 7.8 we see that the total chromaticity range in the u direction possible with colour television phosphors is roughly 0.4. There are consequently about $0.4 \times 13W^*$ CIE units of chromaticity difference in this range. Calculating this quantity for various levels of brightness W^* and plotting the ratio

$$\frac{\text{number of CIE } U^* \text{ units}}{\text{number of CIE } W^* \text{ units}} = \frac{0.4 \times 13W^*}{100}$$

we have the result in Figure 7.10

It can be seen that at high brightness in the picture there are many more steps of detectable chromaticity over the system's reproduction range than there are detectable steps in its brightness range. A point of equality is reached at $W^* \simeq 20$.

Hacking (1966) studied the relative visibility of spatial sine-wave variations of luminance and chromaticity, at 2.2 and 6.7 cycles/degree. Measuring brightness changes as the Weber fraction $\Delta V / V$,

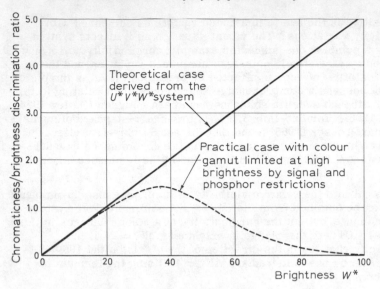

Theoretical case
derived from the
*U*V*W**system

Practical case with colour
gamut limited at high
brightness by signal and
phosphor restrictions

*Figure 7. 10   Ratio of the number of CIE
chromaticity units to the number of CIE
brightness units in a typical colour
television system, as a function of brightness W*.*

where V is luminance, and chromaticity changes in terms of linear
distances on the 1960 CIE-UCS diagram, he found that chromaticity/
brightness sensitivity varied between about 2, and 8, with the higher
ratios (towards 8) being obtained at higher luminances, lower spatial
frequency and increased levels of visibility of the variations. Approximate conversion of these results to the terms in which Figure 7. 10
are expressed again indicate that, at medium and higher brightness,
there are more chromaticity steps in the range of a colour television
system than brightness steps of equivalent visual significance.

These arguments would appear to indicate that chrominance noise in
the system is more visible than luminance noise, because a given
percentage perturbation of the amplitude of a chrominance signal
would tend to be noticed more readily than the same percentage
perturbation of the luminance signal. However, the chromaticity
range of a display CRT is limited at the higher luminances, since one
or two phosphors only are stimulated to produce colours of maximum
excitation purity and this limits the luminance output. Figure 7. 11
illustrates this restriction, as calculated by Schade (1958). The
chrominance signal amplitudes may consequently be scaled to produce
a more restricted range of chromaticity at high brightness than that
assumed in the derivation of Figure 7. 10. Other signal considerations
(Figure 7. 14) further limit this range.

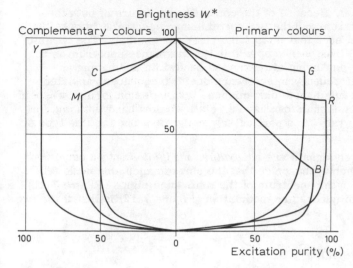

Figure 7.11 Chromaticity reproduction range of a colour CRT as a function of brightness W*, for the red (R), green (G) and blue (B) phosphor colours and complementary two-primary mixture colours cyan (C), magenta (M) and yellow (Y) (after Schade, 1958).

We see therefore that the eye is not inherently less sensitive to chromaticity noise than it is to luminance noise. What determines the relative noise sensitivity of the luminance and chrominance signals is the permitted *range* over which they operate. In broadcast television a lower signal-to-noise ratio can be tolerated in the chrominance channel because at high brightness a given fractional change in the amplitude of the chrominance signal is not permitted to produce a very large change in displayed chromaticity. In a system capable of reproducing a wide range of chromaticities at high brightness this might not be so. In practice there are complicating factors such as the masking of chrominance noise by relatively noiseless luminance transitions, the effect of display gamma, the unequal bandwidths of luminance and chrominance noise signals and the temporal variations of the noise, which tend to make system decisions based on fundamental arguments difficult and recourse to laboratory testing advisable.

Analogue transmission of chrominance information by subcarrier quadrature modulation

In broadcast colour television the two chrominance signals are modulated onto a subcarrier placed within the baseband spectrum of the luminance signal. Because of the comb-like structure of both the luminance spectrum and the two chrominance spectra, it is possible to interleave them such that mutual interference is small. The chrominance 'channel' thus opened up within the luminance spectrum is a relatively poor one, being of restricted bandwidth and having an amount of low-frequency interference due to frequency-translated crosstalk. The luminance—chrominance transmission format, wherein the chrominance signals can have a relatively low bandwidth and low signal-to-noise ratio, is a particularly convenient one for this type of transmission.

The chrominance signals are *quadrature modulated* onto a carrier of frequency f_{sc} hertz, chosen so that the chrominance sidebands fall between peaks in the spectrum of the luminance signal (Figure 7.12). The principle of quadrature modulation (Figure 7.13) is that if the two

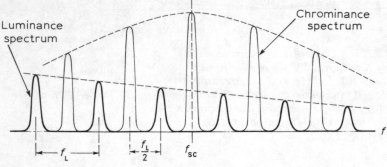

Figure 7.12 Principle of interleaving chrominance and luminance spectra.

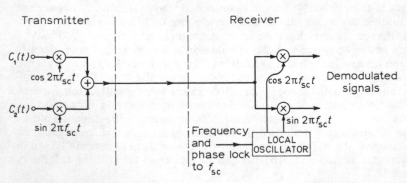

Figure 7.13 Principle of chrominance signal transmission by quadrature modulation and synchronous detection. Not shown is the addition of the luminance signal to the modulated subcarrier signal.

chrominance signals are $c_1(t)$ and $c_2(t)$, the modulated subcarrier $s(t)$ is formed as

$$s(t) = c_1(t) \cos 2\pi f_{sc}t + c_2(t) \sin 2\pi f_{sc}t$$

This equation indicates that $c_1(t)$ is modulated onto a cosine carrier and $c_2(t)$ onto a quadrature sine carrier such that when either signal is of zero amplitude the amplitude of its respective carrier is reduced to zero. When both $c_1(t)$ and $c_2(t)$ are zero, both carrier amplitudes are zero; this happens when the transmitted colour is the reference white of the system

The spectrum $S(f)$ may be found from Table 1.1 using the fact that

$$\cos 2\pi f_{sc}t = \frac{1}{2} \left(\exp[j2\pi f_{sc}t] + \exp[-j2\pi f_{sc}t] \right) \text{ and}$$

$$\sin 2\pi f_{sc}t = \frac{1}{2j} \left(\exp[j2\pi f_{sc}t] - \exp[-j2\pi f_{sc}t] \right)$$

whence

$$S(f) = \frac{1}{2}[C_1(f - f_{sc}) - jC_2(f - f_{sc})]$$
$$+ \frac{1}{2}[C_1(f + f_{sc}) + jC_2(f + f_{sc})]$$

Thus the baseband chrominance spectra $C_1(f)$ and $C_2(f)$ are both frequency-translated to a centre frequency f_{sc} by this process, with the spectral components of $C_2(f)$ being rotated by 90° in the process. Demodulation is accomplished by synchronous detection, i.e. by separate multiplication at the receiver by $\sin 2\pi f_{sc}t$ and $\cos 2\pi f_{sc}t$ to give two recovered signals

$$s(t) \cos 2\pi f_{sc}t = c_1(t) \cos^2 2\pi f_{sc}t$$

$$+ c_2(t) \sin 2\pi f_{sc}t . \cos 2\pi f_{sc}t$$

$$= \frac{1}{2}c_1(t) + \frac{1}{2} c_1(t) \cos 4\pi f_{sc}t$$

$$= \frac{1}{2} c_2(t) \sin 4\pi f_{sc}t$$

and

$$s(t) \sin 2\pi f_{sc}t = c_1(t) \cos 2\pi f_{sc}t . \sin 2\pi f_{sc}t$$

$$+ c_2(t) \sin^2 2\pi f_{sc}t$$

$$= \tfrac{1}{2}c_2(t) + \tfrac{1}{2}c_1(t) \sin 4\pi f_{sc}t$$

$$- \tfrac{1}{2}c_2(t) \cos 4\pi f_{sc}t$$

The high-frequency demodulated products at twice carrier frequency can be filtered out to give $c_1(t)$ and $c_2(t)$.

Figure 7.13 is an idealised representation of quadrature modulation which is complicated in practice by several factors. Not shown in the figure is the addition of the luminance signal before transmission; this introduces spurious energy into the spectra of the demodulated chrominance signals. Since, however, this energy tends to fall in the minimum-visibility gaps between the chrominance spectral components (Chapter 4), the visual effect is not generally serious. Comb filters can be used to suppress undesirable levels of such luminance-chrominance crosstalk (Carnt and Townsend, 1969). Another modification used in practice is that the quadrature-modulated sub-carrier signal is filtered to produce a VSB (vestigial sideband) signal before addition to the luminance signal, so as to allow a greater base-band chrominance bandwidth. The asymmetry of both chrominance and luminance channels produces crosstalk between the two chrominance signals. One feature of PAL as opposed to NTSC is that it reduces the visibility of this kind of distortion (Townsend, 1970).

Adding the modulated subcarrier to the luminance signal increases the amplitude of the transmitted signal (Figure 7.14). The additional amplitude is a function of the excitation purity of the transmitted colours, since the modulated subcarrier can alternatively be written as

$$s(t) = [c_1{}^2(t) + c_2{}^2(t)]^{1/2} . \ \cos(2\pi f_{sc} t - \phi)$$

where

$$\phi = \arctan\left[\frac{c_2(t)}{c_1(t)}\right]$$

The subcarrier is modulated in both amplitude and phase, the amplitude increasing with excitation purity and the phase changing with dominant wavelength.

The situation is worst for both high-luminance and low-luminance colours of high excitation purity; the positive swing of the subcarrier increases the peak positive amplitude of the transmitted signal and the negative swing reduces the lower amplitude limit. Consequently some increase in transmitted power, or some decrease in signal-to-noise ratio for the luminance signal, has to be accepted. In broadcast television with a peak-power channel limitation, a restriction has to be placed on the excitation purity at high luminance (Townsend, 1970), which helps to reduce the visibility of chrominance-channel noise.

Spectrum of the PAL signal

The special feature of PAL as compared with NTSC is that the chrominance signal $v_t(t)$, controlling the red-green direction of

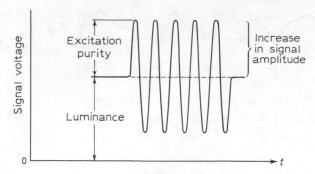

*Figure 7.14 Increase in signal amplitude
due to the addition of colour information to
the luminance signal in the form of a modulated subcarrier.*

chromaticity variation, is inverted on alternate lines. This is a small
yet very significant alteration in the format first proposed by the
NTSC. The form of transmission illustrated in Figure 7.14 means
that the decoded colour is affected by phase distortions in the transmission channel, which may be a function of signal amplitude. By re-
inverting $v_t(t)$ at the receiver and averaging over two lines, the effects
of phase errors are reduced. The loss in the vertical spatial bandwidth of the chrominance information caused by this averaging is not
greatly missed as the vertical bandwidth is excessive in relation to
the horizontal bandwidth.

The transmitted subcarrier in PAL is sometimes written (CCIR Conclusions, 1970) as

$$s(t) = u_t(t) \cos 2\pi f_{sc}t \pm v_t(t) \sin 2\pi f_{sc}t$$

where f_{sc} is the subcarrier frequency. The chrominance signals are
here written using lower case letters, to distinguish them from their
spectra, in upper case letters, which we calculate later. To calculate
the spectrum of $s(t)$ we need, however, to give mathematical form to
the notion of inverting the amplitude of $v_t(t)$ (or, equivalently, of
$\sin 2\pi f_{sc}t$) every line.

Let $q(t)$ be a square wave whose amplitude excursions are ±1 and
whose period is twice line period or $2T_L$ (Figure 7.15). Then the
modulated subcarrier is

$$s(t) = u_t(t) \cos 2\pi f_{sc}t - q(t) . v_t(t) \sin 2\pi f_{sc}t$$

and its spectrum, using the fact that multiplication in the time domain

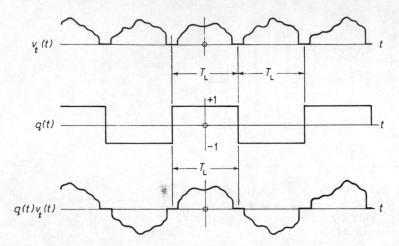

Figure 7.15 Inversion of the amplitude of the $v_t(t)$ chrominance signal every line period T_L in PAL, represented by multiplication by a switching function $q(t)$.

becomes convolution in the frequency domain, is, from Table 1.1,

$$S(f) = \frac{1}{2} \left[U_t(f - f_{sc}) + U_t(f + f_{sc}) \right]$$

$$- Q(f) * \frac{j}{2} \left[V_t(f + f_{sc}) - V_t(f - f_{sc}) \right]$$

where $U_t(f)$ and $V_t(f)$ are the respective spectra of the chrominance signals $u_t(t)$ and $v_t(t)$.

We can calculate the spectrum of the switching function $q(t)$ by writing it as

$$q(t) = 2 \operatorname{rep}_{2T_L} (\operatorname{rect} t/T_L) - 1$$

whence its spectrum is, from Table 1.1

$$Q(f) = \frac{2}{2T_L} \operatorname{comb}_{1/2T_L} (T_L \operatorname{sinc} fT_L) - \delta(f)$$

$$= \operatorname{comb}_{1/2T_L} (\operatorname{sinc} fT_L) - \delta(f)$$

Thus $Q(f)$ has its power concentrated at odd harmonics of half line frequency $f_L/2 = 1/2T_L$.

The spectrum $S(f)$ is seen to consist of the baseband spectrum $U_t(f)$, frequency-shifted to $f = f_{sc}$, plus a more complex spectrum comprising $Q(f)$ convolved with the frequency-shifted version of $V_t(f)$. The effect of the convolution on $V_t(f + f_{SC})$ and $V_t(f - f_{SC})$ is easy to see in outline, though more difficult to draw in detail. The convolution produces spectral smoothing with a sinc function weighting together with a frequency shift of $f_L/2$ in the frequency components of $V_t(f + f_{SC})$ and $V_t(f - f_{SC})$. Since both $U_t(f)$ and $V_t(f)$ are of conventional video spectral structure (Chapter 3) with power concentrated around harmonics of the line frequency f_L, it follows that the U_t and V_t sidebands are spectrally interleaved (Figure 7.16b). In PAL, therefore, sideband peaks are at harmonics of $f_L/2$ and the subcarrier cannot be spaced midway between line harmonics as in the NTSC case, since this would cause spectral coincidence of lumi-

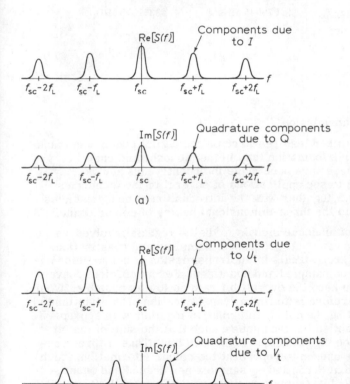

Figure 7.16 Spectral structure around the subcarrier frequency of (a) the NTSC I and Q sidebands (b) the PAL U_t and V_t sidebands, showing interleaving.

nance and chrominance components and maximally visible interference. Instead, the subcarrier is given an offset of $f_L/4$, plus, to minimize its temporal visibility, a further offset equal to the frame frequency f_F. Some parameters of the 525-line NTSC format and the 625-line PAL System I format are summarized in Table 7.2.

Table 7.2 Subcarrier modulation parameters in the PAL System I and NTSC colour television systems

	NTSC	PAL System I
Nominal video bandwidth	4.2 MHz	5.5 MHz
Line frequency f_L	15.734264 kHz	15.625 kHz
Subcarrier frequency f_{sc}	3.579545 MHz	4.43361875 MHz
Relation of subcarrier frequency to line frequency	$f_{sc} = (227 + \frac{1}{2})f_L$	$f_{sc} = (284 - \frac{1}{4})f_L + 25$ Hz

7.3   Digital Transmission

There has been rather less research on the digital coding and transmission of colour information than in the monochrome case, but significant advances have been made in recent years and we may expect the future to see applications of several of the techniques noted in Chapter 5, together with the introduction of new principles specially suited to the three-dimensional nature of colour space.

The conversion of analogue signals to digital signals involves, as we have seen, two fundamental processes: sampling and quantisation. Since there are three signals in the transmission of colour information, each has to be sampled and quantised. For an efficient conversion the aim is to keep the overall bit rate as low as possible. What is of interest therefore is to find a transformation of the tristimulus values representing the colour information together with appropriate sampling and quantisation techniques, such that the sum of the bit rates for the three digital colour signals is low. Thus if three analogue signals are chosen to represent the colour information, which are then sampled at S_1, S_2 and S_3 samples per second and quantised into N_1, N_2 and N_3 bits/sample respectively, the overall bit rate R is required to be as low as possible for a given standard of picture quality, where

$$R = S_1 N_1 + S_2 N_2 + S_3 N_3 \text{ bits/s}$$

Experimental evidence accumulated to date (e.g. Gronemann, 1964; Limb, Rubinstein and Walsh, 1971; Pratt, 1971; Frei, Jaeger and

Probst, 1972) indicates that the luminance-chrominance format is a good one for digital coding. The reason is probably related to the arguments previously considered for analogue transmission, namely that by locating a white or luminance transmission primary Y_t at the approximate centre of gravity of typically occurring colours on the 1960 CIE-UCS diagram, the resulting Y_t signal carries the bulk of the information in the picture. If Y_t is sampled and quantised along the lines described in Chapter 5 to produce a decoded picture of high quality, the chrominance signals may be sampled at a relatively low rate and quantised fairly coarsely, since they carry relatively little information and their defects tend to be masked by the luminance signal. Experimental observations indicate that the chrominance signals together need occupy only about 10-20% of the total digital channel capacity required for the transmission. For low-luminance pictures or for areas of low brightness within a high-luminance picture, fewer bits are in principle required to code the chrominance information, owing to the eye's rapidly increasing sensitivity to chromaticity differences with increasing luminance (Figure 7.10). Since the eye's spatio-temporal luminance bandwidth rises fairly quickly with increasing luminance as well, high-brightness colour displays may require considerably larger digital channel capacities than low-brightness displays.

Although quite a few techniques have been suggested and tried, including basic PCM, differential pulse code modulation (DPCM), which we saw previously was simple and effective for monochrome video signals, has perhaps been the most successful practical method to date of coding broadcast-quality television signals and videotelephone signals (Limb, Rubinstein and Walsh, 1971; Golding and Garlow, 1971). The principle is illustrated in Figure 7.17. The luminance signal

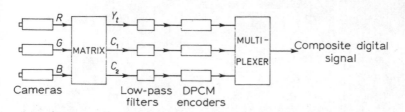

Figure 7.17 Principle of separate DPCM encoding of luminance (Y$_t$) and chrominance signals (C$_1$ and C$_2$).

Y_t is prefiltered to the normal monochrome bandwidth, then sampled at the Nyquist rate or a little less and quantised into 4-5 bits/sample using a standard DPCM encoder. The chrominance signals are each bandlimited to a fraction of the luminance bandwidth, this fraction being of the order 1/3-1/9 depending on the transformation matrix and application. Each chrominance signal is then sampled at an appropriate rate, this rate being about 1/3-1/9 of the luminance rate, and quantised into 2-4 bits/chrominance-sample. The three bit streams are time-multiplexed to produce a composite digital signal. Rates of about 35 Mbit/s for 5.5 MHz NTSC broadcast colour transmissions and about 8 Mbit/s for 1 MHz video-telephone signals have been achieved.

Since the chrominance signals specify the difference in chromaticity between the transmitted colour and the system neutral, and since naturally occurring colours are frequently near the system neutral, chrominance signals tend to be low-level signals with occasional peaks. This makes them well suited to separate DPCM coding. However, the analogue colour signals may not be available in separate form at the point of digital coding; rather than attempting to separate out a composite PAL or NTSC signal with inevitable signal distortion, a more complex form of DPCM may be applied directly to the composite signal (Thompson, 1973). Alternatively straight PCM may be used at 8-9 bits per sample, though this produces higher overall bit rates, of the order of 70-100 Mbit/s for broadcast television pictures.

Chapter 8

SUBJECTIVE ASSESSMENT OF PICTURE QUALITY

8.1 Relationship Between Picture Quality and Channel Capacity

In an ideal picture transmission system the viewer would receive pictures which appeared continuous in space and time, free of distortion and noise, and having as much detail and as many colours as he was capable of seeing.

In practice this ideal condition is never met nor seriously aimed at, not because it is impossible to achieve, but because it is prohibitively expensive. To make the system ideal would, with our present knowledge of electronic techniques, require a very large channel capacity and expensive equipment. Considerable cost savings can be realised if the scanning parameters, noise levels, colour rendition and encoding methods are made somewhat less than the ideal. However, in this case visible impairments are introduced into the picture, whose effect is to lower the overall quality.

The problem which confronts visual systems engineers is that of selecting a suitable point on the quality versus cost curve for any particular picture transmission system which they may be called upon to design. If too high a quality is selected, the system may turn out to economically unattractive; if the quality is too low it may fail to provide effective visual communication. As an aid to the solution of this problem a good deal of effort has been devoted to the study and measurement of picture quality. The purpose of this work, which continues at the present time, is to be able eventually to attach a number to a picture indicating its quality.

8.2 A Numerical Scale for Picture Quality

Communication engineers often use a block diagram such as that in Figure 8.1 to describe communication systems. The number of blocks and their labels vary somewhat according to preference, but they amount to much the same thing. Those in the figure are used quite frequently.

The *source* is in our case the source of pictures, i.e. the visual scene. The *source encoder* is the device which converts the light from the scene into electrical signals, i.e. the camera; its design involves consideration of the principles of scanning and colour reproduction. The *channel encoder* converts the source signal to a form suitable for transmission; it incorporates both modulation and encoding techniques.

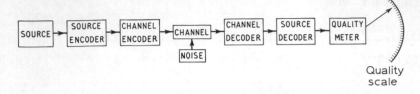

Figure 8.1 *A picture transmission system incorporating quality measurement.*

At the receiver the *channel decoder* performs operations which are inverse to those performed by the channel encoder, while the *source decoder* is the display device which converts the electrical signals to a visible picture.

Visual systems designers are usually confronted with a channel of limited capacity through which they have to send their pictures. They have to consider a number of variables: source encoding parameters such as picture size, number of lines per picture, number of picture elements per line, number of frames per second, interlacing, whether and how to include colour or stereo, together with channel encoding parameters such as analogue or digital transmission, amplitude or angle modulation, etc. Because the number of such parameters is large and experimentation with human subjects a fairly time-consuming process it would be convenient to have an instrument which could quickly assess picture quality (Figure 8.1). The instrument might have stored in its memory extensive information about the human eye and brain and how humans look at and judge pictures. Having ingested a particular series of pictures it would perform some computations and then produce a reading on a scale which indicated the quality of the transmission. The designers could then happily adjust the variables of the system at the transmitter until they had maximised the quality reading; alternatively, they could arrange for the channel capacity to be minimum for a certain tolerable quality level. The instrument could also be used to monitor transmissions on a continuous basis.

We are rather far from being able to construct effective instruments of this kind and in practice it is often simpler and more accurate to involve human subjects, despite their tendency to boredom and fatigue. Designers frequently make initial judgements about picture quality themselves; then, when they feel the system is nearly right, they arrange for a more formal 'subjective test' with a group of independent subjects. The subjective tests provide a final assessment of the system, confirming or disproving the designers' own judgements about it and enabling some fine tuning of the design parameters to be carried out. They also provide means for maintaining an appropriate grade of service once the system is in operation.

Finding a reliable and meaningful way to carry out a subjective test of picture quality is part of the general problem of measuring human reaction to physical stimuli. The field of study of this problem is known as *psychometrics* or *scaling* (Guilford, 1954; Torgerson, 1958). Efforts in the specific area of picture quality measurement have tended to be concentrated on two traditional psychometric methods, *category-judgement methods* and *comparison methods* (Pearson, 1972), of which an account follows. Multidimensional scaling techniques (Shepard, Romney and Nerlove, 1972) have not been applied to any extent as yet but the future will no doubt see their increasing use in this field.

For continuous, in-service monitoring of transmission quality, there has been some progress towards automatic measurement by *wave-form testing*, i.e. by using special test waveforms which are sent over the system; at the moment these could be said to be secondary methods of quality measurement whose reliability and efficacy requires checking by the primary subjective methods. Work continues in all these fields with the ultimate intention of arriving at a simple, general and accurate measurement method (CCIR Conclusions, 1970). Achievement of this objective would bring benefits for the international transmission of pictures as well as in performance comparisons of new systems obtained in different research laboratories at different times.

8.3   Category-judgement Methods

In the category-judgement method, also known as the *opinion-rating, rating-scale* or *quality-grading* method, subjects are required to view an impaired picture and to classify it into one of a small number of categories. The categories usually number between five and seven and are identified by numbers or letters together with some verbal description.

Types of scale

A number of scales are currently in use (CCIR, 1970). In the choice of the verbal descriptions, some scales describe the degree of impairment and others have words which are associated directly with quality *per se*. There has, however, been some limited comparison between scales; the results indicate that, when actually *using* the scales, subjects are not very much influenced by the number of categories or their word descriptions. At the XIIIth Plenary Assembly of the CCIR meeting in Geneva in 1974, a recommendation to use one of the three scales in Table 8.1 was made. The scales comprise a quality scale, an impairment scale and a comparison scale; the comparison scale is for use where an indication of relative quality is sought (for an alternative method, see Section 8.4).

In an actual test, subjects might record their responses on a sheet of paper, at the top of which was printed, as a reminder, the details of

Table 8.1   CCIR-recommended category-judgement scales for the
subjective assessment of television pictures.

I	Quality Scale	II	Impairment Scale
5	Excellent	5	Imperceptible
4	Good	4	Perceptible but not annoying
3	Fair	3	Slightly annoying
2	Poor	2	Annoying
1	Bad	1	Very annoying

III	Comparison Scale
+3	Much better
+2	Better
+1	Slightly better
0	The same
−1	Slightly worse
−2	Worse
−3	Much worse

the scale. The highlight luminance and contrast of the pictures, the
ambient illuminance, the viewing distance and picture size, all of
which can affect judgements, would be carefully set at predetermined
values. Some standardisation has been achieved through the CCIR
(1970); 1974, loc. cit. Other variables which may affect the result,
such as the order of presentation of the impairments, are randomised
in an appropriate experimental design. Around 20 subjects are
normally used for representative results.

Differences in judgements have been found between 'experts' and
'non-experts', where experts are those familiar with the principles
and practice of television or photography. Experts turn out to be
more sensitive to imperfections in pictures, differences of 4-12 dB
in impairment levels having been observed between the two types
(Allnatt, 1971). Organisations have differed on which of these types
to employ, some maintaining that experts give more reliable judgements while others that non-experts are more representative of the
judgements of ordinary people in their homes.

Interpretation of the results

It is a characteristic of all subjective tests that the results prove to be quite variable, this variability being compounded of the variability of each individual subject from judgement to judgement, and the variability between subjects. The spread of category judgements has been studied and can be described by binomial probability models. Although the variability is quite large, the mean score

$$\overline{C} = \frac{\sum\limits_{i=1}^{k} n_i C_i}{\sum\limits_{i=1}^{k} n_i}$$

where C_i is the numerical value associated with the ith scale category, n_i the number of judgements in that category, and k the number of categories, turns out to be a fairly good indicator of the overall quality for any particular impairment. Often the C_i are normalised, with 0 representing the lowest category, 1 the highest, and a linear spacing of the intermediate categories. As the impairment level is increased, $\overline{C}$ is found to decrease from near 1 to near 0 (Figure 8.2), never quite attaining these limits.

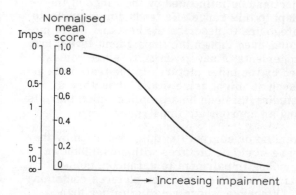

Figure 8.2 Typical regression of the normalised mean score in a category-judgement test with variation of the impairment level.

Lewis and Allnatt (1965) have suggested an alternative scale derived from the mean score $\overline{C}$. This is the *imp* scale, where the number of imps (impairment units) I is given by

$$I = \frac{1}{\overline{C}} - 1$$

This scale is shown alongside the normalised mean score scale in Figure 8.2. Lewis and Allnatt have found that with this transformation, the imp value of a number of different impairments occurring simultaneously can be obtained as the sum of the imp values of the same impairments occurring individually. This rule is not applicable in one or two obvious cases where impairments tend to cancel each other out, e.g. positive and negative echoes.

Deriving a grade of service from category-judgement tests

Category-judgement methods are popular in the field of broadcast television (Mertz, Fowler and Christoper, 1950; Fink, 1965; Weaver, 1959; Prosser, Allnatt and Lewis, 1964) where they are used as an aid to the setting up and maintenance of an appropriate grade of service.

The use of some mean score or imp value obtained in the laboratory for grade of service specification, however, is not altogether straight-forward. Normalised mean scores of around 0.8 ($\frac{1}{4}$ imp) are some-times aimed at, but allowance may be made for factors which make in-service viewing conditions somewhat different from laboratory conditions.

A specific well-known problem with category-judgement scales is that of *adaptation* (Allnatt 1971; Pearson 1972). Faced with a succession of impaired pictures and a scale with descriptions running from very good to very bad, the subject can be influenced by the range of im-pairments he sees and adapt to this range. He tends, for example, to use the top and bottom categories to describe the best and worst pic-tures in a particular session, even though the impairment levels may all be small. Thus his judgements of any given picture are context-dependent, being influenced by the other pictures in the test. With a new type of impairment, such as might arise in the laboratory in bandwidth-compression studies, this can be a problem, since there is no way *a priori* of choosing an appropriate impairment range.

It may be possible to minimise or correct for this adaptation by the use of scale *anchors*. These would be pictures with certain known levels of a commonly occurring impairment (e.g. random noise), which would be included in the same test with the pictures containing the unknown impairment. Of course, where relative rather than absolute judgements are required, as in comparing two or three dif-ferent systems or coding methods, the problem of anchoring need not arise.

8.4   Comparison Methods

Principle

The other commonly used method for picture quality measurement is the comparison method, in which one impaired picture is compared

with another containing a different impairment. The situation is
illustrated in Figure 8.3. Pictures from a camera or other source
are processed in two separate paths, A and B. These might be two
competing digital coding schemes or merely two different impairments such as echo and random noise, artificially generated in the
laboratory and added in controlled amounts to the video signal in each
path.

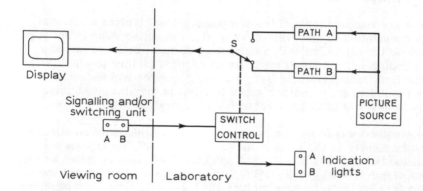

*Figure 8.3 Experimental arrangement for comparison method of
picture quality measurement.*

The setting of the switch S determines which of the pictures, A or B,
is seen by the subject in the viewing room. This switch can be under
the control of the subject himself or it can be timed to switch auto-
matically every few seconds. In either event, the subject sees the two
impairments sequentially in time on the monitor and can readily compare the relative quality of the two pictures. After he has made up his
mind, he signals to the experimenter which of the two presentations
(identified in some way as A and B) he finds of higher quality.

There is some evidence to indicate that comparative judgements of
this kind are less influenced by adaptation and by extraneous factors
such as screen brightness and contrast and ambient illuminance than
are category judgements. This is perhaps not unexpected, since the
subject is merely comparing two pictures, both seen under the same
viewing conditions. Both judgement-to-judgement and subject-to-
subject variability persist in fairly large measure, however, particularly when the two impairments are of a quite different character.

Test procedure

If the two paths A and B are two systems whose parameters have
already been optimised, the comparison test takes on its simplest

form. The judgement as to which system is of higher quality is made by a number of subjects, either individually or in small groups. Some explanation is given to the subjects about what is expected of them; a form of words is required which is clear and which acquaints them with the idea and purpose of the picture transmission systems under test. The result is then obtained as a majority vote in favour of one of the systems. The number of subjects used will depend on the importance of the decision and the difference in character between the two impairments, but will usually be between 10 and 20.

The more common form of the comparison test involves additional experimentation to discover not only which is better, A or B, but *how much* better it is. Typically impairment A might be noise introduced by a coding scheme and B might be an uncoded picture to which a controlled amount of noise from a noise generator had been added. The result the experimenter seeks to elicit is the amount of noise to be added to B to make it subjectively equivalent to A.

The simplest way to do this is to provide the subject with an attenuator which controls the level of noise in picture B^*. He adjusts it until the two pictures are of equal quality. This point is known as the *point of subjective equality* (PSE) and is expressed in terms of the noise level in the reference picture B. This noise level then becomes the measure of quality for the unknown impairment A. The subject could be asked to find a PSE for a number of different levels of the test impairment A, in which case a regression curve of the form illustrated in Figure 8.4 is obtained, the PSEs being averaged over all the participating subjects to give the plotted ordinate and a curve being fitted to the plotted points.

Relation to the category-judgement method

The comparison method has been quite widely used in research and systems engineering studies for evaluating such things as noise visibility (Brainard, 1967), echo impairment (Mertz, Fowler and Christopher, 1950), the effect of channel errors on coded video signals (Huang and Chikhaoui, 1967) and the subjective impairments caused by bandwidth compression schemes (Mounts and Pearson, 1969). However, the curve of subjective equivalence (Figure 8.4) provides a somewhat different form of result from the category-judgement test. In comparing the two an analogy might be made with subjective judgements about height. One way to gauge a subject's height reaction to an object would be to ask him whether it was 'high',

---

* This is known in psychometrics as the *method of adjustment*. In cases where the impairment B is not easily adjustable in this way, other psychometric methods such as the *method of constant stimuli* or the *staircase* method may be more appropriate (Guilford, 1954).

'very high', 'very low' etc. The other would be to hold a measuring stick against it and ask him to read off the height in metres.

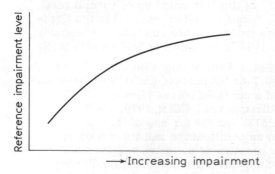

Figure 8.4 Subjective equivalence of test and reference impairments obtained in a comparison test, averaged over all subjects.

In the second case, which corresponds to the comparison method of quality judgement, the result is not always useful unless one knows how high a metre is. But people familiar with the metric system are quite capable of picturing how high a height of one, two or three metres is, and whether this is appropriate to their purposes. In a similar way visual systems engineers gain a working familiarity with signal-to-noise ratio for one or two common types of noise. The statement 'this impairment is equivalent to bandlimited white noise at 30 dB below the peak signal in a 625-line broadcast television picture' would conjure up a standard of picture quality in their mind. Alternatively, they could reproduce this picture in their own laboratory and look at it. It is this aspect of reproducibility which is attractive about the comparison method.

Uncertainty arises with the comparison method, however, when the test impairment A is quite different from the reference impairment B in appearance. It is not known how consistently and meaningfully subjects can compare the two in this case. Certainly in a number of cases of widely-different impairments, subjects have been quite inconsistent in their comparisons, but it is not known how general this is. Further, if they equate A to B and then, for a different impairment C, also equate C to B, would A and C be found to be subjectively equal when directly compared? If they are, then the law of *transitivity* could be said to hold. It is known that transitivity holds if A, B and C are similar, but we do not have sufficient evidence to say under what conditions, if any, it does not hold.

8.5   Waveform Testing

As subjective tests involve careful planning and execution they are
usually fairly time consuming. A need has arisen in broadcast television practice for quick tests of the quality of point-to-point links.
The method which has evolved is the transmission of special test
waveforms over the system. These are often inserted in the field-
blanking period for in-service system monitoring and are termed
vertical interval test signals (VITS) or *insertion test signals* (ITS).

In a composite insertion test signal there might be a combination
of sharp pulses (the so called T or 2T pulses), staircases, constant-
amplitude sections (bars) and modulated pulses (Lewis, 1954; Macdiarmid, 1960; Mallon and Williams, 1968; CCIR, 1970. CMTT
Recommendations 420-2 and 473). At the far end of the channel
the waveform is displayed on an oscilloscope and its distortions
observed. Alternatively it is possible to compare received and
original waveforms using a computer for continuous monitoring
purposes (McKenzie, 1972). Error criteria are used which take
account of the eye's insensitivity to waveform distortions in the
vicinity of sharp brightness changes.

There is a rather tenuous relationship between the distortion in
artificial test waveforms, observed on an oscilloscope, and the
complex viewer-response to impairments during actual picture
transmissions. While waveform testing fulfils a very real need,
experienced engineers in this field take care to confine their application of the method to specific forms of distortion and to check
their conclusions by the subjective testing procedures discussed in
previous sections.

REFERENCES

ABATE, J. (1967), 'Linear and Adaptive Delta Modulation', *Proc. IEEE,* **55,** No. 3, 298-308.

ABBOTT, R. P. (1971), 'A Differential Pulse-Code-Modulation Codec for Videotelephony using Four Bits per Sample', *IEEE Trans. Comm. Tech.,* **COM-19,** No. 6, 907-912.

ALLNATT, J. W. (1971), 'Subjective Assessment of Impairments in Television Pictures', *Appl. Ergonomics,* **2. 4,** 231-235.

ALLNATT, J. W. and PROSSER, R. D. (1965), 'Subjective Quality of Television Pictures Impaired by Long-delayed Echoes', *Proc. IEE,* **112,** No. 3, 487-492.

ALLNATT, J. W. and PROSSER, R. D. (1966), 'Subjective Quality of Colour-television Pictures Impaired by Random Noise', *Proc. IEE,* **113,** No. 4, 551-557.

ARPS, R. B., ERDMAN, R. L., NEAL, A. S. and SCHLAEPFER, C. E. (1969), 'Character Legibility Versus Resolution in Image Processing of Printed Matter', *IEEE Trans. Man-Machine Systems,* **MMS-10,** No. 3, 66-71.

BAILEY, W. F. (1954), 'The Constant Luminance Principle in NTSC Color Television', *Proc. IRE,* **42,** 60-71.

BALDWIN, M. W. (1951), 'Subjective Sharpness of Additive Color Pictures', *Proc. IRE,* **39,** 1173-1176.

BALDWIN, M. W. and NIELSEN, G. (1956), 'Subjective Sharpness of Simulated Color Television Pictures', *J. Opt. Soc. Am.,* **46,** No. 9, 681-685.

BARLOW, H. B., NARASIMHAN, R. and ROSENFELD, A. (1972), 'Visual Pattern Analysis in Machines and Animals', *Science,* **177,** No. 4049, 567-575.

BARSTOW, J. M. and CHRISTOPHER, H. N. (1962), 'Measurement of Random Video Interference to Monochrome and Color TV', *Trans. AIEE,* No. 63, 313-320.

BARTLESON, C. J. (1966), 'Color-Appearance Measurement I. A Colorimeter for Haploscopic Color Matching', *Phot. Sci. Eng.,* **10,** No. 2, 104-110.

BARTLESON, C. J. (1968), 'Color Perception and Color Television', *J. Soc. Mot. Pict. Telev. Eng.,* **77,** No. 1, 1-11.

BARTLESON, C. J. and BRENEMAN, E. J. (1967a), 'Brightness Reproduction in the Photographic Process', *Phot. Sci. Eng.,* **11,** No. 4, 254-262.

BARTLESON, C. J. and BRENEMAN, E. J. (1967b), 'Brightness Perception in Complex Fields', *J. Opt. Soc. Am.,* **57,** No. 7, 953-957.

BARTLESON, C. J. and WITZEL, R. F. (1967), 'Illumination for Color Transparancies', *Phot. Sci. Eng.,* **11,** No. 5, 329-335.

BELL LABORATORIES TECHNICAL STAFF (1970), *Transmission Systems for Communications,* Bell Telephone Laboratories, Inc., N.J., USA.

BENNETT, W. R. (1970), *Introduction to Signal Transmission,* McGaw-Hill, New York.

BENNETT, W. R. and DAVEY, J. R. (1965), *Data Transmission,* Mc-Graw-Hill, New York.

BRACEWELL, R. (1965), *The Fourier Transform and Its Applications,* McGraw-Hill, New York.

BRAINARD, R. C. (1967), 'Low-Resolution TV: Subjective Effects of Noise Added to Signal', *Bell Sys. Tech. J.,* **46,** No. 1, 233-260.

BRAINARD, R. C. (1972), 'Subjective Effects of Noise in Television', in *Picture Bandwidth Compression,* ed. Huang, T. S. and Tretiak, O. J., 31-46, Gordon and Breach.

BRAINARD, R. C., MOUNTS, F. W. and PRASADA, B. (1967), 'Low-Resolution TV: Subjective Effects of Frame Repetition and Picture Replenishment', *Bell Sys. Tech. J.,* **45,** No. 1, 261-271.

BRIEL, L. (1970), 'A Single-Vidicon Television Camera System', *J. Soc. Mot. Pict. Telev. Eng.,* **79,** 326-330.

BRITISH STANDARDS INSTITUTION (1970), *The International System of Units (SI),* British Standard 3763.

BROWN, E. F. (1967), 'Low-Resolution TV: Subjective Comparison of Interlaced and Noninterlaced Pictures', *Bell Sys. Tech. J.,* **46,** No. 1, 199-232.

BROWN, E. F. (1969), 'Television: The Subjective Effects of Filter Ringing Transients', *J. Soc. Mot. Pict. Telev. Eng.,* **78,** No. 4, 249-255.

BROWN, G. H. (1954), The Choice of Axes and Bandwidths for the Chrominance Signals in NTSC Color Television', *Proc. IRE,* **42,** 58-59.

BRUCH, W. (1966), 'Selected Papers II. PAL, a Variant of the NTSC Colour Television System', *Telefunkenzeitung* Special Issue.

BUDRIKIS, Z. L. (1972), 'Visual Fidelity Criterion and Modeling', *Proc. IEEE,* **60,** No. 7, 771-779.

CAMPBELL, F. W. (1968), 'The Human Eye as an Optical Filter', *Proc. IEEE,* **56,** No. 6, 1009-1014.

CAMPBELL, F. W., CARPENTER, R. H. S. and LEVINSON, J. Z. (1969), 'Visibility of Aperiodic Patterns compared with that of Sinusoidal Gratings', *J. Physiol.,* **204,** 283-298.

CAMPBELL, F. W. and GREEN, D. G. (1965), 'Monocular Versus Binocular Visual Acuity', *Nature,* **208,** No. 5006, 191-192.

CAMPBELL, F. W. and GREGORY, A. H. (1960), 'Effect of Pupil Size on Visual Acuity', *Nature,* **187,** No. 4743, 1121-1123.

CAMPBELL, F. W. and ROBSON, J. G. (1968), 'Application of Fourier Analysis to the Visibility of Gratings', *J. Physiol.,* **197,** 551-566.

CANDY, J. C. (1972), 'Refinement of a Delta Modulator', in *Picture Bandwidth Compression,* ed. Huang, T. S. and Tretiak, O. J., 323-339, Gordon and Breach, New York.

CANDY, J. C., FRANKE, M. A., HASKELL, B. G. and MOUNTS, F. W.
(1971), 'Transmitting Television as Clusters of Frame-to-Frame
Differences', *Bell Sys. Tech. J.*, **50**, No. 6, 1889-1917.

CARLSON, A. B. (1968), *Communication Systems: An Introduction to
Signals and Noise in Electrical Communication*, McGraw-Hill,
New York.

CARNT, P. S. and TOWNSEND, G. B. (1961), *Colour Television Vol. 1:
Principles and Practice*, Iliffe, London.

CARNT, P. S. and TOWNSEND, G. B. (1969), *Colour Television Vol. 2:
PAL, SECAM and Other Systems*, Iliffe, London.

CATTERMOLE, K. W. (1969), *Principles of Pulse Code Modulation*,
Iliffe, London.

CAVANAUGH, J. R. (1970), 'A Single Weighting Characteristic for
Random Noise in Monochrome and NTSC Color Television',
J. Soc. Mot. Pict. Telev. Eng., **79**, 105-109.

CCIR Conclusions (1970) XIIth Plenary Assembly, New Delhi, Vol. 5,
Part 2. International Telecommunication Union, Geneva.

CHERRY, E. C. (1942, 1943), 'The Transmission Characteristics of
Asymmetric-Sideband Communication Networks', *J. IEE*, **89**,
Part III, No. 5, 19-42 (1942) and **90**, Part III, No. 10, 75-88 (1943).

CHERRY, E. C. (1962), 'The Bandwidth Compression of Television and
Facsimile', *Telev. Soc. J.*, **10**, 40-49.

CHERRY, C. and CHITNIS, A. M. (1972), 'Picture Bandwidth Compression Research at Imperial College, University of London', in
Picture Bandwidth Compression, ed. Huang, T. S. and Tretiak, O. J.,
285-302, Gordon and Breach, New York.

CONNOR, D. J., BRAINARD, R. C. and LIMB, J. O. (1972), 'Intraframe
Coding for Picture Transmission', *Proc. IEEE*, **60**, No. 7, 779-791.

CONNOR, D. J., PEASE, R. F. W. and SCHOLES, W. G. (1971), 'Television Coding Using Two-Dimensional Spatial Prediction',
Bell Sys. Tech. J., **50**, No. 3, 1049-1061.

COSTIGAN, D. M. (1971) *Fax: The Principles and Practice of Facsimile Communication*, Chilton Book Co., Philadelphia.

CRATER, T. V. (1971), 'The Picturephone System: Service Standards',
Bell Sys. Tech. J., **50**, No. 2, 235-269.

CUTLER, C. C. (1952), 'Differential Quantization of Communication
Signals', US Patent 2, 605, 361; also 2,724,740 (1955).

DAVSON, H. (1972), *The Physiology of the Eye* (3rd Edition), Churchill
Livingstone, London.

DE JAGER, F. (1952), 'Delta Modulation, a Method of PCM Transmission Using the 1-unit Code', *Philips Res. Rep.*, **7**, 442-466.

DE LANGE, DZN H. (1958), 'Research into the Dynamic Nature of the
Human Fovea-Cortex Systems with Intermittent and Modulated
Light. I. Attenuation Characteristics with White and Colored
Light', *J. Opt. Soc. Am.*, **48**, No. 11, 777-784.

DE MARSH, L. E. (1971), 'Color Reproduction in Color Television',
Proc. ISCC Conference on Optimum Reproduction of Color,

Williamsburg Va., 69-97, Graphic Arts Information Services, Rochester, NY.

DE MOUILPIED FREMONT, A. (1971), 'The Mark VIII Colour Camera— Aperture Correction Facilities', *Sound Vision Broadcasting*, **12**, No. 2, 17-21.

DE VRIJER, F. W. (1957), 'The Choice of Chrominance Signals in the NTSC System with a View to the Differential Sensitivity of the Human Eye to Colour', *Acta Electronica*, **2**, Nos. 1-2, 103-109.

DEUTSCH, S. (1971), 'Visual Displays using Pseudo-Random Dot Scan', *Proc. Soc. Inf. Display*, **12**, No. 3, 131-146.

DORROS, I. (1971), 'The Picturephone System: The Network', *Bell Sys. Tech. J.*, 50, No. 2, 221-233.

EASTMAN, F. H. (1970), 'A High-Resolution Image Sensor', *J. Soc. Mot. Pict. Telev. Eng.*, **79**, No. 1, 10-15.

EPSTEIN, D. W. (1953), 'Colorimetric Analysis of RCA Color Tele- vision System', *RCA Rev.*, **14**, 227-258.

FELLGETT, P. B. and LINFOOT, E. H. (1955), 'On the Assessment of Optical Images', *Phil. Trans. Roy. Soc., London*, Series A, **247**, 369-407.

FINK, D. G. (1955), *Color Television Standards, N.T.S.C.*, McGraw-Hill, New York.

FOWLER, A. D. (1951), 'Observer Reaction to Video Crosstalk', *J. Soc. Mot. Pict. Telev. Eng.*, **57**, No. 5, 416-424.

FREI, W., JAEGER, P. A. and PROBST, P. (1972), 'Quantisierung der Farbinformation bei der Bildcodierung', *NTZ*, **9**, 401-404.

GABOR, D. J. and HILL, P. J. C. (1961), 'Television Band Compression by Contour Interpolation', *Proc. IEE*, **108**, Part B, 303-315.

GERRARD, G. A. and THOMPSON, J. E. (1973), 'An Experimental Differential P.C.M. Encoder-Decoder for Viewphone Signals', *Radio Electronic Eng.*, **43**, No. 3, 201-208.

GOLDING, L. S. and GARLOW, R. K. (1971), 'Frequency Interleaved Sampling of a Color Signal', *IEE Trans. Comm. Tech.*, **COM-19**, No. 6, Pt. 2, 972-979.

GOLDMARK, P. C. and HOLLYWOOD, J. M. (1951), 'A New Technique for Improving the Sharpness of Television Pictures', *J. Soc. Mot. Pict. Telev. Eng.*, 57, No. 10, 382-296.

GOODALL, W. M. (1951), 'Television by Pulse Code Modulation', *Bell Sys. Tech. J.*, **30**, No. 1, 33-49.

GOODMAN, J. W. (1968), *Introduction to Fourier Optics*, McGraw-Hill, New York.

GOURIET, G. G. (1952), 'Dot-Interlaced Television', *Electronic Eng.* 24, No. 290, 166-171.

GRAHAM, R. E. (1958), 'Predictive Quantizing of Television Signals', *IRE Wescon Convention Record*, Part 4, 147-156.

GRONEMANN, U. R. (1964), 'Coding Color Pictures', *MIT Research Lab. of Electronics, Technical Report 422*.

GUILFORD, J. P. (1954), *Psychometric Methods,* McGraw-Hill, New York.

HACKING, K. (1957), 'The Choice of Chrominance Axes for Color Television', *Acta Electronica,* **2**, Nos. 1-2, 87-93.

HACKING, K. (1962), 'The Relative Visibility of Random Noise over the Grey Scale', *J. Brit. IRE,* **23**, No. 4, 307-310.

HACKING, K. (1966), 'Colorimetric Analysis of Interference in Colour Television', *BBC Eng. Div. Monograph,* No. 60.

HASKELL, B. G., MOUNTS, F. W. and CANDY, J. C. (1972), 'Interframe Coding of Videotelephone Pictures', *Proc. IEEE,* **60**, No. 7, 792-800.

HEIGHTMAN, A. N. (1967), 'Vertical Aperture Correction for the Mark VII Camera', *Sound Vision Broadcasting,* **8**, No. 1, 31-32.

HEIGHTMAN, A. N. (1971), 'Gamma in Television', *Sound Vision Broadcasting,* **12**, No. 2, 26-30.

HEIGHTMAN, A. N. (1972), 'A High-Performance Automatic Color Camera', *IEEE Trans. Broadcasting,* **BC-18**, No. 1, 1-7.

HENDLEY, C. D. and HECHT, S. (1949), 'The Colors of Natural Objects and Terrains and their Relation to Visual Color Deficiency', *J. Opt. Soc. Am.,* **39**, No. 10, 870-873.

HERRIOTT, D. R. (1958), 'Recording Electronic Lens Bench', *J. Opt. Soc. Am.,* **48**, No. 12, 968-971.

HIGGINS, G. C. and STULTZ, K. (1948), 'Visual Acuity as Measured with Various Orientations of a Parallel-line Test Object', *J. Opt. Soc. Am.,* **38**, No. 9, 756-758.

HOPKINS, H. H. (1962), 'The Application of Frequency Response Techniques in Optics', *Proc. Phys. Soc.,* **79**, 889-919.

HOWELLS, P. W. (1954), 'The Concept of Transmission Primaries in Color Television', *Proc. IRE,* **42**, 134-138.

HUANG, T. S. (1965), 'The Power Density Spectrum of Television Random Noise', *Appl. Optics,* **4**, No. 5, 597-601.

HUANG, T. S. (1972a), 'Digital Transmission of Halftone Pictures', *Proc. Conference on Digital Processing of Signals in Communications,* Loughborough, 113-122, IERE London.

HUANG, T. S. (1972b), 'Run-length Coding and its Extensions', in *Picture Bandwidth Compression,* eds. Huang, T. S. and Tretiak, O. J., 231-264, Gordon and Breach, New York.

HUANG, T. S. and CHIKHAOUI, M. T. (1967), 'The Effect of BSC on PCM Picture Quality', *IRE Trans Inf. Theory,* **IT-13**, No. 2, 270-273.

HUANG, T. S., SCHREIBER, W. F. and TRETIAK O. J., (1971), 'Image Processing', *Proc. IEEE,* **59**, No. 11, 1586-1609.

HUANG, T. S. and TRETIAK, O. J. (eds.) (1972), *Picture Bandwidth Compression,* Gordon and Breach, New York.

HUFFMANN, D. A. (1952), 'A Method for the Construction of Minimum-Redundancy Codes', *Proc. IRE,* **40**, 1098-1101.

HUNT, R. W. G. (1965), 'Measurement of Color Appearance', *J. Opt. Soc. Am.,* **55**, No. 11, 1540-1551.

HUNT, R. W. G. (1967), *The Reproduction of Colour,* Fountain Press, London.
HURVICH, L. M. and JAMESON, D. (1957), 'An Opponent-process Theory of Color Vision', *Psychol. Rev.,* **64,** 384-404.

JESTY, L. C. (1952), 'Television as a Communication Problem', *Proc. IEE,* **99,** Part IIIA, 761-770.
JESTY, L. C. (1958), 'The Relation between Picture Size, Viewing Distance and Picture Quality', *Proc. IEE,* **105,** Part B, 425-434.
JONES, A. H. (1968), 'Optimum Color Analysis Characteristics and Matrices for Color Television Cameras with Three Receptors', *J. Soc. Mot. Pict. Telev. Eng.,* **77,** No. 2, 108-115.
JUDD, D. B. (1940), 'Hue, Saturation and Lightness of Surface Colors with Chromatic Illumination', *J. Opt. Soc. Am.,* **30,** 2-32.
JUDD, D. B. (1960), 'Appraisal of Land's Work on Two-Primary Color Projections', *J. Opt. Soc. Am.,* **50,** No. 3, 254-268.
JUDD, D. B. and WYSZECKI, G. (1963), *Color in Business, Science and Industry,* John Wiley & Sons, New York.
JULESZ, B. (1962), 'Visual Pattern Discrimination', *IRE Trans. Inf. Theory,* **IT-8,** No. 2, 84-92.

KELL, R. D. (1929), British Patent No. 341811.
KELL, R. D., BEDFORD, A. V. and TRAINER, M. A. (1934), 'An Experimental Television System', *Proc. IRE,* **22,** 1246-1265.
KELLY, D. H. (1961), 'Flicker Fusion and Harmonic Analysis', *J. Opt. Soc. Am. ,***50,** 1115-1116.
KELLY, K. L. and JUDD, D. B. (1955), 'The ISCC-NBS Method of Designating Colors and a Dictionary of Color Names, *Nat. Bur. Stand. Circ.* 553, NBS, Washington D.C.
KNOWLTON, K. and HARMON, L. (1972), 'Computer-Produced Grey Scales', *Comput. Graphics Image Processing,* **1,** No. 1, 1-20.
KOLERS, P. A. (1972), 'Reading Pictures: Some Cognitive Aspects of Visual Perception', in *Picture Bandwidth Compression,* eds. Huang, T. S. and Tretiak, O. J., 97-121, Gordon and Breach, New York.
KRETZMER, E. R. (1952), 'Statistics of Television Signals', *Bell Sys. Tech. J.,* 31, 751-763.
KUBBA, M. H. (1963), 'Automatic Picture Detail Detection in the Presence of Random Noise', *Proc. IEEE,* **51,** No. 11, 1518-1523.

LAND, E. H. (1959), 'Color Vision and the Natural Image', *Proc. Nat. Acad. Sci.,* **45,** 115-129 and 636-644.
LE GRAND, Y. (1968), *Light, Colour and Vision,* 2nd Edition, Chapman and Hall, London.
LEVINSON, J. Z. (1972), 'Psychophysics and TV', in *Picture Bandwidth Compression.* eds. Huang, T. S. and Tretiak, O. J., 11-29, Gordon and Breach, New York.
LEWIS, N. W. (1954), 'Waveform Responses of Television Links', *Proc. IEE,* **101,** Pt. III, 258-270.

LEWIS, N. W. (1962), 'Television Bandwidth and the Kell Factor', *Electronic Technol.*, **39**, No. 2, 44-47.

LEWIS, N. W. and ALLNATT, J. W. (1965), 'Subjective Quality of Television Pictures with Multiple Impairments', *Electronics Lett.*, **1**, 187-188.

LIGHTHILL, M. J. (1958), *An Introduction to Fourier Analysis and Generalized Functions*, Cambridge University Press.

LIMB, J. O. (1967), 'Source-Receiver Encoding of Television Signals', *Proc. IEEE*, **55**, No. 3, 364-379.

LIMB, J. O. (1969), 'Design of Dither Waveforms for Quantized Visual Signals', *Bell Sys. Tech. J.*, **48**, No. 7, 2255-2582.

LIMB, J. O., RUBINSTEIN, C. B. and WALSH, K. A. (1971), 'Digital Coding of Color Picturephone Signals by Element-differential Quantization', *IEEE Trans. Comm. Tech.*, **COM-19**, No. 6, Part 2, 992-1001.

MACADAM, D. L. (1954), 'Reproduction of Colors in Outdoor Scenes', *Proc. IRE*, **42**, 166-174.

MACDIARMID, I. F. (1960), 'Waveform Distortion in Television Links', *J. Brit. IRE*, **20**, 201-216.

MALLON, R. E. and WILLIAMS, A. D. (1968), 'Testing of Television Transmission Channels with Vertical Interval Test Signals', *J. Soc. Mot. Pict. Telev. Eng.*, **77**, No. 8, 789-793.

MARSH, A. H. (1972), 'Minimum Legibility Requirements for a High Resolution Graphics Transmission System', *Proceedings of the 6th International Symposium on Human Factors in Telecommunications*, Swedish Telecommunications Administration, Stockholm, Sweden.

MAURICE, D. A. (1958), Discussion of paper by L. C. Jesty (1958), *Proc. IEE*, **105**, Part B, 436-437.

MAURICE, R. D. A., GILBERT, M., NEWELL, G. F. and SPENCER, J. G. (1955), 'The Visibility of Noise in Television', *BBC Eng. Div. Monograph*, No. 3.

MCKENZIE, G. A. (1972), 'Experiments with a Computer in a Television Control and Monitoring Centre', *IBA Tech. Rev.*, **1**, 15-23.

MERTZ, P., FOWLER, A. D. and CHRISTOPHER, H. N. (1950), 'Quality Rating of Television Images', *Proc. IRE*, **38**, 1269-1283.

MERTZ, P. and GRAY, F. (1934), 'A Theory of Scanning and Its Relation to the Characteristics of the Transmitted Signal in Telephotography and Television', *Bell Sys. Tech. J.*, **13**, 464-515.

MILLMAN, J. and TAUB, H. (1965), *Pulse, Digital and Switching Waveforms*, McGraw-Hill, New York.

MONTEATH, G. D. (1962), 'Vertical Resolution and Line Broadening', *BBC Eng. Div. Monograph*, No. 45.

MOON, P. and SPENCER, D. E. (1945), 'The Visual Effect of Non-Uniform Surrounds', *J. Opt. Soc. Am.*, **35**, No. 3, 233-248.

MOUNTS, F. W. (1969), 'A Video Encoding System with Conditional Picture-Element Replenishment', *Bell Sys. Tech. J.*, **48**, No. 7, 2545-2554.

MOUNTS, F. W. and PEARSON, D. E. (1969), 'Apparent Increase in
Noise Level when Television Pictures are Frame-Repeated',
Bell Sys. Tech. J., **48,** No. 3, 527-539.

NEWELL, G. F. and GEDDES (1963), 'Visibility of Small Luminance
Perturbations in Television Displays', *Proc. IEE,* **110,** No. 11,
1979-1984.
NEWHALL, S. M., NICKERSON, D. and JUDD, D. B. (1943), 'Final Re-
port of the O.S.A. Subcommittee on the Spacing of the Munsell
Colors', *J. Opt. Soc. Am.,* **33,** 385-418.

O'NEAL, J. B. (1966), 'Predictive Quantizing Systems (Differential
Pulse Code Modulation) for the Transmission of Television
Signals', *Bell Sys. Tech. J.,* **45,** No. 5, 689-721.

PEARSON, D. E. (1967), 'A Realistic Model for Visual Communication
Systems', *Proc. IEEE,* 55, No. 3, 380-389.
PEARSON, D. E. (1972), 'Methods for Scaling Television Picture
Quality: a Survey', in *Picture Bandwidth Compression* eds. Huang,
T. S. and Tretiak, O. J., 47-95, Gordon and Breach, New York.
PEARSON, D. E. and RUBINSTEIN, C. B. (1971), 'Studies of Two
Systems for Color Reproduction with a White Primary', *J. Soc.
Mot. Pict. Telev. Eng.,* **80,** No. 1, 15-18.
PEARSON, D. E., RUBINSTEIN, C. B. and SPIVACK, G. J. (1969),
'Comparison of Perceived Color in Two-Primary Computer-
Generated Artificial Images with Predictions based on the
Helson-Judd Formulation', *J. Opt. Soc. Am.,* **59,** No. 5, 644-658.
PEASE, R. F. W. and LIMB, J. O. (1971), 'Exchange of Spatial and
Temporal Resolution in Television Coding', *Bell Sys. Tech. J.,*
50, No. 1, 191-200.
PETERSEN, D. P. and MIDDLETON, D. (1962), 'Sampling and Recon-
struction of Wave-Number-Limited Functions in N-Dimensional
Euclidean Spaces', *Information and Control,* **5,** 279-323.
POOLE, H. H. (1966), *Fundamentals of Display Systems,* MacMillan,
London.
PRATT, W. K. (1971), 'Spatial Transform Coding of Color Images',
IEEE Trans. Comm. Tech., **COM-19,** No. 6, 980-992.
PROSSER, R. D. and ALLNATT, J. W. (1965), 'Subjective Quality of
Television Pictures Impaired by Random Noise', *Proc. IEE,* **112,**
No. 6, 1099-1102.
PROSSER, R. D., ALLNATT, J. W. and LEWIS, N. W. (1964), 'Quality
Grading of Impaired Television Pictures', *Proc. IEE,* **111,** No. 3,
491-502.

RECHTER, R. J. (1968), 'Signal Processing and Transmission for the
Surveyor Television System', *J. Soc. Mot. Pict. Telev. Eng.,* **77,**
No. 4, 341-350.
RICHARDS, W. (1972), 'One-Stage Model for Color Conversion',
J. Opt. Soc. Am., **62,** No. 5, 697-698.

RICHARDS, W. and PARKS, E. A. (1971), 'Model for Color Conversion', *J. Opt. Soc. Am.*, **61**, No. 7, 971-976.
ROBERTS, L. G. (1962), 'Picture Coding Using Pseudo-random Noise', *IRE Trans. Inf. Theory*, **IT-8**, No. 2, 145-154.
ROBINSON, A. H. (1973), 'Multidimensional Fourier Transforms and Image Processing with Finite Scanning Apertures', *Appl. Optics*, **12**, No. 10, 2344-2352.
ROBSON, J. G. (1966), 'Spatial and Temporal Contrast-Sensitivity Functions of the Visual System', *J. Opt. Soc. Am.*, **56**, No. 8, 1141-1142.
RUBINSTEIN, C. B. and PEARSON, D.E. (1970), 'Color Perception in Colored Displays', *Proc. 1st AIC Congress*, 157-165, Muster-Schmidt, Göttingen.

SALOMON, P. M. (1970), 'Applications of Slow-Scan Television Systems to Planetary Exploration', *J. Soc. Mot. Pict. Telev. Eng.*, **79**, No. 7, 607-615.
SCHADE, O. H. (1958), 'On the Quality of Color-Television Images and the Perception of Color Detail', *RCA Rev.*, **19**, No. 4, 495-535.
SCHADE, O. H. (1964), 'Modern Image Evaluation and Television', *Appl. Optics*, **3**, No. 1, 17-21.
SCHADE, O. H. (1971a), 'Electron Optics and Signal Readout of High-Definition Return-Beam Vidicon Cameras', *Photoelectronic Imaging Devices*, **2**, 345-399, Plenum Press.
SCHADE, O. H. (1971b), 'Resolving Power Functions and Integrals of High-Definition Television and Photographic Cameras—a New Concept in Image Evaluation', *RCA Rev.*, **32**, 567-609.
SCHREIBER, W. F. (1956), 'The Measurement of Third Order Probability Distributions of Television Signals', *IRE Trans. Inf. Theory*, IT-2, No. 3, 94-106.
SCHREIBER, W. F. (1967), 'Picture Coding', *Proc. IEEE*, **55**, No. 3, 320-330.
SEYLER, A. J. (1965), 'Probability Distributions of Television Frame Differences', *Proc. IREE (Australia)*, 355-366.
SEYLER, A. J. and BUDRIKIS, Z. L. (1965), 'Detail Perception after Scene Changes in Television Image Presentations, *IEEE Trans. Inf. Theory*, **IT-11**, 31-43.
SHANNON, C. E. (1948), 'A Mathematical Theory of Communication', *Bell Sys. Tech. J.*, **27**, 379-423 and 623-656.
SHANNON, C. E. (1960), 'Coding Theorems for a Discrete Source with a Fidelity Criterion', in *Information and Decision Processes*, ed. Machol R. E., 93-126, McGaw-Hill, 1960.
SHEPARD, R. N., ROMNEY, A. K. and NERLOVE, S. B. (eds.) (1972) *Multidimensional Scaling, Vol. 1: Theory, Vol. 2: Applications*, Seminar Press, New York and London.
SHURTLEFF, D. A. (1967), 'Studies in Television Legibility', *Information Disp.*, **4**, No. 1, 40-45.
SPERLING, G. (1971), 'Flicker in Computer-generated Visual Displays;

Selecting a CRO Phosphor and Other Problems', *Behav. Res. Meth. Instrum.*, **3,** No. 3, 151-153.
SPROSON, W. N. and HACKING, K. (1963), 'New Methods of Lens Testing and Measurement', *BBC Eng. Div. Monograph,* No. 50.
STEVENS, S. S. (1957), 'On the Psychophysical Law', *Psychol. Rev.*, **64,** 153-181.

TAYLOR, E. W. and CHAMBERS, J. P. (1971), 'Automatic Compensation in Colour Television Cameras for Changes in Scene Illuminant', *Proc. IEE,* **118,** No. 3/4, 449-459.
TEMPLE, G. (1955), 'The Theory of Generalized Functions', *Proc. Roy. Soc.,* Series A, **228,** 175-190.
THIELE, A. N. (1970), 'Horizontal Aperture Equalization', *Radio Electronic Eng.*, **40,** No. 4, 193-212.
THOMPSON, J. E. (1971), 'A 36 Mbit/s Television Codec Employing Pseudo-Random Quantization', *IEEE Trans. Comm. Tech.*, **COM-19,** No. 6, 872-879.
THOMPSON, J. E. (1973), 'Differential Coding for Digital Transmission of PAL Colour Television Signals', *British Post Office Research Department Report,* No. 361.
TOMPSETT, M. F. (1972), 'Charge Transfer Devices', *J. Vac. Sci. Technol.*, **9,** No. 4, 1166-1181.
TORGERSON, W. S. (1958), *Theory and Methods of Scaling,* John Wiley & Sons, New York.
TOWNSEND, G. B. (1962), 'The Choice of Normalizing Illuminant in Colour Television', *Television Engineering,* (IEE Conf. Report Series 5), 528-536.
TOWNSEND, G. B. (1970), *PAL Colour Television,* Cambridge University Press.

UNDERHILL, W. T. (1972), 'A New Automatic Color Camera', *J. Soc. Mot. Pict. Telev. Eng.*, **81,** 450-454.

VAN DER HORST, G. J. C. and BOUMAN, M. A. (1969), 'Spatiotemporal Chromaticity Discrimination', *J. Opt. Soc. Am.*, **59,** No. 11, 1482-1488.
WEAVER, L. E. (1959), 'Subjective Impairment of Television Pictures', *Electronic Radio Eng.*, **36,** No. 5, 170-179.
WINTRINGHAM, W. T. (1951), 'Color Television and Colorimetry', *Proc. IRE,* **39,** No. 10, 1135-1173.
WINTZ, P. A. (1972), 'Transform Picture Coding', *Proc. IEEE,* **60,** No. 7, 809-820.
WOOD, C. B. B. and SPROSON, W. N. (1971), 'The Choice of Primary Colours for Colour Television', *BBC Engineering,* 19-36.
WOODWARD, P. M. (1953), *Probability and Information Theory, with Applications to Radar,* Pergamon Press, London.
WRIGHT, W. D. (1934), 'The Measurement and Analysis of Colour Adaptation Phenomena', *Proc. Roy. Soc.*, B., **115,** 49.
WYSZECKI, G. and STILES, W. S. (1967), *Color Science,* John Wiley & Sons, New York.

INDEX

AC-coupling 61
Achromatic colour 142, 154-61
Achromatic point 144, 154, 156, 157, 161
Adaptation 39
  chromatic 142, 155-6
  in category judgements 204
Aliasing 21, 56, 60, 74, 81
Amplification factor 22
Analogue baseband transmission 111-13
Analogue transmission, colour information 177-96
Angle of inclination 81
Aperture correction 66
Aperture effect 62-6, 81
Apparent chromaticity 144
Autocorrelation function 25, 107
  impulsive 27
  two-dimensional 25

Bandlimitation 23, 68, 85, 184
  with line broadening 91-3
  pre-scan 60
  sharp optical 62
Bandwidth 20
  eye 48
  limitation. See Bandlimitation
  numerical value of 21
  spatial 20
  strict 21
  2-dimensional 19-23
  3-dimensional 30
Bessel function 16, 64, 93
Binocular vision 44
Blanking for video signal 82
Brightness 36, 38, 41, 108, 142, 144, 154, 160, 187

Camera 54, 199
  aperture correction 66-7
  colour 164
  gamma 87, 180
  matrixing 171-3
  monochrome 54
  optical system 20, 54, 60-3
  single-tube colour 89
  target 67-8
Candela 36-7
Carrier modulation 114

Category-judgement methods of picture quality
  measurement 201-4, 206
CCIR (Comité Consutatif International des Radiocommunications)
  colour television characteristics 134, 180, 186, 193, 196
  monochrome television charteristics 70
  noise weighting 105
  subjective assessment 105, 201-2
  vestigial sideband transmission 114
Character legibility 75
Channel capacity and picture quality 199
Channel decoder 200
Channel encoding 199
Channel gains 173
Chroma 143, 144
Chromatic aberration of the eye 176, 184
Chromatic adaptation 142, 156
Chromaticity 132, 178, 181
  and perceived colour 144-56
  of common objects with daylight illumination 163
Chromaticity/brightness sensitivity 189
Chromaticity coordinates 132-3, 137-40, 157, 161-2, 168-9, 171, 175
Chromaticity diagram
  1931 CIE 132-5
  1960 CIE-UCS 135-8, 144, 157, 161, 162
Chromaticity error 165, 173
Chromaticity noise 187, 189
Chromaticity variation 184
Chrominance 177
Chrominance error 187
Chrominance noise 188
Chrominance primaries 186
Chrominance signal 177, 180-6 189-98
CIE (Commission Internationale de l'Eclairage) 32, 126
  colour matching functions 131
  primaries, non-physical 127-33, 168
  relative luminosity function V_λ 32-8
  standard illuminants A, B, C, D_{5500}, D_{6500}, D_{7500}, E 139-40
  standard observer 34, 131

system of colour measurement
126- 41
uniform colour space U* V* W*
160-1
unit of colour difference E 161
1931 chromaticity diagram 132-5
CIE-UCS (1960) chromacity diagram
135- 6
colour mixture on 136-8
standard illuminants and blackbody radiation on 139
for representation of perceived
colour 144-56
Circular symmetry 15-16
Clamping circuit 112
Coding, digital 114
differential 118
of colour signals 196
pulse code modulation 114
run-length 117
subsampling in 115
transform 119
using frame storage 120
Colorimeter 127
Colorimetry 125-6
Colour 37
chromaticity. *See* Chromaticity
complementary 141
ISCC-NBS method of designating
143
perceived. *See* Preceived colour
Colour balance 156-7
Colour balance point 157, 174
Colour camera 164
spectral sensitivities 168, 172-4
Colour-difference 177
Colour displays 125-61
Colour information
analogue transmission 177-96
digital transmission of 196-8
sampling density 176
scanning 176
Colour matching 126
binocular method 143
Colour-matching functions 131-3,
168
Colour measurement, CIE system of
126-41
Colour mixture on 1960 CIE-UCS
chromaticity diagram 136
Colour names, dictionary of 143
Colour reproduction
criteria for 164
effect of channel gains on 174
principles of 162

Colour space 127-8
Colour television 125, 164, 177,
179-80, 184
display primaries 134, 136, 162
reference white 140, 169
transmission primaries 180
Colour temperature 139, 155, 156, 173
correlated 140
Colour video telephone 164
Colour vision 125
Comb filter 66, 121, 192
Comb function. *See* Woodwards
notation
Comparison methods of picture qual-
ity assessment 204-7
Complementary colours 141
Computer 121-2, 173
Constant-luminance principle 178,
179
Contrast 38
Contrast sensitivity 43
simultaneous 142
spatial 43, 185-6
successive 142
temporal 46
Contrast threshold 38
Convolution 16-18, 57, 83, 88, 195
2-dimensional 16, 17
8-dimensional 30
graphical 18
Correlated colour temperature 140
Crispening 112
Crosstalk 113, 192
CRT display 1, 75, 91, 93, 109, 115,
164, 173

D_{6500} 139-40, 159, 169-72
Delay lines 66, 120
Delta function 2, 55, 57, 59, 61, 79, 83
sifting property of 18
unidimensional 6, 7, 10
2-dimensional 10, 57
3-dimensional 29, 30, 57
Delta modulation (DM) 118
Demodulation 192
Deterministic functions 23
Differential coding 118
Differential pulse code modulation
(DPCM) 118-19, 120, 197, 198
Digital signals 196
Digital transmission 111, 114
colour information 196-8
Dimensionality of information
source 2

Displays 1, 200
  colour 125
  contrast 38, 39
  flicker 47, 96
  Kell factor 94-5
  line broadening 91-3
  luminance 37
  of graphical information 75
  phosphors 95-8, 134, 136, 162-4
  supersampled 93-4
  visual factors in 31-50
Distortion 121, 123
  intermodulation 87
Dither signals 116
Dominant wavelength 140
Dot interlacing 53
Double sideband (DSB) amplitude
    modulation 114

Echoes 113
Electrical matrix 172
Energy density spectrum 25
  two-dimensional 25
Entropy 122
  of image 24
Equal-energy white 130, 140
Excitation purity 141
Eye
  angle subtended at 31-2
  bandwidth 42, 184-5
  chromatic aberration 176, 184
  contrast sensitivity 43-7
  frequency response 42-9, 184-5
  line-spread function 45
  modulation transfer function 42
  properties of 31-50
  relative luminous efficiency V_λ
    35-6
  response to radiant energy 32
  response to spatial patterns 42
  response to temporal patterns 45
  retinal illuminance 42
  spatial-frequency response 42,
    184-5

Facsimile systems, scanning para-
    meters 74
Field 52
Filter-camera sensitivities 174
Filters and filtering 4, 60
  comb 66, 121, 193
  electro-optical low-pass 49, 60-6
    93
  linear-phase 66

low-pass 22, 48, 54, 56, 58, 60, 67,
    68, 90, 93
  optical striped 90
  recovery 22, 30, 56, 60, 68, 92 94
  spatial 16, 43, 60, 62
  2-dimensional 17
  3-dimensional 30, 48
Flicker 46, 72, 102
Flicker sensitivity 46, 47
Flicker threshold 46
Foot candle 37
Foot lambert 37
Fourier-Bessel transforms 16
Fourier transform 2, 17, 57, 67, 107
  multidimensional 3
  negative values of frequency 4
  or circularly symmetric function
    16
  tables of 7, 8-9, 26-27
  unidimensional 2
  2-dimensional 5-6
  3-dimensional 28, 85
Fovea 32
Frame 52
Frame storage, coding schemes
    using 120
Frequency
  horizontal spatial 5, 99
  negative values 4
  temporal (flicker) 102
  vertical spatial 5, 100, 101
Frequency modulation 114
Frequency response 20
  space-invariant or isoplanatic 20
Frequency shift 195

Gamma 41, 87-8, 108-10
  (of typical camera tubes 87)
Gamma correction 109, 115, 179
Gaussian spot 66
Generalised functions 2, 19, 30
Graphical material
  coding 117-8
  display 75
Grey scale 38, 108-9
  visibility of noise over 109-10

Hankel transforms of zero order 16
High-frequency roll-off 112
Hue 142-4
Huffman codes 122

Illuminance 3, 37, 61, 87
Image
    and picture 1
    bandlimitation 20, 23, 68
    entropy of 24
    information content 25
    mathematical analysis 1-30
    of finite spatial extent 23
    representation of 2
    restoration and enhancement 121
    with motion 28, 85
Image spectrum and video spectrum
    77-81
Image transmission as communica-
    tion process 1
Impulse line 57
Impulse plane 10, 79
Impulse response 4, 16, 67
    2-dimensional 23
    3-dimensional 68
Impulse sheet 10, 79
Information theory 122
Insertion test signals (ITS) 208
Interference 113, 121
    sine wave, visibility of 97
Interlacing 52-3, 58-60, 86, 103
Intermodulation distortion 87
Irradiance 37
Ives-Abney-Ule compromise 173

Kell factor 94-5

Light 32
    incoherent 4
Lightness 38
    and luminance 41
Line broadening 91
Line crawl 52
Line interlacing 52-3, 58-60, 86, 93,
    103
Line-spread function 23, 45
Low-frequency roll-off 111
Lumen 37
Luminance 3, 24, 36-9, 41, 131-3, 137,
    138, 156, 163-170
Luminance difference threshold 38
Luminance error 187
Luminance noise 188, 189
Luminance signal 177, 180, 182, 184,
    186, 190, 197
Luminance variation 184, 186
Luminosity 38

Luminous flux 37
Lux 37

Masking, spatial and temporal 48
Mathematical analysis of images
    1-30
Matrixing, in colour cameras 171-3
Matrix inversion 169
Memory method of recording per-
    ceived colour 143
Mesopic vision 38
Modulation transfer function (MTF)
    20, 23
    of eye 42
Moiré patterns 56, 74
Monochrome information, transmis-
    sion of 54, 111-24
Monocular vision 44
Multidimensional functions 3
Munsell Book of Colour 143
Munsell Renotation System 143, 145-
    53

Needle spectrum 85-6
Noise 121, 123, 186, 205, 206
    frozen (stationary) 107, 110
    narrowband 113
    over grey scale, visibility of 109-
        107
    visibility curve 105
    two-dimensional 25, 27, 10
Noise power spectrum 106, 107
Nonlinearity in communication cir-
    cuit 87
NTSC system 134, 136, 162, 169-71,
    170, 177, 180-4, 186, 192, 196
Nyquist sampling rate 115

Opponent-colour theory 180
Optical transfer (OTF) 23

PAL System I 134, 136, 162, 163, 169-
    71, 170, 177, 180-4, 186, 192-6
Parseval's theorem 27
Patterns, two-level 49
Pels 51
Perceived colour 125, 141, 165, 175,
    178
    and chromaticity 144-56
    binocular matching method of
        recording 143

characterisation and measurement 142
influence of surround conditions 158-60
memory method of recording 143
representation on 1960 CIE-UCS chromaticity diagram 144
Perceived hue and saturation 144
Phase distortion 112
Phosphors 95-7, 125, 134, 136, 139, 162-4
Photometric concepts and units 37
Photometry 34
Photopic vision 38
Picture 52
and image 1
interlaced and non-interlaced 52, 99, 101, 102, 103
Picture coding. *See* Coding, digital
Picture elements 51, 156
Picture quality
and channel capacity 199
measurement of, category-judgement methods 201-4, 206
comparison methods 204-7
numerical scale for 199
subjective assessment 199-208
subjective tests 200-1
Picture sharpness 112-13
Picturephone 72
Point of subjective equality (PSE) 206
Point-spread function 23
Power (density) spectrum 25, 27, 107
Prediction 118, 120
Primary colours 125, 138, 162, 164
chromaticities 134, 136, 162
transformation of 127
Principle of superposition 4, 35
Probabilistic signals in two dimensions 23
Probability density function 24
first-order 24
Psychometrics 95, 201
Psychophysical system 36, 43
Pulse code modulation (PCM) 114-5, 197, 198
Purity. *See* Excitation purity
Purkinje effect 38

Quadrature modulation 189-96
Quantisation 38, 114-20, 196
distortion (noise) 110, 115, 117

Radiance 34, 132

Radiometric concepts and units 34
Random noise, visibility curve 105
Raster 51
Rate-distortion function 123
Rate-distortion theory 123-4
Rating scale 201
Rect. function. *See* Woodward's notation
Rep function. *See* Woodward's notation
Resolving-power frequency 108
Retina 31, 42, 176
Ringing 113
Roll-off
high-frequency 112
low-frequency 111
Run-length coding 117

Sampling 6, 19
multidimensional 19
rectangular 21, 30, 56
2-dimensional 19
3-dimensional 30, 55
Sampling density 49, 55-6, 69, 74-6, 176
Sampling frequency 58, 70
horizontal 72, 73
vertical 72, 73
Sampling function 13
Sampling pattern, irregular 21, 30
Sampling process 12, 30
scanning as 54
Sampling theorem 19, 49, 76, 81
rectangular 21, 30, 56
Saturation 127, 142, 144, 163, 165
Scale anchors 204
Scaling 201
Scan, direction of 60
Scan rate 52
Scanning 15, 19, 51-90
as sampling process 54
dot-interlaced 53
ideal form of 55
interlaced 30, 58
line-continuous 57
line-interlaced 86
noninterlaced 51, 58
of images in colour 176
pseudo-random dot 54
spot profile, influence of 62-7
target storage in 67
using charge-coupled devices 55
Scanning devices 55

Scanning parameters 69-76
  aerial surveillance and space
    systems 76
  CRT displays of graphical
    material 75
  facsimile systems 74
  television 69
  visual telephone system 72
Scotopic luminous efficiency curve
  38
Separability 14, 57, 59, 78
Sifting property of delta function 18
Signal-to-noise ratio 108, 189, 192
  207
Sinc function. *See* Woodward's
  notation
Sine wave
  angular alignment of 20
  2-dimensional, 4, 5, 88, 94-5
  3-dimensional 5
Sine-wave interference 97, 113, 121
Single sideband (SSB) transmission
  114
Source 199
Source decoder 200
Source encoder 25, 199, 200
Spatial bandwidth 20
Spatial carrier 88
Spatial carrier modulation 88
Spatial filtering 16
Spatial frequency 5, 20, 31
  conversion table 33
Spatial frequency response 27
  of eye 42
Spatio-temporal domain representa-
  tion 3
Spatio-temporal sine wave response
  in system design 47
Spectral sensitivities 168
Spot profile 63, 81, 93-4
Spot size, finite 62
Spot wobble 90
Standard illuminants 139, 140
Standard observer 34, 131, 132
Subcarrier modulation 189-2
Subsampling 115
Supersampling 93
Surround 39, 158
Switching function 194
Synchronising pulses 82
Synchronous detection 190, 191
System design
  and eye properties 31-50
  spatio-temporal sine wave
    response in 47

System nonlinearities 87

Target response 67
Target storage 67
Telephone, colour video 164
  visual, scanning parameters 72
Television
  colour. *See* Colour television
  scanning parameters 69-72
Time-division multiplexing 55
Tone reproduction 38
Transform coding 119
Transformation matrix 129, 168
Transitivity 207
Transmission
  analogue 111-14
  by carrier modulation 114, 189-6
  digital 114-21
  imperfections 111-13
  information theory considerations
    122-4
  of colour signals 177-98
Transmission primaries 178, 179,
  186
Tristimulus values 127, 128-31, 133,
  135, 137, 138, 143, 168, 169-72,
  182
Troland 42
Two-level patterns 49

U* V* W* system 160

Value 143
Vertical interval test signals (VITS)
  208
Vestigial sideband (VSB) transmission 114, 192
Video bandwidth restriction 111-3,
  184
Video noise spectrum 107
Video signal 1, 23, 55, 76-88
  confusion in 81
  blanking for 82
  demultiplexed 91
Video signal amplitude and image
  illuminance 87
Video spectrum 77-88
  as projection of sampled spec-
    trum 79-80
  of uniform white field 83
Videotelephone 72-4
Video transmission bandwidth 76

Vidicon 87, 109
Viewphone 72
Visibility of noise over grey scale
    109-10
Visibility curve 103-5
    random noise 105
V_λ curve 34

Wave number 5
Waveform testing 201, 208

Weber-Fechner law 39
Weber Fraction 39
Weber's law 39
White noise, two-dimensional 27
Wiener-Kinchine theorem 27
Woodward's notation 6, 13, 15
    2-dimensions 9
    3-dimensions 28

Zero-luminance primaries 130, 182